Laughter
of tl

MICHAEL A. KEECH

Foreword by Anthony Grafton

THE UNIVERSITY OF CHICAGO PRESS

CHICAGO

For Dr. Bernard Curchod of Lausanne
a good friend and the ideal reader

The University of Chicago Press, Chicago 60637
The University of Chicago Press, Ltd., London
© M. A. Screech, 1997
Foreword ©1998 Anthony Grafton
All rights reserved.
The University of Chicago Press edition 2015
Printed in the United States of America

24 23 22 21 20 19 18 17 16 15   1 2 3 4 5

ISBN: 978-0-226-24511-9 (paper)
ISBN: 978-0-226-24525-6 (e-book)
DOI: 10.728/chicago/9780226245256.001.0001

First published by Allen Lane the Penguin Press 1997
Published in the United States by Westview Press in 1999
A version of the foreword was originally published in the *Times Literary Supplement* in 1998.

Library of Congress Cataloging-in-Publication Data

Screech, M. A. (Michael Andrew), author.
Laughter at the foot of the cross / Michael A. Screech ; foreword by Anthony Grafton.
pages cm
"First published by Allen Lane the Penguin Press 1997. Published in the United States by Westview Press in 1999. A version of the foreword was originally published in the Times Literary Supplement in 1998."—Title page verso.
ISBN 978-0-226-24511-9 (paperback : alkaline paper) — ISBN 978-0-226-24525-6 (ebook) 1. Laughter—Religious aspects—Christianity. I. Grafton, Anthony, writer of preface. II. Title.
BT709.S64 2015
233—dc23
2014048344

♾ This paper meets the requirements of ANSI/NISO Z39.48-1992 (Permanence of Paper).

I saw Him—Him—and I laughed at Him
Kundry, in Wagner's *Parsifal*

*This book was written during
my tenure of an Emeritus Fellowship
from the Leverhulme Trust.
I am most grateful to the Trustees
for their generosity.*

M. A. S.

MICHAEL A. SCREECH is an emeritus fellow of All Souls College, Oxford. His scholarship has roots in University College London and the Warburg Institute. He is recognized as a world authority on the Renaissance, especially for his studies on Rabelais, Erasmus, and Montaigne, as well as on Clément Marot, Joachim Du Bellay, Renaissance laughter, and religious ecstasy. His translation of Montaigne was immediately welcomed for its discrete learning and elegance. His concept and practice of translation arose from his living with the Japanese language as a soldier at the end of the Second World War. The same approach marks his subsequent translation of Rabelais. In recognition of his achievements, the French Republic made him a Chevalier dans l'Ordre national du Mérite and then a Chevalier dans la Légion d'Honneur.

Contents

CONTENTS

Illustrations

(PAGES 196–201)

Wisdom preaching from the *Stultifera Navis* ('Ship of Fools'), Io. de Olpe, 1497 (reproduced from a copy in the Codrington Library by courtesy of the Warden and Fellows of All Souls College, Oxford).

Wisdom preaching from *Moriæ encomium* ('Praise of Folly'), Theodore Martens, Antwerp, 1512 (reproduced by courtesy of the British Library, London).

An ignorant fool preaching, hiding the truth, from the *Stultifera Navis* ('Ship of Fools'), Io. de Olpe, 1497 (reproduced from a copy in the Codrington Library by courtesy of the Warden and Fellows of All Souls College, Oxford).

The title page of *La Declamation des louenges de follie* ('Praise of Folly'), P. Vidoue for Galiot Du Pré, Paris, 1520.

The Fool and the Astrologer, from the *Stultifera Navis* ('Ship of Fools'), Io. de Olpe, 1497 (reproduced from a copy in the Codrington Library by courtesy of the Warden and Fellows of All Souls College, Oxford).

The Fool and the Astrologer, from Rabelais, *Pantagrueline Prognostication*, François Juste, Lyons [1532?] (reproduced from a facsimile – in fact a forgery – in private possession).

Foreword

Why is it funny to expose one's genitals or bottom? The Renaissance physician Laurent Joubert had an answer: "Because that action is ugly, yet not worthy of pity, it incites those who see it to laugh." In a full-scale *Treatise on Laughter*, which appeared in 1579, Joubert developed this thesis at length. He tried to fix the boundaries of the laughable. Nothing, he argued, could kill a good joke like pity. "If someone were to come along and put a red-hot iron" on the exposed arse, for example, our "laughter would give way to compassion." But not every branding of an exposed buttock would provoke pity. When the hot iron was applied as the punishment for stupidity and coarseness, its touch would make the onlookers laugh even harder than the victim's bare arse had on its own.

Joubert identified some actions as too harsh ever to be funny: "If, in order to avoid a greater evil, you desire, with or without his consent, to excise a man's penis, it is not possible to laugh because the ensuing pain by which pity surprises us and checks us as, in an ecstasy of displeasure, we contemplate that operation." Readers of the fifteenth-century manual on witchcraft, the *Malleus maleficarum*, will recall the striking passages in which its Dominican authors described castration as a basic practice of witches who menaced European society.

No social task is harder than explaining a joke to someone who does not get it. And no intellectual task is harder than trying to understand what made jokes funny in another society, or in the earlier history of one's own. Confronted with an ironic or satirical work of great originality, like Thomas More's *Utopia*, historians of ideas notoriously find it impossible to agree about which of the stories and proposals it contains were meant only to amuse, which to point up the real horrors of European society, which to suggest concrete remedies for them. Many a PhD thesis forms part of the tribute that modern incomprehension pays to the past humor we can no longer fathom. Can any scholar hope to trace—much less too write—the history of this endlessly mutable, always dangerous subject?

M. A. Screech thinks so. In his lavishly erudite, digressive, provocative *Laughter at the Foot of the Cross*, he seeks to show that laughter played a special—and a vital—role in Renaissance thought and religion. Joubert, he declares, was only one member of the horde of intellectuals who attacked the subject, which they saw as extremely—if not deadly—serious. Philosophers, theologians, and medical writers took laughter as a defining characteristic of the human race, one that had received close attention from the greatest ancient thinkers and that played a vital role in the Bible itself. The Renaissance, Screech argues, witnessed the revival not only of ancient texts and artistic forms, but also of ancient ideas about laughter and ways of provoking it—ideas and forms which, in the explosive context of early sixteenth-century Christianity, helped to provoke a revolution in religious, as well as social, sensibility: "Laughter echoed round the Western Church as it set out to purify itself, and sought its soul."

Michael Screech commands the intellectual and literary history of the sixteenth century. His published works include definitive editions of Rabelais; a delightfully readable translation of Montaigne; and a long series of learned, original essays and monographs on the sixteenth-century intellectuals he has always liked best. A longtime habitué of the great libraries of Europe, Screech is a master investigator of historical and bibliographical niceties as well as an accomplished reader of sixteenth-century Latin scholarship. Rumor has it that he uses the huge volumes of the 1703–1706 Leiden edition of Eramus's complete works as his bedtime reading. No one who works through the erudite pages of his new book would find this story altogether implausible. Its pages buzz with the talk of obscure witnesses—often more obscure than Joubert: "The authors," Screech remarks in a characteristic footnote, "whom I found most useful for the study of Renaissance laughter include Celio Calcagnini, Cardano, J. B. Fregoso, Fracastoro, J. C. Scaliger, Francesco de Vallès, Valleriola, Viret, Vivès, Camerarius, Nicander, Jossius, Politian, Celso Mancini"—and the list goes on. *Laughter at the Foot of the Cross* sums up research on which Screech has been engaged for some thirty years or more. It has been eagerly awaited ever since he and his pupil Ruth Calder gave a preliminary talk on the subject, which appeared in 1970. And the finished book is a provocative, wide-ranging work of cultural history.

Laughter, Screech begins by showing, pervades the Bible—once one begins to look for it. Elijah laughed at the prophets of Baal. Abraham and Sarah laughed when told that she would bear a child—he in joy, she in incredulity. Children laughed at the bald Elisha—and bears killed forty-two of them. Even biblical texts that did not mention laughter turned out to describe it. For the medieval and Renaissance critic, each biblical line acted like a hyperlink on the Internet once trip on any verse in the New Testament and one confronted not twenty-nine distinct damnations, but twenty-nine parallel tags in the prophets and the Psalms. Analyzing the mocking of Christ in the Gospels, Erasmus found evidence in Isaiah and Zechariah that the Jews not only tormented, but laughed at, the crucified Christ. Drawing on the Psalms as well as Paul, Erasmus also found that God the Father laughed—harshly, chillingly—at sinners. Christ himself, another ingenious interpretation showed, poked ironical fun at the apostles who slept at Gethsemane. Screech traces now-forgotten paths across the biblical text, making clear that sixteenth-century readers explored its territories in ways that now seem very strange indeed.

Screech, however, has more in mind than revealing the ingenuity of Renaissance exegetes. The Catholic humanists on whom he concentrates—above all, Erasmus—set out to reform both Church and society. Screech sees them as the soldiers of an army of intellectual liberation. They swarmed into the world of learn-ing in the years around 1500, using the printing press and their own formidable powers of invective to attack the arteriosclerotic habits and habitués of the universities—the culture of scholastic theology which had its principal base at the University of Paris. In their hands, old forms of laughter proved an effective weapon against modern folly and superstition. Lucian's laughing attacks on the superstition of his own time, which horrified the orthodox, gave Erasmus his chief literary model for the satires in which he excelled. The unruly scatology of the Middle Ages gave Rabelais not only central elements of his comic art, but also powerful ways of revealing what it meant not to be a Christian.

Above all—and here Screech returns to themes that have long occupied him—Erasmus and Rabelais saw laughter as the proper response to madness. In believing this, Screech shows, they saw themselves as followers of Plato. In the *Philebus*, Socrates argues that laughter forms the proper response to *agnoia* (ignorance)—or at least, he has done so since Ianus Cornarius emended the text in his influential mid-sixteenth-century edition of Plato's works. The earlier edition by Aldus Manutius, however, left out a gamma, turning *agnoia* (ignorance) to *anoia* (madness). Even though Mar-silio Ficino had followed a Greek text that read *agnoia*, when making his immensely influential translation of Plato, Erasmus and Rabelais, who used the Greek, continued to connect laughter with madness. Not for the last time, a textual error had profound intellectual consequences.

If Christianity had to do with laughter—and laughter with madness, or folly—then Christianity must really represent, as Erasmus argued in his *Praise of Folly*, the rejection of the wis-dom of this world. Man—a creature characterized by the ability to laugh—was naturally designed to be Christian, a belief that Erasmus and other optimistic humanists always cherished. But, in becoming a true Christian, man committed himself to following a code that the wise and authoritative would condemn, and that would condemn them in turn—a belief that underpinned the radi-calism of Erasmus's and Rabelais's satires. The Christian folly for which the humanists stood represented a unique synthesis of the classical and the Christian, the philological and the associative, the subversive and the comforting.

In the end, for Screech, the charitable quality of Christian laughter overcame the Lucianic mockery of fools and villains, Erasmus tried to restrain himself, not always successfully, from personal attacks; Rabelais insisted, in the *Quart Livre*, that the wise man responds even to folly with generous charity. A sketch toward a genealogy connects the Renaissance satirists—who could not bring themselves to revel "in the endless and ingenious torture of the damned" which much later theologians, like F.W. Farrar, who finally rejected the doctrine of eternal torment—and by doing so made it impossible for Christians to "enjoy, from a belvedere in Paradise," the endless panorama of monsters and torture devices over which the theological, poetic, and artistic imaginations had brooded and gloated for centuries. Ancient laughter turns out to be one of the roots from which modern tolerance grew.

Screech takes the reader down many paths in this absorbing book. Many of his arguments—like his wonderful analysis of how publishers and humanists tried to neutralize the radical message of Erasmus's *Praise of Folly*—rest on minute and convincing examinations of texts and images. More important, he makes us see the northern Renaissance, and early modern Christianity more generally, from a new vantage point. The deepest questions of life and death, Michael Screech shows, were for Erasmus and Rabelais literally a laughing matter. By doing so, he makes clear how great a cultural distance stretches between their creative scholarship and our Alexandrian collection of details—between their religion, which knew how to laugh, and our religions, which take themselves and everything else with equal, deadening seriousness; between their age of joyful anger and our age of flame wars, in which the sense of humor and the sense of humanity both seem strange, lost qualities of a better past.

Anthony Grafton

To the Reader

Laughing is fun. Most of us enjoy a good laugh. So did those who heartily laughed at the bruised and blood-strewn wretch hanging on the Cross. In *Messiah* Handel makes their laughter grow from a hesitant titter to an assured guffaw, swelling up in a torrent of jeering from *hee! hee! hee!* to *ha! ha! ha!*

Those scoffers were laughed at in their turn. The Father in Heaven laughed them to scorn.

What can that mean?

There is laughter amongst the Prophets. Jesus may or may not have laughed on this earth, but, say some, he laughs now. At whom?

Joy, happiness and laughter are found in many a Christian home, many a Christian writer. Millions of the faithful follow their daily round with laughter in their hearts. But there have always been Christians who feel ill at ease with happy laughter: 'Can it,' they wonder, 'have any place at all in an evil, unjust, faithless, suffering world?' Yet evil, injustice, heresy and suffering can be laughed away. Many banish joy and laughter from this vale of tears: laughter is for the elect in Paradise. (Some at least of that laughter in Paradise is brutish and nasty.)

Rarely has laughter been more pervasively present than during the Renaissance and Reformation. Laughter echoed round the Western Church as it set out to purify itself, and sought its soul. Erasmus and Rabelais, two of the greatest laugh-raisers ever, lived then, wrote then, thought then, and they influence us still. Both had been monks. Both became secular priests. Both were well aware of the Christian dimension of their laughter. Neither was a prisoner of a narrow view of the Church.

This is not a book on Erasmus and Rabelais – and certainly not a study of the whole range of their laughter – but I look to them for examples. Christian laughter is a maze: you could easily finish snarled up within it. Erasmus and Rabelais often serve here as guides, even as exemplars. That they can do so is, for me, providential: I have lived with them both for almost as long as I can remember. It is enriching to share in Christian laughter as those clerics practised it.

This book is 'all my own work' – or rather, it is all my own work and that of the young people I have taught and listened to over a lifetime. Everything I say about laughter goes back to study and reflection arising from time spent talking and listening in seminars at home and abroad. (The quest started decades ago in the barrack-room during the 1939–45 war.) To all who have listened and argued I am grateful. Experience suggests that these pages will tempt many to get to know Erasmus and Rabelais better, or to look at them afresh. That will be a by-product. It is Christian laughter itself which will, I hope, exercise its fascination.*

M. A. S.

Wolfson College, Oxford
The Feast of Lancelot Andrewes, 1996

---

* In the early 1950s in Birmingham I put a postgraduate on to Laurent Joubert's French treatise on laughter. He drifted away, finishing nothing. He may not have learned much, but I did.

One of the earliest lectures I ever published was on laughter: it was given under my name and that of Ruth Calder, one of my students.

Over the years colleagues have sent me studies. I particularly recall three good books: Joël Lefebvre's *Les Fols et la Folie: études sur les genres du comique et la création littéraire en Allemagne pendant la Renaissance*, Klincksieck, Paris, 1968; Daniel Ménager's *La Renaissance et le Rire*, Presses Universitaires de France, Paris, 1995; and an interesting collective volume, *L'Umanesimo e 'la Follia' – Scritti di Castelli, Bonicati, Mesnard, Chastel, Secret, Klein*, Edizioni Abete, Rome, 1971. Readers might like to compare with them what is said in this book. We have all gone our own way. The most recent article on laughter I have been sent is 'Un Etron dans la cornucopie: la valeur évangélique de la scatologie dans l'œuvre de Rabelais et dans Marguerite de Navarre'. It is by Yvan Loskoutoff and appeared in *La Revue d'Histoire Littéraire de la France*, XCV, no. 6, Paris, 1995, pp. 906–32.

A Note on Translations and Abbreviations

The Bible is quoted when possible from the Authorized Version, except for the psalms, which are normally taken from the Book of Common Prayer. The commentators and glossators from the earliest days of Christianity were working mainly on Hebrew, Greek and Latin texts which might either give different meanings from the ones best known, or else might be open to other meanings and other ambiguities. Different versions are therefore used when necessary, including a few which I have made myself.

Everything in languages other than English is given in translation: the translations are mine unless specifically attributed to someone else.

Some points raised here are developed in another of my books available in a Penguin edition: *Erasmus: Ecstasy and the Praise of Folly* (Duckworth, 1980; Penguin Books, 1988). Reference is also made to a book which I worked on with my wife, Anne Reeve: *Erasmus' Annotations: The Four Gospels* (Duckworth, 1986).

The following abbreviations are used in the footnotes:

TLF: *Textes Littéraires Français*, published by Droz, Geneva. Quotations from Rabelais are normally by chapter and line.
LB: *Lugduni Batavorum*, 'at Leyden': the Leyden edition of the *Opera* of Erasmus, edited by Clericus, 1703–6.
M.A.S.: an allusion to a book or article of my own.

This book has been so written that the footnotes may be completely ignored by any reader who does not want to take matters further.

Introduction

God, the one and true God of Jews and Christians, could easily have become the God of laughter. For the New Israel which is the Church he remains the God of Abraham, of Isaac and of Jacob. And Isaac means 'laughter'. Or so the rabbis and the Fathers of the Church said.

That name was imposed on Isaac by God during the establishment of the Covenant, one of the key moments in religious history. Pronounced 'Isha-ak', it was thought to carry its etymology with it, as clearly as, by the shores of Gitche Gumee, the 'haha' of Minnehaha meant *Laughing* Water.

When God chose the name Isaac and imposed it on a child yet to be conceived, he also changed two existing names. Up till then Abram was the name of the man who was to be Isaac's father; God changed it to Abraham. The constituent parts of the new name declare that Abraham will become the father of a multitude of nations. To believe such a promise required a great act of faith on Abraham's part: he was a childless old man of ninety-nine. The same was asked of Sarai his wife. God changed her name as well: Sarai became Sarah. Her new name means 'princess', a fitting name for the wife who was to enable Abraham's seed to fructify so richly. Divinely imposed names carried deep religious significance in biblical times.

They still did in the Renaissance. The Scriptures were then rediscovered, with their force renewed, in Hebrew and in Greek. To their teachings and assumptions about laughter and proper names were added those of Plato, newly available in Greek and in Latin. Especially important for Christian ideas about laughter is Plato's dialogue the *Philebus*. Centrally important for the half-hidden deeper meanings to be discovered in proper names is his dialogue the *Cratylus*. Plato gave his sanction to the doctrine that any noun, but especially personal names and divine names, is – when properly imposed – full of prophetic meaning. Such doctrines confirmed the practices of the Old Testament.

But although Isaac means 'laughter', the kind of laughter implied is by no means certain. There are three explanations for the imposing of such a laughter-filled name upon Isaac. All three accounts are in Genesis, and they overlap. On two occasions the laughter aroused by God's promise and its fulfilment is normally taken as a sign of joy and happiness. The third is very different. On that occasion the laughter is sceptical and scoffing. As such it merited an awesome rebuke in the name of God.

Happy laughter dominates only part of the time: Abraham realized that he would be a hundred years old by the time that Isaac was born – if God's promise was to be believed. And it was to be believed. His laughter was full of happy wonder: Sarah was already ninety! Indeed, both Abraham and Sarah had every reason to be happy, provided they fully trusted in the explicit promises of God. The aged, shrivelled Sarah was to become 'a mother of nations', 'kings and peoples shall be of her'.

On being told of this future wondrous conception and birth, Abraham fell on his face; and he laughed. By falling on his face, he acknowledged the almighty power of God; his laughter was normally taken to be not mocking or sceptical but joyful and trusting:

'Shall a child be born unto him that is an hundred years old! and shall Sarah that is ninety years old, give birth!'

God, acknowledging that good laughter, said:

'Sarah thy wife shall bear a son; and thou shalt call his name *Isha'ak*.'[1]

The same happy laughter is heard on Sarah's lips once Isaac is born:

---

1. Genesis, 17:15–17.

'God hath made me to laugh; everyone that heareth shall laugh with me.' And she said, 'Who would have said unto Abraham that Sarah would give children suck, for I have borne him a son in his old age!'[2]

That happy laughter of Abraham and Sarah was certainly enough to explain Isaac's laughter-filled name. But embedded between the two joyful accounts is another. Three more-or-less independent tales, told to provide an explanation of the name of Isaac, have been merged together into one. In this other case the promise that Sarah would conceive came indeed from God, but Sarah lacked faith. She did not believe the divine promise; she did not trust in God.

In this account God's promise was delivered by one of three men. They were in fact angels, messengers from God. Sarah, lurking inside the tent, overheard what was promised to Abraham. The sexual implications moved her to scoff: she and her husband were 'old and stricken with age'; it had 'ceased to be with her after the manner of women'. Was she going to lie with her husband again – and fruitfully?

And Sarah laughed within herself, saying, 'After I am waxed old, shall I have pleasure, my Lord being old also?' And the Lord said unto Abraham, 'Wherefore did Sarah laugh, saying, "Shall I who am old of a surety bear a child?" Is anything too hard for the Lord?' [. . .]

And Sarah denied, saying, 'I laughed not.' For she was afraid. And he said, 'Nay, but thou didst laugh.'

Because of that awesome rebuke, Isaac's name recalled for many not Sarah's happy laughter but her faithless scoffing. Exceptionally, St Jerome even read that scoffing back into the laughter of Abraham.[3] Especially perhaps when in none-too-serious a mood, writers on laughter sometimes gave prominence to the happy trusting laughter of Sarah; serious theologians – who were frequently distrustful of

2. Genesis, 21: 6–7.
3. On Genesis, 18:9–15, St Jerome, despite his vast authority, was not widely followed in this. The points are dealt with in, for example, John Eck's treatise, *De Prædestinatione*, Augsburg, 1514, sig. R4vo f. If Abraham's laughter had been sceptical like Sarah's, God would have reprimanded him too. Abraham's laughter was that of astonishment and exultation; 'not doubting but full of wonder, he said, *So you really think a child will be born to a centenarian!'*

women – fixed rather on the disbelieving laughter for which Sarah had been divinely condemned.

Amongst those who directly contributed to an emphasis on Sarah's sceptical laughter was St Luke. He relates in chapter two of his Gospel how the angel Gabriel told Mary that she was to conceive and bear a son. Mary did not laugh outright, but she replied in a sceptical form of words which was for Erasmus typical of Old Testament Jewry. What she replied was, 'How can this be?' She had not yet lain with any man.[4]

But then Mary was told by Gabriel that her cousin Elisabeth had conceived in her old age, and was further reminded – with an echo of God's assurance to Abraham – that 'with God nothing is ever impossible'. Nothing, that is, 'is too hard for the Lord'. Mary thereupon believed; she placed her trust unreservedly in God's promise and sang *Magnificat*.

Mary, who did not laugh in circumstances akin to those in which Sarah did, became the supreme example of true faith, in ready contrast to the sceptically laughing Sarah.

Sarah's good happy laughter could, like Abraham's, be used to justify an explosion of joy. Yet, because of the rebuke in the third account, she could also be cited as proof that certain kinds of laughter aroused God's deep displeasure.

When reading the Renaissance authors who spread their religious ideas by laughter rather than by thumbscrew and stake, we find that they do not limit themselves to the few places in Scripture where laughter is presented as desirable and good. Both theology and their own sense of fun lead them to find laughter from one end of the Bible to the other. But as moralists they were guided by the kind of laughter which they found mentioned with approval there. Some of that laughter is explicit; in other cases it was uncovered by skilful exegesis.

4. In the Latin of the Vulgate, *Quomodo* . . . ? ('How can this be?'). For Erasmus, that and the many episodes where *Quomodo* . . . ? is found in the Old Testament reveal a centuries-old tradition of incredulity, in which, at that moment, Mary shared with so many of her own people. He gathers quite an impressive list of cases where *Quomodo* appears. (See LB, 5, 379D, ff.)

God gave divine sanction to such laughter, but perhaps to no other. Many in positions of power and authority never accepted laughter as a vehicle for Christian joy, Christian preaching, or the propagation of Christian truth. Faced with an Erasmus or a Rabelais they sought to censor, to suppress, to burn book or author. Some never understood what such laughter implied. Some even amongst the censors understood, and laughed despite themselves; others understood, and snarled.

I

Laughter is the Property
of Man

The property of blue litmus paper is to turn pink when exposed to acids. The property of God is, as the Book of Common Prayer reminds us, 'always to have mercy'. The property of Man is to be able to laugh. For well over two millennia that was taken for a fact. It was taught as firmly in Shakespeare's time as in Ancient Greece and Rome. Any human being who is totally unable to laugh is ill or flawed. By never laughing, the Virgin Mary was an exceptional, perhaps an incomplete, human being. Doubtless Mary should be classed with those great mystics who did not laugh because they had risen above their humanity, but most human beings who never laugh have fallen below it.

Rabelais reminded his readers of the basic definition of Man in the verses placed at the beginning of *Gargantua*:

> 'Tis better to write of laughter than of tears,
> Since laughter is the property of Man.

The doctrine goes back in a general way to Aristotle, although it was more strictly formulated later. Aristotle wrote that 'no animal laughs save Man'.[1] That was the starting-point for those who used the commonplace formula adopted by Rabelais, 'laughter is the property of Man'. That conviction was supported by Galen and by Porphyry. As Melchior Sebizius summed it up in the seventeenth century:

---

1. In his treatise *On the Parts of Animals*, X, 29.

I

Following Aristotle in Book III, Chapter 10 of *On the Parts of Animals* and the common opinion of the rest of philosophers, we say that Man alone (the most noble and most perfect of animals) is subject to laughter, for whom laughing is so familiar that Porphyry declared that what he calls in Greek the faculty of laughing is proper to Man alone in the fourth mode.[2]

The support of Galen is stressed by many, not least by doctors, for whom Galen was to remain an important authority throughout the Renaissance.[3]

The actual formula 'property of Man' was spelled out by Ysaac, a ninth-century commentator variously surnamed Arabus or Judæus. His works were eventually printed in 1515, and so were accessible to Renaissance readers. Laughter for Ysaac is firmly confined to the human species. A human being either does laugh, or can laugh. No other creature has that property. The ability to laugh in fact defines mankind, and so gives rise to reciprocal truths: 'Every human being can laugh: every being which can laugh is human.'[4]

Renaissance authors by the score approved of what was said by Aristotle and accepted the formulation of it in Latin to be found in Ysaac, and in French in Dr Rabelais. Those who could read French

2. Melchior Sebizius (Sebisch), *De Risu et fletu*, s.d., p. 37.

3. The number of authors accepting laughter as the property of Man is legion. Amongst others one could cite Celsus Mancinius, *De Risu et ridiculis*, Ferrara, 1591, p. 101 (the beginning of *De Risu*). For Porphyry's *De Quinque Vocibus*: cap. *De Proprio* and for Galen one could consult F. Valleriola's *Enarrationes Medicinales*, Lyons, 1554, pp. 213ff.

4. Cf. Ysaac Judæus (or Arabus, sometimes catalogued under Ishâk ibn Suleiman, Al Israili); in his *Opera*, Lyons, 1515, fol. vii recto col. 1: 'Laughter is found in the whole of the human species (that is, either in potential or in action).' It cannot be transferred to anything else; 'neither is it possible for Man to create anything like him [in this respect] either by intelligence or by art'. Laughter exists in Man in whom it is a property, as does a definition within the thing defined. 'Human' and 'able to laugh' are therefore interchangeable terms:

For you can say, 'Every man is a creature able to laugh, and vice-versa', just as you can say, 'Every man is a living, rational, mortal creature, and vice-versa.'

but not Latin could find it treated in one of the best of all Renaissance books on laughter, Dr Laurent Joubert's *Traité du ris*.[5]

Erasmus was one of the few who had reservations. At least once he does cite the ability to laugh as the property of Man, but on another occasion he points out that it can also be seen in dogs and monkeys. He judged the property of Man to be his ability to speak.[6] Some accepted the contention of Lactantius Firmianus in his *Divine Institutions* that 'those other things which seem to be proper to Man are shared with other animals. The property of Man is to know and worship God.'[7] That in turn was challenged: it was widely thought that elephants worshipped God.

Such reservations are not unimportant, but even they do not deny that Man is a laughing animal: they deny that he alone is such. And the mass of authors certainly come down heavily on the side of Man being the only creature who was created able to laugh.[8]

Vivès goes some way towards accepting Erasmus's contention that other creatures besides Man can laugh, yet in the end he concedes that Man alone truly laughs: other creatures who seem to do so may have cognate emotions to Man's, but, not having human face, cannot correctly be said to do so.[9] And while the Calvinist writer Pierre Viret, in his *Métamorphose chrétienne*, accepts the assertion of Lactantius that Man's true property is to know and worship God,

---

5. Paris, 1579.
6. Erasmus, *De Conscribendis Epistolis*, in LB, 10, 411C: 'A property is what befalls one species only, such as laughter to Man'; *De Ratione Concionandi*, LB, 5, 922BC: 'It is a faulty definition which fits something other than what it defines.' Such is the description 'able to laugh', for 'what is attributed to Man as his *property* seems to be shared with dogs and monkeys'.
7. III, 10.
8. Cf., amongst others, Gentilis de Fuliginio's commentary on Avicenna, *Prima tertii*, cap. IV, towards the end; Gabriel de Tarrega in his long and perversely named book, *Opera brevissima*, Bordeaux, 1520, fol. XC recto, dubio iiii; and F. Valleriola's *Enarrationes Medicinales*, pp. 213f. The list could easily be extended and would include writers of all sorts.
9. J.-L. Vivès, *De Anima*, Lyons, 1555, p. 208.

3

it did not stop him from becoming the laughing face of the *Église Réformée*.[10]

In the Renaissance, Christian laughter swept into prominence, aided by the conviction that Man is a laughing animal. It is right for him to laugh. Doubts, hesitation and limitations remained, but Alain de Lille in his *Anticlaudianus* had long before made laughter part of at least the perfect Man: nature formed for Man a perfect body; but the appropriate soul with its appropriate powers, including the ability to laugh, was bestowed by God. Alain de Lille personified that laughter. Laughter thus personified is neither the derision of malice nor the smirk of ill-will or lasciviousness: embodied Laughter bears herself with gravity, a modest countenance, uttering no deforming guffaws but 'laughter, corrupted by no abuse, appropriate to cause, place, time and person'.[11] An Aristotelian laughter, therefore: Aristotle's ideal of the urbanely jesting gentleman formed part of the bedrock of Christian ethics.[12]

Some laugh-raisers accepted these restraints. Many did not. It is Man's peculiar privilege to laugh. He cannot easily be stopped; laugh he will.

Those ideas are commonplace enough, but they play their role in Christian views on laughter. A consequence of certain conclusions is that laughter is the property of mankind only in a special, limited, physiological sense. Some other animals feel at least some of the same emotions as those which make men laugh, but they show them by different 'signs'. So only in the strictest sense can they be said to be unable to laugh.[13]

10. Pierre Viret, *Métamorphose chrétienne*, 1561 edition, part II, p. 454.
11. Alain de Lille, *Anticlaudianus*, ed. Bossuat, Paris, 1955, VII, lines 102f.
12. *Nicomachæan Ethics*, IV, viii, 1–11 (1127b, end, to 1128b).
13. Bartholomaeus à Medina, *Expositio in Primam Secundae Angelici Doctoris Divi Thomae Aquinatis*, Salamanca, 1588, IX, p. 327. (The first edition was published in 1580.) He points out that man alone can be said to laugh, given that he alone has a face which can testify to emotions in that way. Other animals are also stimulated by a sense of their good or of pleasure and 'emit signs which have the force of laughter and stand in its stead, but since they do not change their faces as we do, they are not said to laugh'. Such ideas have been exploited by many authors.

If that is true, human beings, the laughing animals, may have no special dignity from their God-given property. Man, the one animal with a face which permits of laughter, may feel the same 'exultation' as the many other animals created with faces not adapted to laughter. What some beasts show by frisking about, Man shows by his laughter.

2

Laughter in an
Evil World

Laughter at religious error became widely acceptable. The northern Renaissance was racked by religious wars and oppression; the wonder is that, in the earlier days of the sixteenth century, so many could have made religious error not shocking, but amusing. For many in authority, error was culpable, meriting grievous torture and burning at the stake. Rabelais did not want to burn anyone: that is why some wanted to burn him. If burning heretics was right – and the Sorbonne condemned Luther for saying it was not – then not to burn them was wrong.

There were many Christian sobersides who were persuaded that no place at all should be found for joy and laughter: we live in a wicked world which merits, rather, penitential tears and sorrow:

> The world is very evil;
>   The times are waxing late;
> Be sober and keep vigil,
>   The Judge is at the gate.[1]

For others there was room for the laughter of relaxation but no place at all for laughter in the correcting of religious error: for them such error never aroused amused laughter: it aroused horror.

Ambiguity about laughter was no new thing. It was typical of early Christianity. There is a profound paradox in the very nature of Christianity. Christianity is a religion of joy: 'Rejoice in the Lord

---

1. J. M. Neale's rendering of lines from the *Hora novissima* of Bernard of Cluny. They are perhaps best known from their inclusion in the English Hymnal.

alway, and again I say rejoice.' But the same apostle Paul who wrote those words also wrote, 'I have continual sorrow in my heart.' For Christianity is also a religion of woe. 'Blessed are ye that weep now' and 'Woe to you that laugh now' are sayings from the mouth of Jesus himself. The Christian paradox of joy mingling with sorrow was recognized by Paul: 'sorrowful, but always rejoicing'.[2]

A question hovers over Christendom. Most of us enjoy laughter; but should we? Oliver Goldsmith wrote of the 'loud laughter that spoke the vacant mind'. And over the centuries theologian after theologian rediscovered for himself that the Jesus of Scripture is shown weeping but never laughing.

Yet great Renaissance authors opted firmly for Christian laughter. Such laughter was destined to flourish in England, though in France (which taught Renaissance England to laugh in new ways) it was destined to wither.[3] Two of the world's greatest laugh-raisers, Erasmus and Rabelais, were fully ordained religious who had ditched their monasteries but not their convictions or their priesthood. Loud laughter came at times from another ex-monk, Luther, and amongst the Reformed theologians from Pierre Viret. They were not alone. Laughter flourished in the soil of Renaissance Christian controversy.

The influence of such men is alive today, but the world of ideas which they inhabit can seem strange and remote. For them, to raise laughter with a good conscience posed specific problems. Those problems were not merely literary: laughter must serve theological and moral purposes. It was not enough to be good at telling jokes at table or in the pulpit, or to excel at writing amusing pieces which others enjoyed. Laughter echoed far and wide. It changed the religious beliefs of men and women. The laugh-raisers and their supporters justified their laughter with the help of their Bibles, and with the help of some of the greatest writers and thinkers known to Renaissance scholars.

Such scholars were Humanists. 'Humanist' is a term in no wise

2. See the excellent study by Edwyn Bevan, 'A Paradox of Christianity', in his *Hellenism and Christianity*, London, 1921, pp. 157f.
3. Boileau's *Art poétique* may be cited as an example of a work which has so bleak a conception of Christianity that laughter can have no place in it.

opposed to 'Christian'. A Humanist is devoted to 'politer literature' – to all those many kinds of writing which were known in Renaissance Latin as *litteræ humaniores*. That literature was mainly in Greek and in good, not barbarous, Latin. The Greek and Latin antiquity in which Renaissance scholars sought artistic guidance and truth in almost all fields of human inquiry was not coterminous with pagan antiquity. It extended right on into the heady world of the Greek and the early Latin Fathers.

As for classical Antiquity itself, it had its allotted role in the divine economy of salvation.

3

Christian Humanists

Wherever readers rejoice in laughter, Erasmus and Rabelais are held in high honour. They dominate these pages; they are the best of finger-posts and the best of guides. They taught first Europe and then the world to laugh afresh. Both were Christian Humanists, both loved and studied the literature of Greece and Rome and both were evangelical Christians, not only in their writings but in their lives. Both became secular priests; they had set out on their earthly pilgrimage as religious – Erasmus as an Augustinian monk, Rabelais as a Franciscan friar who, with canonical legality, became a Benedictine monk when the Franciscans proved hostile to his study of Greek. Both left their convents with support from their patrons, but both, at first, without canonical approval from the Vatican. Both eventually legalized their apostasy (as it was called) by getting the Curia to establish them as secular priests. As priests living in the world, both brought men and women to laugh at what they saw as ugliness and error within the Church.

Neither Erasmus nor Rabelais laughed in a void. As Christian Humanists they went back to what were for Renaissance thinkers the very springs of truth and wisdom: the Bible and the Ancients. 'Return to the sources' was the battle-cry of Renaissance humanism.

During their lifetime the New Testament had become virtually a new book. For centuries scholars in the West had read it and glossed it in Latin. It had been overwhelmingly the private hunting-ground of clergymen who had no knowledge of the language in which it had been written. Erasmus produced the first Greek New Testament in 1516 to accompany and to justify his new and more accurate Latin version. He supplied it with annotations which are no strangers to laughter. Both text and notes he kept up to date in ever-expanding editions until his death in 1535.

Rabelais's giant Gargantua talks of a period dominated by the 'infelicity of the Goths'. That was, for Humanists at least, the later Middle Ages, the period before the recent restoration of learning. Now that that 'gothick' ignorance had been dismissed with scorn, it was a disgrace that a Greek-less man should dare to call himself learned. That giant's judgement, typical of Humanist convictions, condemned to inadequacy many of the leading figures in all the professions, as well as those they taught. After centuries of neglect, Greek-based thinking was now the passion of many a scholar in his study, many a doctor in his surgery, many a lawyer in his chambers, and many a controversialist in print and in pulpit. Some of Erasmus's deepest notions of laughter come from his reading of the Bible in Greek.

Hebrew scholarship also provided new insights into the Old Testament, although it gave rise to some aberrations. In medieval times Jewish converts to Christianity made great contributions to Christian thought and exegesis. Nicholas of Lyra (who was probably a convert) and Geronimo of Santa Fè (who certainly was) made a deep impact on their Christian brethren. So too did a converted friend of Erasmus, Paulus Israëlita, surnamed Riccius. The Renaissance saw a rapid expansion of Hebrew learning among some of the best theologians of all Churches. Even the generally educated reading public had often picked up a light smattering of Hebrew, enough to understand, say, some fairly specialized jests in Rabelais. But Hebrew remained a poor second to Greek in the culture of most Renaissance scholars. Erasmus never mastered it and was anyway much more attracted aesthetically to Greek.

Thanks to Erasmus among others, the Greek Fathers also came to the fore, almost replacing the Latin Fathers and their medieval successors for some Humanists. Thomas More was one who valued the Greek Fathers above the Latin. Humanists tended to dismiss the medieval Latin writers out of hand, but it is wise not to swallow their dismissive propaganda uncritically. The influence of the medieval scholastics and mystics remained powerful and, at times, uniquely authoritative.

The ancient Greek translation of the Jewish Bible was also read with zealous interest. (Montaigne had a copy.) For some it was equal in authority to the Hebrew original. It was named the Septuagint, 'the Seventy'. That was because over seventy inspired scholars, working in isolation for King Ptolemy Philadelphus, had independently produced an identical Greek version of the Hebrew original. An old wives' tale? Or a miracle, vouched for by St Augustine in the *City of God?*[1] There was a new realization – now that the Old Testament was available in Hebrew and both Testaments in Greek – that Christ and the New Testament writers often quote the Hebrew Scriptures from the Greek. That fact gave to the Septuagint a special place as an inspired text.

Its influence extended beyond the learned. In the *Quart Livre de Pantagruel* of Rabelais – who was indeed learned – we can see that influence at work unexpectedly in a minor detail. The coarse Benedictine monk, Frère Jean, alludes in an amusing passage to Potiphar, whose wife tried to seduce Joseph, his honoured slave:[2]

'Breviary matter!' replied Frère Jean. 'Why was Potiphar – the master-cook of Pharaoh's kitchens, the man who bought Joseph and whom Joseph could have cuckolded if he had wanted to – made Master of the Horse for the whole kingdom of Egypt?'[3]

The comic answer to that question lies in the monk's wider account: Potiphar, a master-cook, was good at downing meaty chidlings, and chidlings personified are the enemies of meatless Lent. But the joke remains opaque and mysterious if we do not know that Potiphar is indeed described as Pharaoh's master-cook, but only in the Greek Septuagint. You will look for it in vain in the Latin Vulgate, and

1. XVIII, 42.   2. Genesis, 39.
3. Rabelais, *Le Quart Livre*, TLF, XXXIX, 8ff.

without that description Frère Jean would have had no call to spin his yarn as he did.[4]

That is a detail, but the Bible in several learned and vulgar languages played a central and a vital role for thinkers of many kinds. Renaissance Evangelicals turned naturally to it to learn about the moral and religious status of laughter. For Christians of all persuasions the Bible was the book of books. It told them how to die and how to live so as to gain eternal life. But it did not stand alone; it was glossed by the Fathers of the Church and by a mass of exegetes, and its doctrines were seen as intertwined from the earliest times with the highest reaches of Gentile thought.

The earliest Christians may well have been predominantly Jewish, but once the Church began to spread throughout the Roman Empire it had to come to terms with Greek and Latin thought in all its forms. Those early Christians had either to reject the wisdom of Athens, of Alexandria and of Rome and her vast empire, or else to modify it, moulding it into an ally of Christian truth. For Justin Martyr, about A.D. 150, the best of ancient thought had been divinely inspired: does not *Logos* in Greek mean both word and reason? He saw Christ not only as the newly incarnate Word but also as the eternal *Logos*, in the sense of that divine Reason which had guided Socrates and others like him. Those others soon included Plato and Aristotle. Long before the Incarnation the wisdom of the best of the Ancients had been guided by the Son, who, with the Father and the Holy Ghost, exists from all eternity. Those Ancients no doubt saw the truth about God partially and darkly, but they had genuinely glimpsed it:

We are taught that Christ [. . .] is the *Logos* of whom the whole human race partakes: and those who live according to Reason are Christians, even though they are accounted atheists. Such were Socrates and Heraclitus amongst the Greeks, and those like them.[5]

Even philosophies which were rivals to Christianity could be turned

4. Even some quite unlearned authors of French farces somehow knew that Potiphar was once a master-cook.
5. Justin Martyr, *Apology*, I, xlvi, 1–4. Cf. Henry Bettenson, *Documents of the Christian Church*, second edition, Oxford, 1974.

into allies: St Jerome noted that Stoics and Christians agree over many things.

Renaissance Humanists rejoiced in the mutual compatibility of much ancient philosophy and Christian truths. In this they were the conscious heirs of some of the Greek Fathers, and this sense of inheritance also enabled them to turn towards the Fathers for possibly inspired guidance, not least where laughter was concerned.

Humanists were also – less gratefully – heirs to medieval saints and scholars. In the thirteenth century, Aristotle, translated into Latin from the Arabic, became so naturalized within Christendom – not least through the works of Thomas Aquinas – that he became, in his Latin versions, *the* Philosopher. Scholars who wrote *Philosophus dixit* (the Philosopher said) or even simply *Ipse dixit* (*He* said) were alluding self-evidently to him. What he wrote of laughter could not be ignored. It was the pillar on which whole edifices of thought were raised.

With Plato, things were different. Until the late fifteenth century he had to contend with a widespread ignorance of Greek and a limited acquaintance with what he wrote. Nevertheless even in the most blighted of periods some platonic and neo-platonic thought persisted in the West. As for good scholars in more favoured periods, they might well know no Greek yet some of Plato's doctrines filtered through to them from their Latin authors. Socrates and Plato were known through intermediaries; platonism was known mainly through the 'Dream of Scipio' (part of the Sixth Book of Cicero's *Republic*) or from allusions in a range of authors. There was a legend of Plato and a legend of Socrates well before Plato's works became available again in the West.

When, in the early fifteenth century, Leonardo Bruni translated into Latin several platonic dialogues, Plato provided powerful support for the doctrine of the immortality of the soul, but still did not contribute to the theory or practice of laughter. The dialogues translated did not then include the *Philebus*, the major source of Plato's relevant doctrines.[6]

6. For Plato's influence on the doctrine of the immortality of the soul, see Giovanni di Napoli, *L'Immortalità dell'anima nel Rinascimento*, Turin, 1963.

Ever since the Council of Florence (1438–9) had tried unsuccessfully to mend the great schism which split Christian East from Christian West, there had been a growing desire to learn the Greek language and to read not only the New Testament in Greek, but Plato as well. Thanks to the influence of the Byzantine scholar Gemistus Pletho, an Orthodox churchman at the Council of Florence, Plato's thought came to the West already largely christianized, and in such company as Plotinus and the legendary Hermes Trismegistus.[7]

Marsilio Ficino took that process further; it was he who made Plato's works widely known in the West by translating them into Latin and then writing commentaries upon them, as well as by original works of his own. His Plato is subtly brought into near conformity with Christianity.

It was first of all to his translations that scholars eagerly turned for Plato's thoughts on laughter. Many Renaissance scholars, including Erasmus and Rabelais, were syncretists, welding together apparently disparate systems of thought and art. They sought to take over and to christianize much of the philosophy, theology, wisdom and literature of Greece and Rome. The Socrates of Ficino and of the Florentine Platonists, of Erasmus and Rabelais, was a divinely inspired thinker. Like Plato he had, by special grace, anticipated Christian truth. The great French scholar Guillaume Budé believed that Plato had even been vouchsafed knowledge of Christ as *Logos*. If so, that was quite exceptional.

Sages as impressive at that can be allowed to guide Christian laughter.

---

7. Hermes Trismegistus, who was dated from the time of Moses, was admired and followed by those who believed that his works contained that inspired *prisca theologia* which was both a preparation for the Gospel and a complement to it. (Not everybody venerated the mythical Hermes. Erasmus thought him an impostor; for Rabelais he served as an excuse for laughter.)

4

Jewish and Gentile
'Schoolmasters'

It was part of God's plan that the prophets, patriarchs and law-givers of Israel should serve as 'pedagogues' – as moral tutors guiding the Children of Israel and preparing them for Christ. As Paul wrote to the Galatians: the law of Moses was 'our schoolmaster to bring us to Christ' ('our pedagogue', literally).[1]

Philosophy, it was held, played the same role for the Greeks. At the beginning of the second century Clement of Alexandria was convinced that the best of the Greek philosophers had been inspired.[2] Their philosophy was indeed 'a schoolmaster to bring the Greek mind to Christ, just as the Law had brought the Jews'.[3] Such ideas gained a wide currency. They were reinforced by, among others, Eusebius Pamphylus, the third-century historian of the Church. He wrote a book, *On the Preparation for the Gospel*, which was deeply attractive to many Renaissance thinkers. It taught and showed that the Ancient world had been led, under grace, by thought and deed, to Christ.

Erasmus read much of Plato and Socrates into his Christianity, and much of Aristotle too. He never compromised the absolute uniqueness of Christ, but it was for him the height of faith and reason to gloss Paul with Plato, and Plato with Paul.

1. Galatians, 3:24. A 'pedagogue' did not so much teach as guide and protect his charge. He was often a slave. The Authorized Version has made 'schoolmaster' the usual term.   2. *Stromateis*, I, v, 28.
3. Cf. Henry Bettenson, *Documents of the Christian Church*, second edition, Oxford, 1974, p. 6, for excerpts from relevant texts. Paul and Clement both use the word 'pedagogue' – Clement clearly echoing Paul.

What the Old Testament says about laughter mattered. What Socrates and Plato said about it mattered too. They were inspired pedagogues and they were mutually compatible. But the bedrock remained the teachings and the example of Christ.

5

The Mocking of
the Crucified King

'He trusts in God! Let him deliver him if he will have him!'[1]

Even in translation the sneering laughter comes across like a slap on the face. Christ was memorably scoffed at as he hung in agony on the Cross. After Christians had meditated upon the Crucifixion, never again could laughter be thoughtlessly seen by them – if ever it had been – as a sign of simple joy and buoyant happiness. Laughter is one of the ways in which crowds, thoughtless, cruel or wicked, may react to the sight of suffering.

Such laughter may surface at any time. What applies to crowds may also apply to individual men and women. Montaigne was amazed that Frenchman could torture Frenchman for the sheer fun of it during the Wars of Religion, amusing themselves by 'enjoying the pleasant spectacle' of the anguished twitching of their enemies as they slowly tortured them to death.[2]

In times of war as in times of peace, pain and suffering can readily evoke mocking laughter. Perhaps most forms of laughter involve an element of cruelty. The laughter directed at Christ in his agony came from a crowd revelling in the sight of a harsh punishment righteously inflicted upon an idealistic blasphemer.

What are Christians to make of it all?

Moralists found that it may be right and proper for us to laugh at the misfortunes of our enemies. Socrates did; in the *Philebus* he

---

1. Matthew, 27:42.
2. Michel de Montaigne, *Essays*, Allen Lane, 1991, Book II, ch. 2, 'On Cruelty' (also in *Essays, A Selection*, Penguin Books, 1993, p. 181).

asks whether it is 'wrong or envious to rejoice in the ills' which befall our foes. He gets the answer that he expects and requires: 'No; not at all.'[3]

Christians do not necessarily come off much better. It was agreed that the damned constitute the vast, indeed the overwhelming majority of humankind. Enjoying a 'perfect view' of their tortures is one of the pleasures St Thomas Aquinas holds in store for the elect. (As Erasmus reminds us, the Greek proverb said, 'To laugh at the enemy is the sweetest of laughter.') Thomas's ringside view helps the elect to appreciate more fully their blessedness, and they certainly enjoy it; they do not appear actually to laugh, though they might.[4]

For Peter Lombard they probably do: God's elect, he tells us, go forth to gaze on the excruciating tortures of the damned; they are not moved by such unutterable suffering. Quite the contrary: at the sight of it 'they are replete with joy'.[5]

3. Plato, *Philebus*, 39D.
4. The Greek proverb 'To laugh at the enemy is the sweetest of laughter' is cited by Sophocles and quoted by Erasmus in his *Adages* (II, III, XXXIX: *Optimum aliena insania frui*). For the assertion of Thomas Aquinas, see *Summa Theologica*, III, Suppl., qu. 94, art. 1: anything is best appreciated by a comparison with its contrary; therefore the elect will more greatly appreciate their blessedness, and be even more grateful to God for it, by being vouchsafed a perfect view of the punishment of the impious.
5. Peter Lombard (the Master of the Sentences), *Sententiæ*, IV, dist. 5, 9. Those two encouragements to enjoy gazing on torture from Heaven are cited together in Archdeacon F. W. Farrar's revolutionary book against the horrors of the doctrine of Hell, *Eternal Hope*, London, 1892, p. 66, n. 1.

6

The Old Testament Gospel

We know that Christ was laughed at as he writhed in agony on the Cross, but how do we know it? What texts supply the evidence?

When we turn to the accounts of the trial and Crucifixion of Jesus in the four Gospels we find that words for laughter are rare. In the original Greek of the Gospels the laughter is implied rather than specified. It was not so much in the New Testament that Christians found thinly veiled references to mocking laughter directed against Jesus during his trial and Crucifixion: it was in the Old.

Indeed they found Christ throughout the Old Testament. It was standard practice to do so: for example, the title 'Man of Sorrows' comes from Isaiah, 53:3, not from Matthew, Mark, Luke or John. It is not found anywhere in the New Testament. Humanists enthusiastically accepted that Christ was to be found, half hidden, half revealed, in the Jewish Scriptures. In fact it was the only reason Erasmus found for reading them.

In the New Testament Jesus was mocked twice during his trial and Crucifixion. The texts to which the Church turned for infallible guidance did not allow for that laughter to have been a matter of chance. It formed an essential part of God's plan for the redemption of mankind. To the mind of the Church, reading the Old Testament through a Christian prism, the mockery of Christ was providential; it was foretold, not least in the psalms. The laughter at Christ was prophetically foreseen and therefore did occur.

In the New Testament, as then read, and as related by Matthew, the first mocking of Jesus took place in the official Roman residence:

Then the soldiers of the Governor took Jesus into the Residence and they gathered unto him the entire battalion. And they stripped him, and put on him a scarlet robe. And when they had plaited a crown of thorns, they put it upon his head, and a reed in his right hand: and they bowed the knee before him, and mocked him, saying, 'Hail King of the Jews!'

And they spat upon him, and took the reed, and smote him on the head. And after they had mocked him, they took the robe off him, and put his own raiment on him, and led him away to crucify him.[1]

The account in Mark is very close indeed to Matthew's, not only in the actions related but in the very words employed:

And the soldiers led him away into the hall named the praetorium, and they called together the whole battalion. And they clothed him with purple, and plaited a crown of thorns, and put it on him. And they began to salute him, 'Hail, King of the Jews!'

And they smote him on the head with a reed, and did spit upon him, and bowing their knees paid homage to him. And when they had mocked him, they took off the purple from him, and put his own clothes on him, and led him out to crucify him.[2]

Luke does not recount that particular humiliation. John does, stressing the actions but very effectively leaving the hearer to infer the mocking laughter, of which no word is said:

Then Pilate therefore took Jesus, and scourged him. And the soldiers plaited a crown of thorns, and put it on his head, and they put on him a purple robe, and said, 'Hail, King of the Jews!' And they smote him with their hands.[3]

Biblical critics and theologians are now overwhelmingly convinced that Matthew's Gospel derives in part from Mark: the standard conviction, which dominated all approaches to the Gospels until comparatively recent times, was that Matthew came first – hence its place in our Bibles – and that Mark is essentially an abbreviation of it. Many modern biblical scholars put John's Gospel later than was

1. Matthew, 27:27–31.　　2. Mark, 15:16–20.　　3. John, 19:3.

traditionally the case, and a few place it very much later. They detach it more or less completely from the other three Gospels, which recount events from the same optic.

Most Renaissance scholars remained comfortably within the traditional conviction that the Bible is true and self-consistent: for them, nothing in the Old Testament, properly understood, can ever contradict anything whatever in the New, properly understood; for them, all four Gospels are in complete agreement in every detail. Renaissance theologians, in their *Harmonies* or *Concords*, wove the four Gospels into one seamless cloth. Theologians further enriched accounts of events in the New Testament with details derived from the Old – details unveiled by an inspired Christian understanding of their texts. Modern scholars no longer tend to compile such *Harmonies* or *Concords*. Many scholars are distinctly ill at ease with the idea of unveiling Christian truths to which others are blind. In many ways that is a loss: Paul had no such qualms, and neither did the four Evangelists, nor the Fathers, Greek or Latin.

The Renaissance, on the contrary, was the age in which *Harmonies* and *Concords* triumphed. The accounts in the four Gospels, in Acts and in the Epistles, were pored over; they were then ingeniously fitted together like parts of a puzzle or mosaic. What was missing in one source was supplied by another. Two of the most authoritative of such works were the *Harmonie* of John Calvin and the *Commentaries on his own Concord* of Cornelius Jansen, Bishop of Ghent. Calvin needs no puff; Cornelius Jansen of Ghent is now almost forgotten, yet he is still considered by many to be the most outstanding Roman Catholic biblical scholar of his age. Both Calvin and Jansen were good Greek scholars and their harmonies show it. Jansen moreover wrote with works of Erasmus open before him.[4]

Erasmus was one of the best textual critics. His methods are for the most part the ones still used today. He was a good historian, sceptical of legend and the accumulated bric-à-brac of popular piety. We can, thanks to his command of matter and style, savour the

---

4. That Cornelius Jansen is often confused with his more celebrated namesake of Jansenist fame, who was Bishop of Ypres.

qualities that imbue his life's work: Christ is the Word of God; nowhere is that Word more readily found than in the Gospels and Epistles read in their original tongue. Erasmus strove to make freshly accessible those texts, 'in which that celestial Word, who once set out to us from the heart of the Father, lives, breathes, acts and talks for us still, so that nowhere else, in my opinion, is he more effective or more present'.[5]

Exceptionally, Erasmus did not believe the Bible to be correct in all its detail: for example, there is blatantly a human error in Matthew's account of the visit of the Magi. In it the Evangelist misquotes Micah. 'Christ, for reasons unknown to us, wanted something human to remain,' even in the authors of the Gospels.[6] Yet Erasmus too expected the Bible to be absolutely true and self-consistent on all matters of importance. That applied to the trial and Crucifixion of Jesus, so vital for Christian attitudes to laughter. He succeeded quite late in fully harmonizing the accounts in all four Gospels.[7]

The practice of enriching one Gospel with another was centuries old. Some scribes tampered with their texts in order to make them more complete. Words, they thought, had been dropped out by accident. They inserted into one Gospel words taken from another. Even the majority who respected their texts took over the mocking of Jesus in Matthew and Mark and mentally supplied it to Luke; they also read explicit laughter into the implicit mocking found in John. Everything related in one Gospel actually happened, whether it is mentioned in the other Gospels or not.

Erasmus introduced a new element with his emphasis on the force

---

5. See the Introduction by M.A.S. to the first volume of *Erasmus' Annotations*, ed. Anne Reeve, Duckworth, 1986, p. xvi.

6. See Michael Heath (ed.), *Some Renaissance Studies* (THR CCLXII), Droz, Geneva, 1992, pp. 239–41.

7. So urgent was Erasmus's conviction that he had solved a worrying problem which, unsolved, could harm Christian truth that he held up the 1527 edition of his *Annotations on the New Testament* and had a leaf specially reprinted in order to add a note on the very last page. See the Introduction to *Erasmus' Annotations*, ed. Anne Reeve, Duckworth, 1986, III, pp. 3ff. Erasmus drew his new matter from St Cyril, adding, 'This reading brings the Gospel writers into harmony (*in concordiam*).'

of the original Greek. The Latin Vulgate was still authoritative, supremely so for some, but it no longer stood alone. Once the annotated New Testament of Erasmus appeared in 1516 – with four ever-expanding editions to follow – it was no longer possible to limit theology and scriptural exegesis to the text of the Vulgate.

7

Words and their Meanings

The terms used for the mocking of Christ in the Latin Vulgate are ones well understood in the Latin-educated Renaissance. They are basic to any study of Christian laughter.

In both Matthew and Luke the Latin Vulgate word for 'to mock' is *illudo*. It is a compound word, containing within it the verb *ludo*, to sport, to play, to amuse oneself. It means that the scoffers made sport of Jesus, mocked him, made a laughing-stock of him. It is a harsh and emotive term. In context, the laughter implied by it is cruel.

Erasmus naturally gave absolute priority to the original Greek terms which he himself had made accessible. For him it was a joy beyond compare to drink the old wine of the Gospel in the freshly restored original tongue. We cannot cherish the actual words of Christ in his native Aramaic; the Greek is the nearest we can come to them and to him; we must not neglect it. So for the full force of the mocking of Christ one should turn to the Greek.

The Greek word for 'to mock' used by Matthew and Mark is *empaizō*. It means to mock in the sense of to scoff as a child scoffs, to trifle with. Erasmus was quite satisfied with the verb used in the Vulgate: in his own Latin version he changed the grammatical construction but kept the verb.

The Greek implies that Christ was mocked with a laughter akin to the pitiless laughter of children. (When thinking of laughter it is wise not to sentimentalize over children: the fabulist La Fontaine baldly stated of childhood, 'That age is without pity.')

The second mocking of Jesus occurred when Christ was actually hanging from the Cross. Once more, Matthew and Mark are in close agreement; Mark can be thought of as abbreviating Matthew. Phrases in Matthew but not in Mark are put in italics in the following passage:

And they that passed by reviled him, wagging their heads, and saying, 'Thou that destroyest the Temple, and buildest it in three days, save thyself. *If thou be the Son of God, come down from the cross.*' Likewise also the chief priests mocking him, *with the scribes and elders*, said, 'He saved others; himself he cannot save. If he be the King of Israel, let him come down from the cross, and we will believe him. *He trusted in God: let him deliver him now, if he will have him: for he said, "I am the Son of God".*'[1]

Mark is clipped but at one point more colourful. He borrowed in his Greek the Latin ejaculation '*Va!*' and inserted it after 'wagging their heads, and saying'. That Latin monosyllable is close in meaning to our 'O!' or 'Ha!' or 'Aha!'. It can imply amazement; here it is used to deride what was seen as the empty boasting of Jesus, or so St Jerome maintained.[2]

This time Luke joins the other two Gospel-writers in bringing into prominence the mockery at this key moment of Christ's agony:

And the people stood beholding. And the rulers also with them derided him, saying, 'He saved others, let him save himself, if he be the Christ, the chosen of God.' And the soldiers also mocked him.[3]

Once more the verbs are ones suggesting the harsh laughter of scoffing. The verb for 'to revile' in Matthew and Mark is *blasphēmeō*, which means that the people reproached Jesus, calumniated him or railed at him. The verb which both Matthew and Mark use here for 'to mock him' or 'to scoff at him' is one we have already met, *empaizō*: Christ was taunted as a cruel child might laugh and taunt for the sheer fun of it.

1. Matthew, 27:39–44. Cf. Mark, 15:29–32.
2. Theodore Beza, Calvin's successor in Geneva, maintained that it expressed detestation rather than mockery. For various interpretations see, ad loc., Matthew Pole's *Synopsis Criticorum*, Utrecht, 1686.
3. Luke, 23:35–36.

The verb Luke uses for 'to deride' is another one again, *ekmustēr-izō*. It is connected with the Greek word for nose. It implies that Jesus in his agony was sneered at by a mob laughing down their noses at him. It is the kind of laughing you hear from someone who mockingly thrusts forth his tongue, nose and finger behind your back.[4]

Luke uses that same verb for 'derided' (verse 35) and *empaizō* (verse 36) for 'to mock', but again, John omits the mocking.

The final stage of this laughing at the crucified Jesus comes from the robbers who were crucified with him:

And the thieves also which were crucified with him taunted him.

And they that were crucified with him taunted him.

And one of the malefactors which were hanged railed on him, saying, 'If thou be Christ, save thyself and us.'[5]

Two thieves were crucified with Jesus. In John they are mentioned, but remain silent. The word which Matthew and Mark use for 'taunted' is *oneidizō*: Jesus was reproached, upbraided or reviled; people cast in his teeth favours which they had received from him. (Here Luke again uses *blasphēmeō*, in the sense of 'to rail at'.)

So a small cluster of powerful verbs are used in the Greek Gospels for the mocking of Christ. All of them imply laughing: none specifically emphasizes the act of laughing or isolates it. None tells us straightforwardly that the people simply opened their mouths and sniggered, tittered or guffawed.

The same applies in general to the Vulgate Latin. There the verbs corresponding to the Greek ones we have already met are *impropero* (Matthew, 27:44) – the mockers reproach, upbraid or taunt Jesus; *convicior* (Matthew, 15:32) – the mockers revile or rail at him; *blasphemeo* (Matthew, 27:27; Mark, 15:29; Luke, 23:39) – a churchy word in Latin, meaning that the mockers both reviled and blasphemed. The verb *ludo* is particularly emotive (Mark, 15:31); in that

---

4. Cornelius à Lapide in his *Commentary on Paul*, Lyons, 1660, fol. 432, ii D.
5. Matthew, 27:44; Mark, 15:32; Luke, 23:39.

case the scoffers play about with the dying Jesus. It has links with the verb *illudo*, already met (Matthew, 27:41). Jesus was treated in his agony as an object of fun.

In one case the Latin Vulgate does bring out the actual laughter where the Greek original does not. In Luke, 23:35 we find the verb *derideo*; it is a compound of the verb *rideo*, 'to laugh', and it implies that those who mocked Jesus laughed him to scorn. Erasmus avoided that suggestion in his own Latin version. He renders the Greek verb here by *convicia dicere*: for him the scoffers hurled insults at Jesus; they reviled him.

The translation of Erasmus never superseded the Vulgate. The nasty explicit laughter implied by that single verb *derideo* continued to work its way into the other accounts.

It also mentally linked the mocking of Jesus at his trial and Crucifixion with other episodes where the same verb is employed. For example, in Matthew and Luke, Jesus asserted that a maiden was not dead but asleep; the reaction was one of derision: 'they laughed him to scorn'.[6] So too when Jesus taught that no servant can serve two masters, 'the Pharisees, who were covetous, laughed him to scorn'.[7]

In life as in death Jesus provoked the kind of laughter encapsulated in that verb *derideo*: he was scoffed at.

6. Matthew, 9:24 and Luke, 8:53.
7. Matthew, 16:14, re-translated from the Vulgate. The Authorized Version says they 'derided' Jesus, also strongly bringing out the laughter.

8

The Mocking of Christ in
the Old Testament

The Renaissance Christian scholar or his predecessor across the centuries, having piously collected all the places in the New Testament where Christ is laughed at, would still have much to do. Certainty about the humiliation of Jesus was also to be sought from the Old Testament.

Already the accounts of the mocking of Christ in the four Gospels take readers back to more ancient texts and to additional and deeper meanings. Those deeper meanings are to be uncovered in echoes of Old Testament texts and from prophecies hidden within them. (Some of them remain well known, thanks to Handel's *Messiah*.)

The New Testament writers cite their ancient Bible for specific prophecies duly fulfilled in Christ. Those prophecies were held to convey facts as historical as the details given by the Gospel writers themselves: they too were Gospel truth. They supplement and complement the testimony of the Apostles. The same applies to many other prophecies not specifically cited in the New Testament but recognized by the Church. As the years rolled by, pious scholars uncovered them.

Echoes of the Old Testament in the New are not simply literary ornaments. For the Renaissance Christian such echoes and veiled prophecies were God-given correspondences, not backdated prophecies. It was not a case – as a cynic might suppose – of Gospel writers manipulating evidence, arranging the details of the Saviour's death so as to turn it after the event into the fulfilment of ancient prophecies. For Erasmus, those who are vouchsafed the grace to discover the New Testament veiled in the Old are driven outside themselves; they

28

glimpse the unfolding of God's providence. So astounding are the implications that, once the veil is even partly lifted, glimpses of unutterable truth send the privileged Christian into an ecstasy of amazement.[1] It is in such glimpses that deeper testimony to men's laughing at Christ is to be found.

The cry of dereliction, 'My God, My God, why has thou forsaken me', is a quotation by Jesus from the opening verse of the twenty-second psalm. That psalm, in all its detail, was seen as a shadow, providentially cast beforehand by the supreme reality which is the Crucifixion. As such, the psalm can gloss the texts of the Gospels; it can fill in gaps and supply details not given in the New Testament, details otherwise unknowable.

Witness the account of the Crucifixion in Matthew, when looked at in this light:

And they that passed by reviled him, wagging their heads and saying: 'Thou that destroyest the temple and buildest it in three days, save thyself. If thou be the Son of God, come down from the cross.'

Likewise also the chief priests mocking him, with the scribes and elders, said, 'He saved others: himself he cannot save! If he be the King of Israel, let him come down from the cross, and we will believe him! He trusted in God, let him deliver him now, if he will have him!'[2]

Such railing and wagging of heads was foreshadowed in that twenty-second psalm:

'All they that see me laugh me to scorn: they shoot out their lip, they shake their head, saying: "He trusted on the Lord that he would deliver him: let him deliver him, if he delight in him".'[3]

'Laugh me to scorn'; that phrase, duly unveiled in its context, was taken as proof that the insulting of Christ, the making sport of him and otherwise reviling him mentioned in Matthew's Gospel, had taken the form of laughing at him. That laughter, implicit in the New Testament, is explicit in its foreshadowing.

1. Cf. *Erasmus: Ecstasy and the Praise of Folly*, Penguin Books, 1988, p. 66.
2. Matthew, 27:39–43.   3. Psalm 22: 7–8.

That explicit 'laughing to scorn' of the psalmist adds a new fact to the facts given in the Gospels. It is every bit as authoritative, as true, as the Gospel itself. The crowd who massed together at the foot of the Cross to enjoy the spectacle and who saw Jesus hanging there laughed him to scorn. We know they did: the psalmist said so, under a veil. He foretold it. The very events he wrote about foreshadowed it. There are literal meanings to the psalms as to any other part of the Old Testament: there are higher, deeper and more spiritual readings to be found under the guidance of grace.[4]

Handel's librettist chose to put on to the Messiah's lips the words of the psalmist rather than those of Matthew. He was quite entitled to do so.

Again, in Matthew, 27:34 Jesus was offered in his agony wine mingled with gall. In Mark, 15:23 it was wine mingled with myrrh. In John, 19:29 it was vinegar upon hyssop. Luke, 23:35–36 stopped exegetes from thinking that we might be witnessing an act of mercy, a drugged cup kindly offered to deaden the pain:

And the rulers also scoffed at him saying, 'He saved others; let him save himself, if this is the Christ of God, his chosen one.' And the soldiers also mocked him, coming to him, offering him vinegar and saying, 'If thou art the King of the Jews, save thyself.'

That action had been foreshadowed in Psalm 69, where we find:

Reproach hath broken my heart: and I am full of heaviness: and I looked for some to take pity, but there was none; and for comforters, but I found none. They gave me gall for my meat; and in my thirst they gave me vinegar to drink.

St John, 19:28 tells that this was done 'so that the Scripture might

---

4. The literal meaning is accompanied by three others: the allegorical, which applies to beliefs; the moral, which applies to conduct; the anagogical, which leads to the mystical and the spiritual. They are accepted by Erasmus together with the great majority of exegetes. The traditional four senses of Scripture are often summed up in a Latin jingle: *Littera gesta docet, quid credas allegoria,/Moralis quid agas, quo tendas anagogia* ('The letter teaches what was done; the Allegory, what you should believe,/the Moral what you should do; the Anagogical whither you should tend').

be fulfilled'. It was all part of that scoffing prophetically fore-shadowed.

The 'wagging of heads' by the scoffers at the foot of the Cross also increases the rain of laughter falling on the mocked and abandoned Christ. It echoes Isaiah, 37:22, where we find:

The daughter of Zion hath despised thee and laughed thee to scorn, the daughter of Jerusalem hath wagged her head at thee.

Other examples of wagging or shaking of heads in the Old Testament indicate that such a gesture was redolent of scorn.[5]

The Septuagint on one occasion emphasizes laughter in an unexpected way. John, 19:37 cites Zechariah, 12:10. He follows the Hebrew: 'They shall look upon him whom they pierced.' In the Greek Septuagint that same text reads, 'They shall look upon me because they mock me.'

Erasmus was influential in encouraging the seeking of Christ and the Gospel in Hebrew Scripture. He goes to the very end of that road. He is the heir to a long tradition, already running for a millennium and a half after the Gospels were written.

Shadows are cast by realities, not by other shadows. For Erasmus and other Platonizing Christians the reality is the New Testament: the shadows which it throws form the Old Testament. It is in that sense that the Old Testament quite literally foreshadowed the New. Well before they took place, New Testament realities cast their shadows not only on to the text of the Old Testament but on to the very events related there.

For Erasmus, that paradox could be understood by means of Plato's most famous myth, the myth of the cave. In a cave dwelt a people who mistakenly took for realities the shadows they saw upon its walls. Those shadows were in fact cast by realities permanently outside the mouth of their cave. The light which projected those shadows came from a fire further off than the realities themselves. One day, a lover of truth ventured out of the cave; he glimpsed the

5. Cf. Jeremiah, 18:16; Lamentations, 2:15; Ecclesiasticus, 12:18. Commentators sometimes linked them together.

realities. He came back in order to reveal the truth to his fellow cave-dwellers, but they mocked him and rejected him. Back in the dark he seemed confused. Worse: he told them of spiritual things, things they had never seen. He must be mad![6]

For Plato, myths were a means of teaching moral or spiritual truths. Erasmus accepted those truths. His evangelism and his scriptural theology are steeped in them. To remain content with the literal meaning of the Old Testament is to remain locked within Plato's cave. It is part of the divine plan that the Old Testament should foreshadow the New. Those who act upon that conviction must expect to be laughed at. They are the ones who venture outside its beguiling shadows into the dazzling reality beyond, where all is bathed in light. They discover glorious truths; but they may well be dazzled. Carnal men are content to be bound by the horizons of their imprisoning cave. When sages return and tell of the reality which throws the shadows, they may be mocked as madmen.

For Erasmus, David, say, is a shadow thrown by the reality who is Christ. And that shadow conveys miraculous truths. It is not simply that the life of David was so related as to invite us to see correspondences with the life of Christ: by divine providence, David so lived his life that it foreshadowed the life of Christ. With the help of David we can see how we should expect Christ to be laughed at mercilessly as a lunatic.[7]

6. It can be read at the beginning of Book VII of his *Republic* (Plato, *Republic*, 515D–516A). Erasmus alludes to it many times.
7. For acceptance of this myth by Erasmus within his Christianity, cf. *Erasmus: Ecstasy and the Praise of Folly*, Penguin Books, 1988, pp. 80, 88ff. For the prefiguring of Christ, ibid., pp. 224–5. For Christ prefigured in David's madness, see below, ch. 22.

9

Unholy Railing

'Ya! Baldy!'

Jesus was laughed at as a misguided man. In Scripture another man was once made an object of fun: Elisha. Taunting a man for his baldness is nothing new. It was known to ancient Rome, and it was found in ancient Israel. Crowds of boys, not necessarily wicked, can be found in any society laughing and mocking at passers-by. But they had better not mock a holy man such as Elisha!

And Elisha went up from thence to Bethel: and as he was going up by the way, there came forth little children out of the city, and mocked him and said unto him, 'Go up thou bald head! Go up thou bald head!'

And he looked behind him and saw them, and cursed them in the name of the Lord. And there came forth two she-bears out of the wood and tare forty-two of the children apart.

And Elisha went from thence to Mount Carmel.[1]

That example of the quick punishment of mocking laughter was a famous one. It preoccupied theologians and moralists. It is one of the very few episodes of the Old Testament to give guidance on matters of laughter, and as such it was cited over and over again. The Vulgate uses here the same verb as Matthew uses for the mocking of Christ by the High Priests. It is open, then, to link the mocking of Elisha with the mocking of Jesus.[2]

1. II Kings, 2:23–25.
2. The Greek translation of the Septuagint uses *katapaizō*, a verb which does not figure in the New Testament. The Latin verb for 'to mock', linking II Kings 2:23, to Matthew, 27:41, is *illudo*.

So here is a grim warning: the mocking laughter even of children may merit punishment at its most extreme. That account of mauling to death is the word of God: nobody who venerates it as such can shrug off as innocent even the laughter of naughty boys. Not that this mangling of the little hooligans did not cause some disquiet. Tough-minded believers in exemplary punishment sometimes judge such culling of a mob of jeering youngsters to be a trifle severe. Many defended it, of course, and all exegetes who explained it strove to justify it. St John Chrysostom in his treatise *Against the Vituperators of the Monastic Life* was sure that those children had reached the age of discretion and should rightly answer for what they did. They were at least ten years old.

Such an argument still had force for Augustin Calmet in the eighteenth century.[3] As late as 1905 a principal of St John's College, Battersea, cited – unruffled – a comment of Fuller on the savaging of those boys:

No doubt the chickens crowed as the cocks had learned them, and followed the precedents of their idolatrous parents.[4]

Peter Martyr Vermigli, the prior turned reformer who lectured in Oxford and Zurich in the 1540s, firmly defended God's punishment of those cheeky boys. God cannot be cruel. That is axiomatic. Therefore he was not cruel here. Peter Martyr mentions and condemns at this point the Manichean heretics in the early Church who rejected the Old Testament God as an abomination precisely because he and his worshippers were so cruel. Such reasoning, he pointed out, would lead to rejecting the God of the New Testament too: in the New Testament Paul by his curses caused Elymas the Sorcerer to be blinded, just as Peter caused the death of Ananias and his wife.[5] That was justice, not cruelty.

3. Augustin Calmet, *Commentaire littéraire de la Bible*, Paris, 1724, III, p. 814.
4. Cited from Fuller's *Pisgah Sight of Palestine*, II, xii, 22, in Evan Daniel's *The Prayer-Book: Its History and Contents*, twenty-first edition, London, 1905, p. 113. Daniel was in fact interested exclusively in Fuller's traditional use of 'to learn' as a transitive verb.
5. Matthew Pole, *Synopsis Criticorum*, Utrecht, 1686, Acts 5 and 13, ad loc.

Those children – often assumed to be boys – were laughing at a holy man of God. Laughing at God or his prophets is no trivial matter. Piscator stressed that those children were actually not mocking a man but, through him, God himself, whose prophet he was. Peter Martyr reminded the faithful that Elisha did not act out of human vindictiveness but was directly inspired by God; those cheeky boys were all children of idolaters who worshipped the golden calf; the ones who were selected to be torn apart were the worst of the lot. They had been egged on by their parents. God was punishing those wicked parents through their children. Elisha himself was all kindness: he knew that if those boys were not punished there and then, they would grow up to be worse still and would merit damnation at its harshest in the hereafter. He knew that God would be satisfied with this temporal punishment, since the children did not fully understand what they were doing.

None of that lessens the importance of their wicked laughter. By the slaughter which came out of it, God intended to fix irrevocably in men's minds the respect due to elders and to his ministers, who are *in loco parentis*. They must not be laughed at.

Such justifications enjoyed wide currency. They can leave no one indifferent to an act of mockery addressed to the servants of a God who 'is not mocked' and never with impunity laughed to scorn.[6] Children or not, their laughter merited death. The hooligans who jeered at Elisha, and the soldiers and crowds who jeered at Jesus, were mocking God. Their actions gave to all such laughter a grim dimension. The crime of the little boys was horrendous: with their jeering cry 'Go up! Go up!' were they not insulting the miracle which God had performed when taking Elisha's master Elijah up – up in a fiery chariot?

And they mocked Elisha for his baldness. Augustine recognized

6. Those and additional judgements by Piscator, Malvenda, Sanctius, Cornelius à Lapide, Osiander and others can be read in Matthew Pole's *Synopsis Criticorum*, I, 598, ad loc. 'God is not mocked' is St Paul's warning (Galatians, 6:7); Paul uses here the verb *muktērizō*, which is cognate with *ekmuktērizō* found in Luke, 23:25.

that as providential. It prefigured the mocking of Christ: Jesus, stripped and mocked, was made, as it were, bald for our sakes. And as a baldy he was laughed at.[7]

7. Texts and references in Christopher Wordsworth, *The Holy Bible with Notes*, London, 1868, III, ad loc.

IO

Good Holy Railing

But there is another side to the coin. This time it concerns Elijah, not Elisha. The evil must not rail at the good. True: but the good may rightly rail at the evil.

The setting for that lesson is the contest between the fanatical priests of Baal and Elijah, the prophet of the God of Israel, related in I Kings, 18:22–24:

Then said Elijah unto the people, 'I, even I only, am left a prophet of the Lord; but Baal's prophets are four hundred and fifty men.

'Let them therefore give us two bullocks; and let them choose one bullock for themselves, and cut it into pieces, and lay it on wood, and put no fire under: and I will dress the other bullock, and lay it on wood, and put no fire under.

'And call ye on the name of your gods, and I will call on the name of the Lord: and the God that answereth by fire, let him be God.' And all the people answered and said, 'It is well spoken.'

The inability of the frenzied devotees of Baal to bring forth divine fire under their altar, despite their wild self-mutilation, produced jeering comments from Elijah:

And the priests of Baal took the bullock which was given them, and they dressed it, and called on the name of Baal from morning even until noon, saying, 'O Baal, answer us.' But there was no voice, nor any that answered. And they leaped about the altar which was made.

And it came to pass at noon, that Elijah mocked them, and said, 'Cry aloud! for he is a god! Either he is musing, or he is gone aside, or he is on a journey; or peradventure he sleepeth, and must be awaked!'

And they cried aloud and slashed themselves with knives and lancets till the blood gushed out upon them.

Their fanatical zeal took over. They gashed themselves and pranced about until the evening oblation. All in vain: 'there was neither voice, nor any to answer, nor any that regarded'. Elijah, of course, won the contest. He even drenched his altar with water, yet the Lord kindled the fire under it.

The laughter of the good, like the laughter of the evil, can end in death. Elijah's God won. We then learn how the laughter of a great prophet, like the laughter of the evil boys, can end in slaughter. This time the slaughter was good. The people turned against the priestly prophets of Baal, and Elijah urged them on:

'Take the prophets of Baal. Let not one of them escape.' And they took them: and Elijah took them down to the brook Kishon, and slew them there.

All four hundred and fifty of them.

Elijah's mocking of the priests of Baal in their ghastly frenzy, ending as it does with merciless slaughter, is not without analogies with the mockery directed at the flogged and crucified Christ. The Vulgate uses here the same verb for 'to mock' as Matthew uses for the mocking of Jesus by the chief priests, scribes and elders. In the first case the mockery is absolutely good: in the second case it is absolutely bad.[1]

The Septuagint has Elisha wrinkling up his nose or laughing down it in derision.[2] It chooses the same verb as Luke uses of the covetous Pharisees who laugh at Jesus for his teaching against mammon.[3] Poring over the words of the Holy Ghost who had inspired their Bibles, scholars felt invited to make both a comparison and a contrast between Elijah's righteous deriding of the priests of Baal and the blasphemous deriding of Christ.

That applied even more powerfully to the moment when the

---

1. Matthew, 17:41. The verb is again *illudo*.
2. It uses here the verb *ekmuktērizō*.
3. Luke, 16:14.

people and the rulers of the synagogue laughed down their noses at Jesus on the cross: 'He saved others; let him save himself, if he be the Christ, the chosen of God.'

II

Diasyrm

Harsh, railing satire combines disparagement and ridicule. It is technically called diasyrm. The basic meaning of that term implies tearing a man apart.[1] The example of Elijah and the priests of Baal gave to diasyrm a privileged place – perhaps the most privileged place – among Christians. The glossators and exegetes make that abundantly clear. For Grotius, diasyrm is not unfair when used against those who are truly enemies of piety or corrupters of the people.

Mocking at Jesus was wrong because he is the Son of God: mocking at the priest of Baal was right since they were idolaters and the mocker who revealed their impotence was a prophet of the Most High.

Christians might well have been led to reject all cruel laughter by meditating on the railing against Christ from the foot of the Cross. But the Bible as once read would not allow it. Holy Writ unambiguously showed that the very kind of laughter which is abominable when aimed at Elisha or at Christ can be directed – and as Renaissance theologians continued to insist, be rightly directed – at error, and especially at heresy and blasphemy. The jeering at the priests of Baal became a proof-text justifying harsh laughter of all sorts.

Such laughter is frequently found on Christian lips during periods of controversy. In 1641 it appears, for example, in a satirical tract, *Romes ABC*. The butt of the laughter is the Archbishop of Canter-

---

1. From the Greek *diasurmos* (or the Latin form, *diasyrmus*).
It has an accepted place amongst rhetorical devices.

bury, William Laud, then held prisoner under threat of execution on Tower Hill. Hence the fuller title of the pamphlet: *Romes ABC. Being a short perambulation or rather auricular accusation of a late tyrannical Oppressour, with a petition to the Archbishop of Canterbury, now prisoner in the Tower.*[2] The pamphleteer reminds the Archbishop not to forget his mortality: 'which wee thinke you should not, your chamber having so faire a prospect towards Tower-hill'.

A telling taunt.

Such diasyrm is inseparable from the history of Judaeo-Christian laughter.

2. A copy was recently acquired by Lambeth Palace library. See their *Annual Review*, 1994, p. 16. (Article by Dr Richard Palmer, Librarian of Lambeth Palace, who notes, 'Where wit ran out, pamphleteers could still gloat.')

12

A God who
Laughs to Scorn

Commentators such as Gejerus emphasize that, while God is not subject to emotions of any kind, in the Scriptures he is shown as laughing at the 'insane strivings of evil men'.[1] By such a figure of speech God, who is actually tranquil and impassible, is warning mankind of the consequences of sin. It is for sound reasons of teaching and morality that the Old Testament attributes such human motives and actions to God (the technical name for which is anthropopathy). God is rightly portrayed as 'laughing' sinners 'to scorn'; his 'laughter' teaches a salutary lesson.

All are in the hands of Christ.

Œcolampadius, in a sermon which for him was an example of how to be joyful at Eastertide, invokes Pilate by name: 'You laughingly proclaimed *Behold your King.*' More: 'Not lacking in witticisms you made a lampoon against Christ', fixing that sarcastic title above his Cross: *Jesus of Nazareth, King of the Jews.* 'See whom you were mocking, while that Rome of yours also acted like a madman.' Jesus is indeed King of kings, Lord of lords. What Pilate wrote in mockery will be for ever true. 'He is indeed the God of gods', he does indeed have a Name which is above all names:

In short, crowned with an angelic crown, he, dwelling in the heavens, will laugh you too to scorn and break you in pieces like a potter's vessel.

The allusion is to verses 4 and 9 of the second psalm, 'Why do the heathen so furiously rage together?':

1. Cf. Gejerus in Matthew Pole, *Synopsis Criticorum*, Utrecht, 1686, psalm 2, verse 4, col. 513.

42

He that dwelleth in the heavens shall laugh them to scorn: the Lord shall have them in derision. Thou shalt bruise them with a rod of iron: and break them in pieces like a potter's vessel.

Handel's *Messiah* makes the same connection as Œcolampadius between the mocking of Christ by the infidels and God's own infinitely more terrifying mocking of them prophesied in the psalm.[2]

'We read,' Gejerus pointed out, 'that in the Old Testament God laughed but never wept: in the New Testament he wept but never laughed.' The idea of a Jesus who never laughed here on earth is challenged by many, including Erasmus. Anyway, that saying of Gejerus is admirably pithy and even sounds convincing, but it will not do. It will not even do if restricted to God the Father in the Old Testament and God the Son in the New. It ignores the assured conclusions of exegesis. It ignores the laughter of the Father hidden within the New Testament. Above all it is totally unaware of the mocking laughter of the ascended Christ which was prophesied in many places, including that psalm. Until the end of time Christ's mocking laughter at the wicked rolls down from the heavens.

2. Cf. Martin Luther, cited below, p. 55.

13

Erasmus on Diasyrm

Erasmus takes great pains in his excursus on the second psalm to explain that God's laughter in the Old Testament is a metaphor but not an empty one. The implications of that laughter are terrifying. God the Father is indeed always calm and unmoved. No emotion of mind or body can be found in him. Nevertheless,

God is said to laugh at the wicked whenever their efforts recoil on them in another way: when they strive to do evil to others and are caught in their own snares. [. . .] Hear now how 'He who dwelleth in the heavens may laugh them to scorn': *A man made a pit and digged it, and he fell into the ditch which he made.*[1]

You can hear the same voice of derision in another psalm:

The pain is turned back against the man, and his iniquity falls upon his own head. *Even the sons of men, whose teeth are spears and arrows, and their tongue a sharp sword.* You can hear the roaring and the threats of the plotters. But so that you may understand that He who dwelleth in the heavens is above human counsels and power, the psalmist adds, *O God! exalt thy glory above the heavens and above all the earth.* Then see how divine wisdom laughs to scorn their wicked efforts: *They have prepared a net for my steps; and bowed down my soul: they have digged a pit before me and have fallen into it themselves.*[2]

In the Book of Proverbs God's laughter is mercilessly direct:

1. Citing psalm 7:15.
2. 'In psalm fifty-six' (which is for us psalm 57, verses 4, 5 and 6).

44

'I also will laugh in the day of your calamity. When your fear cometh as a storm, and your calamity cometh as a whirlwind; when distress and anguish come upon you, I will mock.'[3]

Then shall men call upon God, but he will not answer.

The laughter of God in the Old Testament holds the promise of his dreadful retribution to be visited on the wicked. For Erasmus, even a profane poet such as Homer conveyed similar and valid warnings.[4]

God is God. But, with provisos, his human followers may also rightly laugh as he does. Elegant mockery and witty satires are not illicit, provided that we use them not for wreaking vengeance and so on but for condemning. That is what Elijah did.[5]

Calvin, a fine student of the classics, insisted that all human laughter should be restrained by the virtue of moderation rightly preached by the Ancients; it should never be at the expense of the innocent. As for bad, un-Christian laughter, we know all about that from everyday experience. Even when we are moved to laugh at the enemies of God, we should do so with sobriety. In that way we may properly laugh at our enemies.

At all events I confirm that God does offer us an occasion for laughter at the tears of our enemies, provided that it be not too lavish, but moderate and temperate and, for that reason, holy and approved of by God; and such that we know that we are not to rejoice at the ills of wretched men.[6]

Calvin's moderation and relative pity are not always respected even within the Reformed Church. When, sometime before 1544, Pierre Viret, the Reformer of Lausanne, planned to publish his *Disputations chrestiennes* in which laughter plays a large part, Calvin hesitated. He counselled against dedicating the work to Messieurs

---

3. Proverbs, 1:26–28.
4. Erasmus, on psalm 2, 'Why do the heathen so furiously rage together', in LB, 5, col. 211.   5. In Matthew Pole, *Synopsis Criticorum*, ad loc.
6. John Calvin, *Sermon on I Samuel XXX*, in *Corpus Reformatorum*, vol. 58 (*Calvini Opera*, vol. 30), col. 699.

de Berne, who held sway over Lausanne. He offered to write instead a prefatory letter certifying that the book's satirical laughter was not merely justifiable but actually praiseworthy. The offer was accepted. Viret also wrote a long introduction to his book, defending the right to laugh. He quotes the saying of Horace, 'What is to stop us from telling truth with a smile?' Horace had also judged the highest literature to be that which 'mixes the useful and the pleasant'. The Bible is still more authoritative; it cannot be treated with too much reverence:

But I would like you also to consider that the word of God is not so severe and glum that it does not have, when the matter so requires, its ironies, its decent jests, its brocards and witty sayings which accord with its gravity and majesty. Whoever would make the experiment, let him consider how God himself sometimes talks, and Jesus Christ too, that great Orator from Heaven, when reproving his disciples, the hypocrites and the reprobate.

Pierre Viret has a section headed 'Joyful manners of speaking in Holy Writ'. The most enlightening example is Elijah's railing against the priests of Baal.[7]

7. See R. M. Calder and M.A.S., 'Some Renaissance attitudes to laughter', in *Humanism in France*, ed. A. Levi, Manchester University Press, 1970. The points made by Viret are repeated by Marnix in his tedious but would-be funny *Tableaux des differens de la religion*.

14

The Laughter of Jesus
and the Laughter of the Father
in the New Testament

One of the received ideas often encountered from very early times is that Jesus is known to have wept but is never known to have laughed. One is tempted to return to it over and over again.

Joannes Lorinus, a Jesuit biblical scholar from Avignon, summed up the standard position in his *Commentary on Ecclesiastes*. His starting-point is the verse, 'Laughter I counted an error: and to mirth I said, "Why do you vainly deceive?"'[1]

Lorinus accepts that laugher is permissible to the Christian. It is indeed the property of Man: 'There is a time to weep: and a time to laugh.'[2] What Scripture frequently reproves is laughter when too effusive or importunate. Not only did wise Gentiles condemn intemperate guffawing, but so did the Fathers of the Church:

Chrysostom provided the example of Christ, of whom we read that he wept but never laughed. That fact is also recalled by Augustine, Basil, Bernard and the author of the *Sermon to his Brothers in the Desert* in Augustine.

Christ is an infinitely 'truer and holier' exemplar than Plato (and the many philosophers to whom Lorinus gives specific references). He adds:

1. Joannis Lorini, Avenionensis Societatis Jesu, *Commentarii in Ecclesiasticen*, Moguntiae, 1607, pp. 61f; gloss on ch. 2, verse 2. His Latin version reads here, '*Risum reputavi errorem: & gaudio dixi: Quid frustra deciperis.*' The R V reading is, 'I said of laughter, It is mad: and of mirth, What doeth it?'
2. Ecclesiastes, 3:4.

Chrysostom points out that neither Paul nor any other Saint ever laughed, as Scripture tells us, except for Sarah, who was rebuked for it, and the son of Noah, who was condemned to slavery because of it.[3]

The Chrysostom mentioned here is Pseudo-Chrysostom. (He was quite possibly an Arian.)[4]

The reference to Noah's son Ham, the father of Canaan, might seem puzzling to those who read their Bibles free from glosses. But Noah was the first to plant a vine and the first ever to experience the effects of wine taken to excess. Ham stumbled across him naked and drunk. For that he was cursed and enslaved to his brothers. But did he laugh? Genesis does not say so, but commentators do. Many follow Nicholas of Lyra; he explains that Ham 'told his two brethren without' about their father's nakedness, doing so 'in order to incite them to derision'. Such derisive laughter brought down on to that unfilial head the divinely ordained enslavement of Ham and his entire progeny. Rightly so; deriding one of God's elect, even when he is drunk, cannot be condoned. A stern warning against random laughter.

Lorinus notes that Chrysostom omits the example of Abraham 'who also laughed', as he himself conceded in his *Commentary on Genesis*.[5] 'Scholars,' he adds, 'normally praise that laughter and, on the contrary, condemn Sarah's – save for Jerome, who believes that Abraham laughed out of a certain incredulity.'[6]

Lorinus leans towards the toleration of good, moderate, joyful laughter. What Ecclesiastes condemns is loud jeering laughs, *cachinni*, and the kind of boisterous joy which involves throwing oneself about. That, he claims, is the sort of laughter which Christ also condemned. The laughter which Scripture approves of is produced by joy and gaiety 'arising from good things in the mind'.[7] That is

---

3. Genesis, 9:20–28.
4. He is best known as the author of the influential *Opus imperfectum in Matthæam*.
5. This refers to the real Chrysostom. Lorinus, with many others, confounds the pseudo and the genuine Chrysostom.
6. The reference is to Jerome's treatise, *Against Pelagius*.
7. His terms are *laetitia* and *festivitas*.

why Jesus in Luke bade Christians rejoice.[8] Christ 'exulted in the Holy Spirit, from joy overflowing from his soul into his body'.

Laughter from false gods is another matter. Zoroaster is said to have been born laughing. If that is true, then his birth was monstrous and portended evil. Man is born weeping and, as Aristotle stated, children do not laugh a normal laugh before their fortieth day.[9] The human face was made for smiling, not for guffawing. We are reminded that Sixtus, pope and martyr (or was it Sixtus the philosopher?), as well as Maximus the Confessor, are cited with approval by St Bernard when treating of sight and facial decorum; both included laughter among the good things of life.

The neo-Platonist philosopher Philo went further in his book *On Rewards and Punishments*: 'Laughter is the most creditable of the emotions, being the one which makes the whole soul replete with tranquillity and assurance.'[10]

When writing on 'There is a time to weep: and a time to laugh', Lorinus too is reminded of that famous verse of Horace in his twelfth Ode:

> *Dulce est desipere in loco;*
> [It is sweet to be foolish at the right season][11]

But Vossius is careful to insert a warning: the poet is alluding to what is *honestum* (honourable, decent, creditable).[12] Considerations such as those would allow the incarnate Christ to show signs of joy. He may even have laughed. It would be part of his full incarnation as a man to do so: laughter is the property of Man.

Vossius, having rehearsed most of the arguments also found in Lorinus and others, concludes his reflections with an open mind. Whether Christ ever laughed we do not need to know. What we do need to know is the mercy towards us of the Lord who came down

---

8. Luke, 10:21.   9. Aristotle, *History of Animals*, X.
10. Lorinus, op. cit., p. 62.   11. Ecclesiastes, 3:4; Horace, *Odes*, XII.
12. Lorinus is cited as a compiler, not as an original thinker. Much the same material is used also by Gerard Joannes Vossius in his *De Theologia Gentili, et Physiologia Christiana*, Amsterdam, 1700, pp. 358ff. Neither is an original thinker: their value here lies in their being compilers of standard commonplaces.

from Heaven for us miserable sinners, assuming the form of a servant, humbling himself in order to exalt us, expiating our sins by his passion and death. There are certainly quite a few places where Scripture tells us that 'laughter is not evil by nature'. God in the psalm tells the nations to clap their hands and rejoice.[13] If 'laughter were vitiated by nature' it would never have been attributed to God in Holy Writ.[14] Jesus himself said: 'Blessed are ye that weep now: for ye shall laugh.'[15] Laughter can be good. In ancient times, as Vossius reminds us, the Blessed Sabina had that verse of Scripture especially in mind,

when, asked by the temple-warden at Smyrna and his guards why she was laughing, she replied: 'It pleases God. For we are Christians, and they who are in Christ with a firm and constant faith will laugh with everlasting laughter.' She was bending her thoughts to the fact that after this life Christian *hilaritas* (joy or merriment) will be everlasting: in this life, the firmer the faith the greater the laughter.

St Basil, commenting on actual words of Jesus, stressed that it was immoderate laugher which he condemned, not clean merriment. What else should we want or expect? 'Laughter is the property of Man, as Porphyry relates in his *Isagoge*.'

Well before Vossius, Erasmus had found Christ's satirical laughter at evil men prophetically adumbrated in the second psalm: 'He that sitteth in the heavens shall laugh: the Lord shall have them in derision.'[16] Erasmus notes that Hilarius had found divine laugher there too.

Like others, Hilarius ignores Hebrew parallelism in poetry, by which the same thing is said in two similar ways. Erasmus passes lightly over that defect. For Hilarius the verse cited from the psalm means that two persons of the Trinity are laughing. The first half of the verse, 'He that sitteth in the heavens', refers to the Father; the second half, 'the Lord shall have them in derision', refers to the Son,

13. Psalm 47:1.
14. Vossius cites Psalm 2:4: 'He that sitteth in the heavens shall laugh'; Proverbs, 1:26: 'I also will laugh in the day of your calamity', etc.
15. Luke, 6:21.   16. Psalm 2:4.

our Lord. Those whom the Father laughs to scorn, Christ our Lord derides. Both are laughing in derision at sinners.[17]

A stunning and chilling conception. The risen Lord does not intercede for sinners – not for all. Some, like the Father, Christ laughs to scorn.

Erasmus did have some idea of the role of parallelism in Hebrew poetry. He admits to doubts about the detail of Hilarius, but essentially he accepts what Hilarius says:

The Father therefore laughs to scorn: the Son derides; but the laugher-to-scorn is the same: the derision is the same.

Whether or not that idea is to be found in that particular verse of that particular psalm, Erasmus accepted the general truth of what Hilarius taught. After passing in review some specific cases of the Father's laughter in the Old Testament – some of it very harsh – Erasmus gives an example of Jesus likewise laughing in the New Testament, even while on earth:

For in the Gospel too that rich man is mocked, who, having filled his barns, decided to live for himself at ease. What did he hear, if not derision from God? 'Thou fool! This night thy soul shall be required of thee. And then whose shall those things be that thou hast gathered together?'[18]

Erasmus found the mocking God the Father of the Old Testament still fully at work in the New. (That vital extension of Old Testament anthropopathy was anchored in tradition.) Erasmus was guided in this by a text of St Paul, a text which, ever since the *Praise of Folly*, was central to his mature theological convictions: 'God hath made foolish the wisdom of this world.'[19] Erasmus believed that the scornful laughter of God the Father directed against sinners was vouched for by prophecy. With it the Father underpinned the whole course of Jesus's life on earth:

17. Erasmus, *Enarratio Psalmi 'Quare fremuerunt'* ('Why do the heathen so furious rage together'), in LB, 5, col. 212: *'Similiter & his quos irridet alter, alter subsannat'*. The first *alter* is the Father, the second, the Son.
18. Luke, 12:20. 19. I Corinthians, 1:20.

If anyone would compare the Gospel story with that prophetic saying, he will readily perceive how often, and in how many ways, the Lord in the heavens laughed at the impious counsels of men and had them in derision.

Erasmus tells in expansive detail of the visit of the Magi and the slaughter of the Innocents. Herod, donning first the skin of a fox and then that of a lion, achieved none of his aims. By massacring those innocent babes he merely supplied Christ with his first martyrs; Jesus, whom he sought to capture, escaped. Thus Herod was made sport of, outplayed (*deluditur*). The Holy Child was taken unharmed to Egypt. That country was then riddled with demonic superstition: Jesus was unharmed by it. He was unharmed by the Devil, by the snares of Pharisees, scribes, elders and priests; Judas was bought with silver. And so on, to the end of Christ's life on earth. All Christ's enemies were mocked that way by God the Father, the Lord who dwelleth in the heavens. All were laughed to scorn.[20]

While the Father laughed in the heavens as his prophets did on earth, Jesus the Lord, incarnate amongst men, also laughed and in the same way. Erasmus directly linked the ironical laughter of Jesus to that mocking by Elijah of the frenzied priest of Baal:

Perhaps you doubt whether irony can rightly be found in the apostolic writings and in the Gospels, although there is no doubt that it can be found in the Old Testament, indisputably in the Third Book of the Kings, chapter eighteen. Elijah, laughing in ridicule at the priests of Baal, said, 'Cry louder! for he is a god; perhaps he is having a conversation; perhaps he has gone into an inn, or is on a journey; or might indeed be sleeping and must be awakened!'

And, according to the opinion of Theophylact, the Hungarian bishop, irony can be found in the words of Christ: 'Sleep now, and take your rest.'[21]

(Those last words were spoken by Jesus to the drowsy disciples in the Garden of Gethsemane at a solemn climax leading to his betrayal.)[22]

Again in chapter six of Paul's First Epistle to the Corinthians the words

20. Erasmus, *Enarratio Psalmi*, cols. 213–14.
21. The word rendered as 'laughing in ridicule' here is *irridens*.
22. Matthew, 26:45.

Set them to judge who are more despised can appear to have been said ironically, especially since there follows, *I speak to your shame*. And perhaps these words of Christ are not far from irony: *It is not meet to take the children's bread and cast it to dogs.*[23]

Nor are these:

I came not to call the righteous but sinners, for he did not mean those who are genuinely righteous but was rebuking those who appeared to be so in their own sight.[24]

Those are not passing interpretations for Erasmus, nor indeed for theology in general.[25] The ironical possibilities of the words of Jesus to his disciples at Gethsemane are expounded by him in his *Annotations on the New Testament*:

Whilst safeguarding other interpretations, Christ's words [at Gethsemane] may have something of irony in them: 'So far I have not been able to get you to stay awake awhile with me; now the event itself will arouse you, when you shall see my suffering and your peril.' And that squares with what follows, 'Arise, he [Judas] is at hand.'

That was in the first edition of 1516. In 1519 Erasmus adds,

This opinion of mine begins to displease me less since I have discovered that Vulgarius states it emphatically.[26]

---

23. I Corinthians, 6:4–5 (Vulgate readings); then, Matthew, 15:26.
24. Matthew, 9:13.
25. Erasmus, *Methodus compendio perveniendi ad veram theologiam*, LB, 5, col. 123. The very same examples of irony are taken up yet again by James Hastings, J. A. Selbie and J. C. Lambert in *A Dictionary of Christ and the Gospels*, Edinburgh, 1906; s.v. *Laughter*. That shows how long the examples given by Erasmus remain authoritative.
26. In his commentary on Mark. See *Erasmus' Annotations*, ed. A. Reeve, Duckworth, 1986, I, p. 104. By Vulgarius Erasmus means Theophylact, Bishop of Orchrida, whom he at first wrongly identified as an Ancient called Vulgarius and antedated when he read him in Basle. Then, after thinking for a while that the author was the great Athanasius, he eventually realized he was a learned medieval Greek bishop. He continued to exploit him as a major exegete, partly as an 'abbreviator' of Chrysostom.

15

More Irony from Jesus

The discovery of ironical laughter in the mouth of Christ became an important aid to exegesis. It could explain some otherwise disturbing words of the Master. For example, a grave problem was set for Luther by the reply to the lawyer who, to try Jesus, asked what he must do to inherit eternal life. Jesus asked what was written in the law of Moses. The lawyer told him. Jesus said, 'Thou hast answered right: this do, and thou shalt live.'

Can that possibly mean what it appears to say? Can a man be saved by keeping the Mosaic law? If so, what happens to Paul's doctrine of salvation through faith? What happens to Luther's basic tenet that man is saved by faith alone?

'This do, and thou shalt live' became a bone of fierce contention. In its Latin form. '*Hoc fac, et vives*', it became famous in sermon and controversy. Can a man be saved by keeping the Ten Commandments? By keeping them, can a man at least contribute to his own salvation? But that would subvert the teaching of Paul, and Luther's entire theology. Luther returns to those words more than once; they had to be made to conform to salvation by faith alone.

Now, if Jesus can laugh and resort to irony, all is well. Paul's and Luther's certainties are safe. When Luther lectured in Wittenberg on Galatians he devoted much effort to explaining the real meaning in its context of Christ's approving reply, 'This do, and thou shalt live.' He does so again when commenting on Galatians, 3:10, 'And the Law is not of faith: but, the man that doeth them shall live in them.' Although lecturing in Latin, he breaks occasionally into homely German to make his point.

The man that doeth them shall live in them. I understand that clause to be irony. Although it can be explained morally: that those who keep the law 'morally' (that is, without faith) live in it (that is, are not punished but obtain corporeal rewards by it). But I take that text to be, in kind, a sort of irony or mockery, like that saying of Christ's, *This do, and thou shalt live.*

And then comes the homely German: '𝔍𝔞 𝔱𝔥𝔲𝔢 𝔢𝔰 𝔫𝔲𝔯' – 'Go on! Just try it!'[1] The word used by Luther for mockery here is *irrisio*. It implies derisive, mocking laughter.[2] Such derisive laughter is attributed by Luther – and by many of those who followed him – to Jesus.

When Luther came to turn such laughter on to the papacy the effect was devastating. For Luther the papacy was so vastly wicked and hypocritical that it called for much more than human laughter. It merited the omnipotent and divine derision of God the Father, as mentioned in the second psalm; God, through such derision, will 'by hell-fire and ineluctable judgement expose the entire papacy to the laughter and derision of all creatures', for the Pope is the would-be rival to God prophesied in II Thessalonians. Human laughter is merely a foretaste of Christ's laughter to come.[3]

The laughter that Erasmus, Luther, Œcolampadius and, indeed, a whole culture found in the New Testament was not limited to innocent joy. It is often the same as the terrible laughter attributed to the Father, who, from the heights of Heaven, laughs men to scorn.

In Heaven as on earth Jesus laughs at times the same derisive laugh as the Father.

1. *Luthers Werke. Weimarer Ausgabe,* XX, p. 425 (*Commentaries on Galatians*).
2. '*quædam Ironia seu irrisio*'.
3. This is a theme of Luther's work *On the Papacy of Rome, the construct of the Devil.* Rabelais read it before completing the *Quart Livre.* It was twice translated into Latin; Rabelais could have read it in the version of Justus Jona, *Contra Papatum Romanum, a diabolo inventum,* 1545, sig. B5vo – B6ro. (In II Thessalonians, 2:5 – 12, Luther saw a prophecy of the pope, 'who sitteth in the temple of God, setting himself forth as God'.)

16

Pitiless Laughter at Ugliness

But why do the Father, the Son and Elijah, let alone Luther, Erasmus or Œcolampadius, laugh? What is it that provokes laughter against anyone in God or in Man? What made those boys laugh at Elisha? What made Elijah laugh at the priests of Baal? What were the springs of the irony of Jesus? What made his enemies taunt and laugh at him? What makes anyone laugh?

The Bible vouches for the laughter but does not explain it. For answers to such questions Renaissance Humanists turned to their classical authors. A substantial body of moral doctrine on that topic came from Aristotle and Cicero, and was codified by Quintilian. Doctors explained the physiology of laughter. Throughout the Renaissance laughter was treated as a medical problem and was discussed in many a medical treatise.

Quintilian valued laughter highly in the legal orator: Demosthenes is criticized for having had a poor sense of humour, while Cicero is praised for having a good one. Unfortunately, laughter is often aroused by lies and distortions. The reaction of juries to such laughter is unpredictable. Quintilian did not believe that anyone had explained the nature of laughter anything like adequately: he does not claim to do any better. Laughter can be aroused by actions, words, or touch. 'There is so much variety': we laugh not only when words are uttered and actions performed 'acutely or wittily, but also when they are uttered or performed foolishly, angrily or timorously'. Quintilian held that laughter was never far from derision.[1]

1. Quintilian, *Institutio Oratoria*, A.D. 96, VI, iii, 8: *ideoque anceps eius rei ratio est quod a derisu non procul abest risu'*. All of VI, iii, is relevant; part of it is summarized above.

Cicero probed deeply into the causes of laughter when he held that laughter arises from our perception of deformity and ugliness. Since the word used for ugliness is *turpitudo*, ugliness can include foulness, baseness and turpitude. The ugliness may be physical, moral, spiritual; the scope is wide. A large but not dominant place is given to folly, yet folly's range is limited: folly applies above all here to wit which turns against the one who aims to be witty.[2] A copy-book example of such folly is Panurge's encounter with the German magician 'Her' Trippa in the *Tiers Livre de Pantagruel*. Panurge throws at Her Trippa the proverbial lore against self-love gathered together by Erasmus in the *Adagia*; it all turns back to him. Her Trippa can be laughed at as a monomaniac egotist: but not by Panurge, himself the very embodiment of self-love.[3]

Plato apart, virtually everything that had been written on laughter by the Ancients had been retrieved, digested and commented on in the Middle Ages. During the Renaissance it became the common stock of knowledge. Some of the doctors, especially the Italian ones, were very learned men. Scholars had scoured the writings of Aristotle, especially – at first – in Latin translation. Such general ideas and assumptions can be confidently supposed to have been known to Erasmus and Rabelais. But they really do not get to the core of laughter as those great laugh-raisers came to see it.[4]

The consensus amongst Renaissance Aristotelians, who also followed Cicero, is that laughter is indeed provoked by the ugliness of which Quintilian spoke. There is a proviso: that ugliness must be made to appear trivial and unthreatening. Pity has to be kept well away, since pity dries up the springs of laughter. Great ingenuity was devoted to classifying as ugly anything which aroused laughter.

Dr Joubert, of the generation after Rabelais, is a good example

2. ibid., citing Cicero, *De Oratore*, II, lviii, 236.

3. Cf. M.A.S., 'Rabelais, *Le Tiers Livre de Pantagruel*, Chapter 25', in *The Art of Criticism*, ed. P. Nurse, Edinburgh, 1969, pp. 28–39.

4. For further brief details on this section one could consult an article by R. M. Calder and M.A.S., 'Some Renaissance attitudes to laughter', in *Humanism in France*, ed. A. Levi, Manchester University Press, 1970, which contains papers read at a colloquy in Warwick.

of learned medical reflection and scholarship. For him too the ridiculous is a subdivision of the ugly. We laugh at what is defective,
deformed, or ugly, but not threatening or destructive. Whatever we
see to be ugly, deformed, indecent and so on provokes our laughter,
'provided that we are not moved to compassion':

An example. If one happens to uncover those shameful parts which we are
accustomed by nature or public decency to hide, because that action is ugly
yet not worthy of pity it incites those who see it to laugh.

The absence of pity is vital. Circumstances might compel us to feel
pity. When they do, there will be no laughter:

If, in order to avoid a greater evil, you desire, with or without his consent,
to excise a man's penis, it is not possible to laugh because of the ensuing
pain by which pity surprises and checks us, as, in an ecstasy of displeasure,
we contemplate that operation.

    It is similarly indecent to bare one's arse and so, when there is no injury
which forces our sympathy, we cannot hold back a laugh. But if someone
were to come along unexpectedly and put a red-hot iron on it, the laughter
would give way to compassion – unless that evil deed is made to seem light
and trivial, for that increases the laughter, seeing that the man is duly
punished for his stupidity and displeasing coarseness.[5]

A great deal of laughter is aroused by such means, not least in
Rabelais. But it is far from exhausting laughter as the great laugh-
raisers conceived it.[6]

    The Humanists found in Plato something fresher, newer, deeper.

    The mob laugh at Jesus stubbornly hanging in agony from a cross.

5. Laurent Joubert, *Traité du ris*, Paris, 1579, pp. 18ff.
6. The authors whom I found most useful for the study of Renaissance laughter
include Celio Calcagnini, Cardano, J. B. Fregoso, Fracastoro, J. C. Scaliger,
Francesco de Vallés, Valleriola, Viret, Vivès, Camerarius, Nicander, Jossius, Politian, Celso Mancini, Erycius Puteanus, João Rodrigues de Castello Branco (the
Jewish doctor Amatus Lusitanus), to whom should be added commentators, major
and minor, on Aristotle, Galen, Avicenna and so on. The list of writers on laughter
could easily be very much extended; such a list would include literary critics such
as Vincent Madius on Aristotle's *Poetics* and Turnebus on Cicero. Probably the
majority of authors of works on laughter write as specialists in medicine.

For them he was a mere man, absurdly and blasphemously convinced that he was the Messiah and the Son of God. Elijah laughed at the priests of Baal because he was sure that they worshipped a false god. Sarah laughed at God's angels because to her it seemed simply absurd to promise that she would bear a child when she was ninety and her husband ninety-nine.

But why laugh? Would not contempt or wrath be more appropriate? What Socrates and Plato had to say about laughter was novel and heady. Their ideas had for a millennium remained unknown in the West. The dialogue of Plato which was to prove most fruitful for establishing the basis for laughter was the *Philebus*. It is concerned above all with the nature of the good, and the relation to the good of knowledge and pleasure. It recognizes that many emotions can be good, bad or mixed. Socrates places laughter amongst the mixed emotions. That was because we enjoy laughing at someone, but also feel awkward about doing so. The conclusion that Socrates elucidated from that observation is that laughter is a kind of 'schoolboy malice'. The term he used for it is *paidikos phthonos*. It recognizes a man's false conceit of wisdom. Since *phthonos* is a somewhat dubious quality, we cannot be laughing at an enemy. If we were, there would be nothing to be dubious about; it is natural to laugh at an enemy, unless he is powerful and terrifying. It is qualities in the weak which are most naturally ridiculous.

Since Christians are taught to speak out without fear but also to love their neighbours as themselves, in a sense all Christian laughter ought to fall into the category of laughing at friends. It is the sin that should be hated, not the sinner. The thought is certainly relevant to Christian laughter, much of which is directed at the errors of other Churches and other Christians.

That is one way of looking at it, but there is another. If one thing is certain from the Scriptures, it is that Christians have enemies. That fact cannot be dodged. The sinful enemy has a duty to repent. If he is not a repentant sinner but, say, a real or potential torturer or oppressor, then he remains an enemy of all that is good and true. Mocking at such foes in their distress may be right, and for many it knows no bounds.

59

Laughter for Socrates was a mixed emotion, at least among the wise. For many Christian laugh-raisers the Socratic notion that the butt of a wise man's laughter remains a friend led them to temper the harshness of their laughter, and to take something off its cutting-edge.[7]

7. Plato, *Philebus*, 49A – 50C.

17

Ignorance or Madness?
The Importance of a Gamma
More Socratic Laughter in
the Philebus

The ideas expounded by Socrates in the *Philebus* – a delightful dialogue – first became more known from the Latin translation of Marsilio Ficino (1433–99), the Florentine Platonist. His translations from the Greek as well as his original works published in posthumous editions reached a wide audience. Ficino alone did not produce Renaissance platonism, but he was one of the most important of the conduits through which Plato and the platonizing learning of Byzantium passed into Western Europe.

Just as many scholars knew their Aristotle only in Latin translation, many first knew Plato almost exclusively in Latin. Soon Greek editions and other intermediaries helped to expound Plato's ideas on laughter more accurately; but the Latin came first. Ficino's Latin does not always correspond in detail to the Greek texts that were eventually made available.

What, then, did the 'divine' Socrates say about laughter in the *Philebus*? Why, for him, do we laugh? Our answer will depend upon which text or translation we use. Ficino's Latin version – and most modern translations into English or other languages – give one answer. The earliest printed Greek text gives another. When Ficino's Latin translation is used, there is no problem: the motor of laughter is our perception not of ugliness (as Aristotle was to say) but of ignorance. The playfulness of Socrates produces some deliberate obfuscation, but he neatly isolates the two misfortunes or evils which naturally provoke laughter. The first is ignorance; the second is silliness or clownishness. (Both qualities can often be taken together as clownish ignorance.)

The Greek term rendered as 'silliness' or 'clownishness' is *abelteria*. There was no disagreement over that word. The Greek term rendered as 'ignorance' is *agnoia*. For those who accept that reading, laughter in God and Man comes from the perception of ignorance in the butt of their laughter.

That word *agnoia* proves to be of seminal importance. In Greek it is written ἄγνοια. How that one Greek word was copied, read, emended and translated has exercised an immense influence over Western ideas, affecting raisers of laughter as diverse as Erasmus, Rabelais, Molière, the Goons and the Marx Brothers.

Socrates was having one of his usual one-sided discussions, in this case with Protarchus.[1] The discussion turned to laughter, which he saw as a 'mixed' reaction. It is indeed the mixed reaction to *agnoia* and *abelteria*.

This is how the great Jowett renders it:

Socrates: And ignorance, and what is termed clownishness, is surely an evil?
Protarchus: To be sure.
Socrates: From these considerations learn to know the nature of the ridiculous.
Protarchus: Explain.
Socrates: The ridiculous is in short the specific name which is used to describe the vicious form of a certain habit; and of vice in general it is that kind which is most at variance with the inscription at Delphi.
Protarchus: You mean, Socrates, *Know Thyself*.
Socrates: I do; and the opposite would be, *Know not Thyself*.

All recent English translations agree that Socrates maintained that we are moved to laughter by our perception of someone's ignorance, by his *agnoia*. And so we find as translations of the first sentence:

Socrates: Now ignorance, or the condition we call stupidity, is an ill thing.
(R. Hackforth, 1972)

and:

1. The relevant part of the *Philebus* is section 48C.

62

Socrates: And ignorance and silliness, as we call it, is a misfortune. (Taylor, ed. R. Klibansky, 1972)

and:

Socrates: And surely that ignorance which we call a state of silliness is a misfortune? (J. C. B. Gosling, 1975)

All agree with the Latin translation of Ficino. Socrates is talking of ignorance. From Ficino's day to our own most hold that Socrates, with the almost mythical authority with which he was endowed, explained laughter as a natural reaction to perceived ignorance.[2]

The fine Greek scholarship of the Renaissance doctor Cornarius remains influential, and modern students of Plato still follow him. He too talks of *ignorantia* here. It is specifically his reading of the Greek which is cited to this day by editors of the *Philebus*.[3]

Ever since the Council of Florence Plato had become progressively integrated into some of the most learned and persuasive doctrines of Christianity. Plato is a principal source of the dogma of the immortality of the soul.[4] It was normal to refer to him as *divinus Plato*, and both he and Socrates were taken by many to have been specially favoured, directly inspired by the one true God. Plato might be truly prophetic. Guillaume Budé, with his great legal mind, was one of a host of philosophers and theologians who were convinced that Plato and Socrates had been inspired by special grace to adumbrate the doctrine of the *Logos*, the Word of God, and even of the Trinity. That placed them in a most privileged band; they were in

2. The words used by Ficino are *ignorantia* and *stoliditas*. The point at issue throughout this book concerns only the first of those terms. The second is uncontroversial. The quotations are taken from Plato's *Philebus*, trans. R. A. Hackforth, Cambridge University Press, 1972, p. 95; Plato, *Philebus and Epinomis*, trans. A. E. Taylor, ed. R. Klibansky *et al.*, New York and London, 1972, p. 167; Plato, *Philebus*, trans. J. C. B. Gosling, Oxford, 1975, p. 47.
3. Ianus Cornarius, Medicus, Physicus, *Platonis Atheniensis Philosophi Summi ac penitus divini Opera quae ad nos extant omnia Latina lingua scripta*, Basle, 1561, fol. 233 recto.
4. Aristotle is ambiguous on the immortality of the soul; as for the Bible, it teaches not the immortality of the soul but the resurrection of the dead.

the same category as David or the Patriarchs, inspired pedagogues preparing the way for the Lord.[5] But that adjective 'divine' applied to Plato and Socrates, not to Ficino or Cornarius. What Socrates said about laughter is authoritative. But supposing scholars misread him? Ficino's or Cornarius's readings of Plato could be challenged. They were.

Where Ficino talks of *agnoia*, ignorance, as the stimulus to laughter, the first edition of Plato in Greek has a different reading: not ἄγνοια but ἄνοια – not, that is, ignorance (*agnoia*) but madness (*anoia*). That makes a world of difference. And it all hangs on the presence or absence of a single letter: γ (gamma), the Greek g.

The present or absent gamma changes the whole picture. Once we read *anoia*, not *agnoia*, the cause of laughter for Socrates and Plato is not perceived ignorance but perceived madness.

That reading had the greatest authority behind it: Plato's Greek as first edited (there was no suggestion anywhere of a variant reading). The first edition of Plato's works appeared in 1513 from the press of Aldus, the Humanist printer of Venice. The scholar who edited the text was the much admired Aldus Pius Manutius. He dedicated it to Pope Pius X, the man who, three years later, was to give his invaluable and lasting support to Erasmus's New Testament.

As the right reading of the divine Plato's Greek, 'madness', not 'ignorance', held sway throughout the laugh-raising lives of Erasmus and Rabelais. Not until 1561 did the medical philosopher Cornarius arbitrarily change 'madness' back to 'ignorance', firmly emending the Greek by putting a gamma into *anoia* and translating accordingly.[6] He defends his emendations in a learned commentary entitled

5. Guillaume Budé, *Commentarii linguae graecae*, in *Opera Omnia*, Basle, 1557 (Gregg reprint, Farnborough, 1966), p. 243; when explaining the various philosophical meanings of *Logos*, Budé affirms, 'No one can however doubt that Plato was talking about the Son of God, if only he would read his letter to Hermias . . .'
6. See his monumental edition of the Complete Works of Plato in Greek and Latin, *Omnia Opera Platonis*, Aldus, Venice, 1513. For the readings ἄγνοια instead of ἄνοια see fol. 168, eleventh line from the end; fol. 169, line 11. The key phrase cited above in English reads (fol. 168, loc. cit.): Σω κακὸν μὴν ἄνοια, καὶ ἦν δὴ λέγομέν ἀβελτέραν ἕσιν. See also fol. 223, line 8. On fol. 228, line 33, one finds neither ἄγνοια nor ἄνοια, but ἄνια – also with the sense of 'madness'.

Eclogue. The emendations seem to have been based purely upon reason: he cites no Greek manuscripts to sustain his case. (Has any editor ever done so?)[7]

Jean de Serres (1578) manages to get the best of both worlds. He emends the Greek text throughout to read *agnoia*, 'ignorance', but keeps *amentia*, 'madness', in the Latin translation of the key passage![8]

---

7. There is a useful separate edition of that *Eclogue*, published in Leipzig in 1741 and edited by O. F. Fischer: *I. Cornarii eclogae in Dialogos Platonis omnes.* Cornarius arbitrarily changes ἄνοια to ἄγνοια throughout the *Philebus* and also in other key passages of Plato: in the *Phaedo* (cited by Cornarius on p. 9); in the *Gorgias* (p. 78), and the Eighth Book of the *Laws* (p. 124). By such means, the vital role of madness in the theories of Socrates is not merely weakened: it is obliterated.

8. See Joannes Serranus, *Platonis Augustiss, philosophi omnium quae extant operum tomus secundus*: he gives two important marginal notes. Against 34D (where he strangely gives *amentia* in the translation, yet emends to ἄγνοια in the Greek) he writes (p. 48):

Another and more accurate explanation evokes *ignorantia* and *dementia* for that mixture of pleasure and pain in us: that is, ἄγνοια and ἄνοια, which is a grievous admixture in the theatre of human life in which tragedy and comedy are variously enacted.

Again (p. 49) against ἄγνοια γὰρ (rendered *ignorantia enim*) Jean de Serres comments:

In previous editions ἄνοια. And twice afterwards ἄνοιαν is read for ἄγνοιαν. Again later we find in those same editions, κακὸν μὴν ἄνοια, where ἄγνοια was first corrupted to ἄνοια and then further corrupted to ἄνια. Ficino everywhere follows the readings [ἄγνοια, etc.] given here.

As far as I am aware, no evidence other than the conjectures of Cornarius is ever cited by modern editions for their emending of ἄνοια and ἄνια to ἄγνοια. Cf. the notes of I. Bekker in his *Platonis Scripta Graece omnia*, vol. 5, London, 1826, p. 513; he cites Stephanus, Cornarius and Ficino. The reading ἄνοια he arbitrarily condemns as *pessime*. See also Gotfredus Stallbaum, *Platonis Philebus*, Gothae, 1841, p. 36n, p. 279n., where the emendations given on the authority of Cornarius are claimed to be the reverse of bold, since a confusion of ἄνοια and ἄγνοια 'is so common elsewhere'. Only ἄγνοια should be retained, despite Winckelmann. 'It is to be understood therefore' that Socrates is not talking of *dementia* or *insania* but of *ignorance*. The notes of Klaus Widdra, and others, *Platon: Timaios, Kritias. Philebos*, Darmstadt, n.d., pp. 383–5, and Cambridge, 1972, p. 120, § 48c2, come down heavily in favour of ἄγνοια.

An abyss awaits the unwary: Erasmus and others read those texts so as to bring out not the ignorance, *agnoia*, but the madness, *anoia*.

But whatever later scholars might conclude to their own satisfaction, readers of Plato's Greek in the first half of the sixteenth century would have found unambiguously in their texts *anoia*, not *agnoia*. Not ignorance but madness. Socrates, then, is taken to have sought the source of man's perception of the ridiculous in the mixed feelings we experience in the presence of madness.

But there is a limitation, as Socrates saw: great people do not like being laughed at. To laugh at a madman you must first be convinced that he has no power to harm you.

Making folly, madness, the trigger was a great enrichment of both the theory and practice of laughter-raising. Ignorance does not include folly; folly can certainly include many kinds of ignorance – especially ignorance of the self on the part of the butt of our laughter. Plato's allusion to the inscription at Delphi, KNOW THYSELF, made sure that it did.

The clash of readings in Ficino's Latin and the *editio princeps* of the Greek doubtless led to some readers first accepting ignorance as the cause of laughter and then folly, with at least self-ignorance thrown in. Some readers fused madness and ignorance together. In the judgement of Socrates the most ridiculous man is one who is so mad as to be totally ignorant of his own nature; such a man is acting flat contrary to the great injunction on the tympanum of the temple at Delphi. The monomaniac magician Her Trippa in Rabelais's *Tiers Livre de Pantagruel* is a good example.[9]

So, at the time when the two most successful laugh-raisers of the Renaissance were living and writing, laughter was held to be provoked by madness, folly.

The best modern scholarship may well rightly conclude that, 'except perhaps in the case of the weak', folly is not an apt word for summing up what is said by Socrates in the *Philebus*.[10] In our days *agnoia* triumphs over *anoia*, ignorance over folly. The practice

9. *Tiers Livre*, ch. xix.
10. Cf. Plato, *Philebus*, trans. J. C. B. Gosling, Oxford, 1975, p. 120, § 482c: 'Reading ἄγνοια (ignorance) here, as in 492c, 49d9, 49e6, instead of ἄνοια (folly), since it is opposed to a form of γνῶσις (*gnosis*: knowledge, c 10), and that it is clear that what is in question is a form of ignorance about oneself (48d8 *seq.*). It

of Erasmus and Rabelais in their maturity shows that they thought otherwise. For them, what above all provokes laughter is folly, madness, insanity, coupled no doubt with ignorance. But of course laughter is a pleasure. We like to laugh. We do not wait for pure madness to present itself. The degree of seriousness in the charge of madness suggested by our laughter can greatly vary. Accusations of madness may be made lightly, paradoxically, provocatively, joyfully.

Folly – the orator of Erasmus's *Moria* – jokingly comments that men and women who marry, who choose to thrust their necks into a halter, must be a bit mad. There they are, happy married lunatics making that mad contract the be-all and end-all of their lives! Folly comments:

So you can see how much you owe to me, if you owe your life to your marriage, and your marriage to my handmaiden *Anoia*.[11]

Banter; but also a deep bow towards Socrates.

But the madness which provokes laughter is often searingly real. The very word 'folly' has taken on for us a cosy ring. The folly that Erasmus and, in his maturity, Rabelais lead us to laugh at is not restricted to amiable eccentricity; it includes it but is not limited to it. We heartily laugh also at genuine madness. In the Renaissance, that *anoia* guided those who set out to arouse the deepest forms of laughter.

But madness lies in the eye of the beholder. Those who, from the foot of the Cross, laughed at Jesus in his anguish did so because they took him for a fool.

---

is a state of false belief that is said to be ridiculous in weak people, dangerous in the strong. "Folly" is not an apt word for summing up what is said except perhaps in the case of the weak, but *ignorance* does precisely.' (Again, the emendation is not supported by any manuscript authority and is not that of Erasmus and many others in his day.)

11. *Moriæ encomium*, ed. I. B. Kan, p. 15; Amsterdam 1898, p. 80.

18

Madman Laughs at Madman

'But the mad laugh at the mad, each providing mutual enjoyment to the other.' It is Folly speaking in the *Moria* of Erasmus.

Madness is the key. Elijah laughed at the frenzied priests of Baal because he knew with prophetic certainty that they were mad; the hooligan boys who laughed at Elisha did so because they thought he – and his God – were mad. High priests, soldiers, crowds and thieves laughed at Christ during his trial and passion, sure that the wretched fellow was mad: he had insane delusions about rebuilding the Temple in three days and being the Son of God (just as today cartoonists may sketch a madman as someone who believes he is Napoleon).

As for God the Father and God the Son, from the heavens they laugh at the wicked: they know infallibly how mad they are. Christ's irony while on earth was no different. It was a form of *irrisio*. Jesus laughed or jeered at those who deserved it. The rich man in the parable was about to die, yet he went on planning to build barns in which to amass even more of this world's goods; many, like him, are irrational, mad.

Such ideas remained in force long after Plato's 'madness' had been arbitrarily changed to 'ignorance'. The ideas were satisfying; they explained so much, and they had acquired a momentum of their own. In the time of French Classicism, Molière's great comic figures are less wicked than insane. They are monomaniacs – single-issue fanatics – or, like Alceste, the melancholy misanthropist, they are medically mad.

These ideas were not restricted to Court or town: they found their way into the austere world of the Jansenists of Port-Royal.

Port-Royal was beset by enemies in Church and state. In that clannish and deeply religious house there was a moment of Christian laughter that throws a broad beam of light on the nature of Christian laughter over the ages.

The Jansenists had enemies who were zealous and highly placed. Formidable among them were the Jesuits. The Jansenists at Port-Royal were under a cloud, suspected by Louis XIV of indulging in dubious mystical practices. Cardinal Richelieu thought they were claiming superior insights from ecstasies and visions. Hoping to catch them out, the Cardinal, in hugger-mugger, dispatched his judicial commissioner to spy out the land. That commissioner was Laubardemont. (He is best known to English readers from Aldous Huxley's *Devils of Loudun*; he played a ghastly role in the exorcism of nuns said to be diabolically possessed.)

Laubardemont sneaked up one morning, hoping to catch the wise Le Maistre and his fellow Jansenists on the hop. He failed. Fontaine, who tells us of the event, writes that 'among the silly questions that the commissioner thought he was bound to ask was whether he, Monsieur Le Maistre, had ever had any visions'. Fontaine adds:

We then saw what St Jerome said of those who serve God and those who serve the world: 'Each to the other we seem insane': *Invicem insanire videmur*. There is a never-ending duel between the two.

There we find, expressed very neatly, one of the key ideas of Erasmus. Fontaine goes straight on to show how Le Maistre laughed at this snooper and his un-Christian ways. Laubardemont persisted: 'Had he ever had any visions?'

Le Maistre coldly retorted, 'Yes, he had indeed seen visions: whenever he opened one of his chamber-windows, which he pointed to, he had a vision over the hamlet of Vaumurier, and, when he opened the other window, he had a view over the hamlet of Saint-Lambert. Those were his only visions.'

His reply, taken down word for word, was seen in Paris and caused laughter at the expense of the one who had deserved it![1]

1. *Mémoires pour server à l'histoire de Port-Royal par M. Fontaine*, vol. I, Strasbourg, 1753, pp. 304, 306; followed up by C.-A. de Sainte-Beuve, *Port-Royal*, Paris, 1867, p. 496.

Invicem insanire videmur: Each to the other we seem insane. The idea, but not the actual form of words, is certainly that of Erasmus. Had Fontaine confused him with Jerome?

No. St Jerome did indeed hold that conviction. Fontaine was quoting from memory. His source is a celebrated letter of Jerome written when under a very black cloud. He addressed it to his modest, religious woman-friend Asella. Erasmus had certainly read it; he produced a famous edition of Jerome's works in which it appears with a brief introduction. He might have found in that letter, when he first read it, the germ of his own fruitful idea: he could certainly find support for it there.[2]

The famously celibate Jerome had been accused of illicit sexual relations with another of his nunnish followers, the austere and aristocratic Paula.[3] When about to shake the dust of Rome from his feet in disgust and migrate with her and her third daughter to Jerusalem, Jerome wrote a very personal letter to Asella. In it he contrasts his own austerities and those of Paula with the self-indulgent life of his unnamed accuser – a man who has a bath every day, quaffing wine and belching as he stuffs himself with duck and sturgeon; Jerome and his followers are content to fill their bellies with water and beans. His accuser lives grossly and incredibly happily within the present world: Jerome and Paula believe the Scriptures,

---

2. Migne, *Patrologia Latina*, vol. XXII, *Hieronymus Stridonensis Epistolæ*, letter XLV, *Ad Asellam*, para. 5: '*Par pari refertur, et invicem nobis videmur insanire.*' It will be seen that Jerome linked his assertion to a classical Latin proverb, *Par pari referre* ('To return like for like'). Terence cites it in his *Eunuch*, from which it appears in the *Adages* of Erasmus. I once read the whole of Jerome with that phrase of Le Maistre's in mind, but failed to spot it. (I learned a lot, though!) The phrase was turned up in no time by means of the database of Migne's complete *Patrologia Latina* in the Bodleian Library. That was done for me by Mr John Britnall, a young friend who is now an undergraduate at St Anne's College.

Curiously, Erasmus has no note on that phrase in his edition of Jerome. Nor does he allude to Jerome in his commentary in the *Adages* on *Par pari referre*.

3. Erasmus wrote a short introduction to this letter stating that Jerome had drawn obloquy on himself by persuading Paula to adopt the monastic life; 'nor was there lacking the suspicion that he was in love with her'. (He can be read in his edition of *Omnes quae extant D. Hieronymi Sindonensis Lucubrationes*, II, fol. 362, Froben, Basle, 1537.)

hold on to the Resurrection and yearn for the life hereafter. Then Jerome rhetorically invokes his accuser:

'What is that to you! But your life, on the contrary, displeases us. Go and fatten yourself up! I delight in leanness and pallor. You judge us to be wretched: we think you are more wretched still. Like is returned for like: in turn each to the other seems insane.'

The mature Jerome can be disapproving of laughter, but he knew what laughter was. As a young man he was convulsed with laughter in the lecture-room: he reminds a friend of that in a letter.[4] He was a great stylist who could indulge is diasyrm against enemies such as Jovinianus.[5] In his scriptural exegesis he is critical of present, worldly laughter. He nevertheless apparently retained an idiosyncratic laugh of his own which grated on others: in the same letter to Asella he complains that his enemies even condemned 'his very gait and his laughter'. There were others who pretended to sympathize with him in his troubles, yet in their hearts they were glad; they kissed his hand while calumniating him 'with a viper's tongue'. That echo of Job, 20:16 led Jerome straight to the second verse of the second psalm: they would not get away with it, 'The Lord saw them, and had them in derision'.

It was a source of strength to Christians to know that the sinners who laughed at them were in turn laughed at, not only by good men but by God.

Erasmus held Jerome's conception of Christian laughter to be true. Such Christian laughter within the Christian life became a pillar of his art and thought – not only in the *Moria*. But Jerome was a fourth-century Roman who accepted the norms of Roman law. He had less confidence than Erasmus in the ultimate efficacy of laughter: his calumniator was duly tortured at the behest of an ecclesiastical court – successfully, in a sense, since he went back on his evidence. But that retraction did little good to Jerome, as that saint bitterly complains; people do not believe his attacker now:

4. The letter now numbered LXVI.
5. The *Contra Jovinianum* makes sad reading today. Erasmus was so disturbed by its diasyrm that he prefaced it by an Antidote in his own edition of Jerome.

They believed him when he lied: well, why do they not believe him now that he retracts? He remains the same man! The man who now says I am innocent formerly said I was guilty, yet torture certainly squeezes the truth out better than laughter does.

With that final certainty Erasmus would not have agreed. But men like Erasmus were ill at ease in a world where Christian laughter was fighting a losing battle against Christian thumbscrews.

Jerome's notion of the mutual laughter of worldly fool and Christian fool helps us to appreciate the lasting qualities of Christian laughter as Erasmus understood it. It would have been recognized for what it was as much in fourth-century Rome as in seventeenth-century Paris.

In 1509 Erasmus had rushed to England. The promise of Andrew Ammonius and his eulogies of the young Henry VIII had led Erasmus to expect a glittering future. But he was deceived. For two long years he lived in Thomas More's house, all but invisible. There were rumours on the Continent that he was ill, perhaps dying. When he emerged from his obscurity and silence, it was with the *Moria* written in its shorter original form and with a new penchant for laughter. From now on, laughter might appear in anything he wrote – even his *Annotations on the New Testament*.

By 1511, during that long and puzzlingly silent stay in the house of Thomas More, Erasmus had produced a complex literary masterpiece. It is a comic and satirical eulogy, a praising of folly by Folly. Its original title is partly in Greek: *Moriæ encomium: stultitæ laus*. That has led to the *Praise of Folly* being conveniently called the *Moria*.

Erasmus chose the word *moria* because of its echoes. *Moria* ('foolish things') and *moros* ('fool') are words found in the Greek New Testament applied to Christians and their doctrines. *Moroi* ('fools') may be good or bad. The good are those men and women who are chosen by God yet are accounted idiots or madmen by the world. The work is dedicated to Thomas More, known by the Latin form of his name, *Morus*. Erasmus plays on the assonance of *Morus*, *moros* and *moria*: Thomas More, as his name showed, was a fool, a sound Christian one. *Moria* and *stultitia* are both rendered now-adays as 'folly', but both have far stronger senses than folly has now. They imply derangement of mind, madness, mania. Such are the defects attributed to Christians by the worldly-wise. And vice-versa.

Erasmus placed the words with which this chapter began quite early in the *Moria*. He put into the mouth of Folly words which show how deeply he agreed with St Jerome:

But the mad laugh at the mad, each providing mutual enjoyment to the other.

Although the mutual laughter may seem six of one and half-a-dozen of the other, it is not. The Christian is profoundly mad merely by the standards of the world. To the world the wicked seem wise, but are mad in the sight of God. The Christian is touched by the Infinite and will not only have the last laugh at the end of time: even now he laughs more insanely than the worldlings:

And you will often see that the greater madman laughs more distractedly at the lesser.[6]

That 'greater madman' is the Christian fool – a fool touched by God.

How much deeper a concept that is for Jerome and for Erasmus than lines of Horace which both would have known and which are sometimes cited to explain them:

Now hear why.
All who call you mad are as insane as you are.[7]

For the Renaissance Horace remained the arbiter of literary greatness. But Christian folly fingers its way into what is genuine madness for

---

6. '*Sed vicissim insanus insanum ridet, ac mutuam sibi voluptatem invicem minis-trant. Neque raro fieri videbitur ut major insanus vehementius rideat minorem.*' (In the edition of I. B. Kan, p. 72, 'Chapter 38'. In the Amsterdam edition, it is to be found on p. 118. Cf. also C. Miller, in his English translation of the *Praise of Folly* for Yale University Press, 1979, p. 60.)
7. Horace, *Satires*, II, 3, 46–7.

worldling and Christian alike. And the link of ideas between Erasmus and Jerome is much stronger than any link of either with Horace. Folly's words gain special force from their balanced repetition: *insanus insanum ridet*: maniac laughs at maniac; lunatic laughs at lunatic; madman laughs at madman. The *Moria* is built round that concept.

Erasmus brings out that mutual insanity very clearly in his theological writings. A rich example is his *Enarratio* on the first verse of the first psalm. In the Prayer Book, which follows the Hebrew, that verse reads,

Blessed is the man that hath not walked in the counsel of the ungodly, nor ˹tood in the way of sinners: and hath not sat in the seat of the scornful.

Erasmus was well aware that the Latin Vulgate talks of 'the seat of pestilence' not 'the seat of the scornful'. His *Enarratio* touches on both readings. The mutual laughter of madman at madman Erasmus sees underlying both the mocking of Elisha and the mocking of Christ. He emphasizes the *dementia* of those who 'scoff at Holy Writ'.

They do not fear to assail the simplicity of pious men with their jests, nor do they abstain from occasionally scoffing at Christ nor from impious or heretical words. What St Jerome says to be the sense of the Hebrew text here, *In the seat of the scornful*, squares well with that meaning. The blessed Jeremiah also gloried in the fact that he had never sat in the council of the scoffers. The voice is that of those who chanted *Go up, thou bald head. Go up thou bald head!* and, *If thou be the Son of God, come down now from the cross!* And the same is found in the Book of Wisdom.[8]

There, in Wisdom, we meet the foolish reprobate, astonished on the Day of Judgement to find in eternal glory the very folk whom they had once mocked in this world as maniacs.

'These were they whom we formerly held in derision and we accounted their lives madness.'[9]

8. The references are to Jeremiah, 15:17, II Kings, 2:23 and Matthew, 27:40.
9. Wisdom of Solomon, 5:3–4. (The whole chapter is relevant to mutual folly.)

For 'madness' the Vulgate uses *insania*. The worldlings had thought the elect to be mad; after death they realize that they themselves were the madmen. That passage of Wisdom was a vital text for Erasmus, a scriptural guarantee of the immortality of the soul.

'Madman laughs at madman' was no mere literary device. In matters great and small, mutual accusations of madness forever fly between the two sorts of madmen, the mad followers of Christ and the mad followers of the world. One critic took grave exception to what Erasmus wrote on Philippians, 4:8, to explain St Paul's injunction: 'Whatsoever things are pure: think on these things:

> What I wrote a certain person attacked with great guffaws and great insults, denying that I was in my senses when I wrote that. [. . .] May God grant to such slanderers that they may at some time come back to themselves.'

The Latin of that retort contains specific accusations of the kind of madness caused by a dislocation of body and soul. For his opponent Erasmus was not *apud se*, not 'at home', not in his right senses; not sane. For Erasmus it was, on the contrary, his opponent who needed to *ad se redere*, 'to come back to himself', to cease to be madly beside himself. Those are the self-same terms that Folly uses in the climax to the *Moria*.[10]

When Lopis Stunica, an editor of the Complutensian Polyglot Bible, violently attacked Erasmus for his *Moria*, it was of folly – madness – that he accused him. Having cited with horror some of the more outspoken satires in it, Stunica exclaimed that he would pass over the rest of that 'most long and most impious book'; it

---

10. *Erasmus' Annotations*, ed. Reeve, Duckworth, 1986, III, p. 631, s.v. *Hæc cogitate & agite* (addition of 1522):

Hunc locum quidam magnis cachinnis magnisque conviciis insectatur, negans me esse apud me cum hæc scriberem. [. . .] Det Dominus talibus sycophantis, ut aliquando ad se redeant.

The phrases *negans me esse apud me* and *ad se redeant* are idioms found over and over again in Erasmus and in Renaissance writers generally. Their implications are clear. They allude to various kinds of madness (including good ecstatic madness) caused by the soul's quitting, or striving to quit, its body. Erasmus was accused of being quite simply out of his mind.

was written by a man whose 'mind is disturbed and worthy to be restrained by Hippocratic fetters'.

If Julian the Apostate who in derision called Christians Galileans; if the blaspheming Porphyry or the Epicurean Celsus; if, finally, all those Gentiles who attacked the Church of Christ with curses and insults should come back from Hell: why! all of them together would not disgorge such bitterness and virulence as it spewed forth against all orders of Christians in that one single book, by Erasmus of Rotterdam alone.[11]

But Erasmus, too, in the *Moria* had found theologians such as Lopis Stunica to be insane, mere devotees of worldly folly. That is why the wise, personified Socratic-Christian Folly laughs at them.

Stunica, for his part, was convinced that Erasmus was a case for the straitjacket. For him Erasmus was so mad that doctors should get out their manacles and force them upon him. Erasmus, for his part, judged the railing against Jesus to have been 'insane commotions'. Stunica's accusations against him were of the same kind. Men who rail thus are paid back in kind: God laughs them to scorn.[12]

Biblical scholarship strengthened such a contention. The preacher in Ecclesiastes says of laughter, 'It is mad.' In his *Commentary on Ecclesiastes*, Lorinus explained that the Vulgate talks of 'mindless madness' here. The Chaldean version uses a term meaning derision or scorn. The Greek Septuagint should perhaps read 'insanity'.[13] In Ecclesiastes laughter is personified:

The original Hebrew word is a particle addressed to Laughter: 'You are mad'; or, 'You cause madness'; or, 'You are driven mad'. It derives from *halal*, from which is formed *Hallelujah*, which is a most happy chant fringing on madness – a madness which is spiritual and holy.

It was of such laughter that Gregory of Nyssa used the word *insania*.[14]

---

11. H. J. De Jonge, 'Four unpublished letters on Erasmus', in Jean-Pierre Massaut (ed.), *Colloque érasmien de Liège*, Paris, 1987, p. 160.
12. *Enarratio in psalmum II*, LB, 5, col. 211C: '*Illi insani tumultus*'.
13. The terms used are *amentia*, *derisio*, and *paraphora*.
14. The principal verse is Ecclesiastes, 2:2 Cf. J. Lorinus, *Commentarii in Ecclesiasticen*, Moguntae, 1607, pp. 63–4.

St Jerome was sure that the laughter condemned by Ecclesiastes as mad is laughter such as Jesus said would be turned to weeping. There is a time for laughing: 'Blessed are they that weep, for they shall laugh'. That time is not in this world: it is in the world to come.[15]

Viguerius, who accepted Erasmus's conception of worldly wisdom as sheer madness, puts it almost epigrammatically:

Such wisdom is contrasted with good folly – with that contempt for the things of this earth for which Christ, who despised things earthly and worldly, was called a fool.[16]

Luther laughed at those idiots who took literally Christ's reply to the lawyer who cited the Ten Commandments: 'This do, and thou shalt live.' But of course, as he was the first to acknowledge, his opponents laughed back at him: they turn Christ into Moses and God's free grace into a new Mosaic law. The 'papists and the fanatics' do nothing but that. It is their entire doctrine:

They laugh at us who, with such diligence, inculcate and encourage faith saying, 'Ha! ha! Faith! You just wait until you get to heaven by faith!'[17]

They laugh at Luther, sure that he is mad: Luther, certain that he has God on his side, finds those 'papists and fanatics' even more laughable.

15. St Jerome, commenting on Ecclesiastes 2 and 3.
16. J. Viguerius, *Institution of Natural and Christian Theology*, Antwerp, 1565, p. 130: '*Huic sapientia opponitur stultitia bona, quae est contemptus terrenorum, de qua Christus, qui terrena et mundana contempsit, dicitur fuisse stultus.*'
17. *Luthers Werke. Weimarer Ausgabe*, XL, p. 250 (*Commentaries on Galatians*, 2:17).

19

Laughing at Christ and
Laughing at Carabba

As we read Erasmus or Rabelais centuries later their laughter at madness may pose few moral problems. The people held up to ridicule are removed from us by time, dress and manners. We are not the people being called insane by Jerome, Erasmus, Luther, Stunica, Rabelais, or by any of the great tribe of theological laughers. Yet if 'madman laughs at madman', laughter – past as well as present and future – touches all folk everywhere. For those who believe in the truth of that saying, all of us are mad in one sense or another.

The laughter directed at Christ on the Cross is deeply disturbing because it involves us. The laughers show no pity: neither do they deserve any. Pity is incompatible with laughter welling up at the foot of the Cross. The mad laughs at the mad. And we are all mad. What makes laughter good or evil is its target.

The laughter at Jesus as a madman as he writhed on the Cross is evil: Jesus is supremely good; Jesus is King. But what if he had been clinically insane? What if he had been simply deluded? A fool convinced he is supremely good and insane enough to believe he was a king can rightly be laughed at, or so it was believed. That can be seen from the long section on laughter in the *Harmoniae evangelicae* of Gerard Vossius. The opinions he expresses were widely held.

Gentiles, we are told, are accustomed to laugh at Christians, 'who place their trust in the Crucified'. The example given of a scoffing pagan is Lucian, in his *Passing of Peregrinus*. Let him mock: Paul knew nothing but Christ crucified. Christ was given a crown of thorns in mockery: yet he is King indeed.

Vossius identifies four categories of people who mocked at Jesus. In the first were those who wagged their heads and taunted him about rebuilding the Temple in three days, laughing, and urging him to come down from the Cross. The second comprises the chief priests, who scoffed, saying, 'He saved others: himself he cannot save.' They acted 'impiously and, indeed, stupidly'.[1] Men in their position must have known that it is not normal for prophets and holy men who place their trust in God to be miraculously snatched from present perils. In the third are the soldiers who said, 'If thou art King of the Jews, save thyself.' The final category contains one of the thieves who, in Luke 23, railed at him, 'If thou be Christ, save thyself and us.'

At this very point Vossius chooses to relate what for him is a funny story. He tells of a case of acceptable mockery to be contrasted with the wicked mockery of Jesus on the Cross; he invites us to make a comparison. To compare with the mocking of Christ 'what Philo of Alexandria relates about a man called Carabba, may be neither useless nor unenjoyable':

Carabba was not quite *compos mentis*; day and night, put off by neither heat nor cold, he would walk naked at the crossroads. He was the butt of the laughter of boys and of youths with nothing to do.

They once propelled that wretched man towards the school and placed a papyrus crown on his head, draped his shoulders with a rush-mat as with a purple mantle and thrust a reed into his hand to act as a sceptre. Having thus made him into a comic king, the youths crowded round him, bearing him on their shoulders as though they formed his retinue. Some bowed to him; others begged him for justice; others consulted him on matters of state. Afterwards they stood round him crying *Makim*, which in Syria means *Lord*.

But now to get on with Christ . . .[2]

---

1. The words he uses are *impie profecto, atque etiam stulte*.
2. Vossius, *Opera*, Amsterdam, 1701; vol. VI, *Harmoniae Evangelicae*, II, v, § 22–3; p. 194, § 46; II, viii, §§ 12–17. Vossius cites this 'from Philo's book *Against Flaccus*'.

20

Laughing Back

Christians are both laughed at and laughing. Few things would be easier than to pile up, from pagan and Christian writings drawn from many cultures over many centuries, proof that, for many, the fundamental teachings of Christianity are insane and laughable. Not only the doctrines of the Resurrection and the Kingdom of God can be condemned as mad or foolish by pagans, heretics or atheists: almost everything in the Bible, the Creeds and mature theology can be, has been, and is.

In the Christian sources, expressly or implicitly, such scoffing is of course deemed to be wrong and often daft. The shepherds who came to the manger seemed foolish, but Christians know better:

The shepherds thanked God they had seen Christ, although in the depth of his humiliation; as afterwards the cross of Christ, so now in his *manger*, though to some it was *foolishness* and a *stumbling-block*, yet others saw in it, and admired, and praised the *wisdom of God*, and the *power of God*.[1]

If Erasmus is right in his contention that madman laughs at madman, then those who laugh at Christians must positively be seen to be mad. Their madness may not be as obvious as that of the world-renouncing followers of Christ. If they cannot be shown to be mad, all the laughter is one way: from the world to the Church and her Master.

The Scriptures themselves provide ample texts to embroider with

---

1. Matthew Henry, *Commentary*, on Luke, 2:8–20. Matthew Henry's great nonconformist commentaries first appeared in 1708–10.

this theme. In the Old Testament, 'fool' often implies sinner; 'folly' and 'foolishness', sinfulness.[2]

The greatest obstacle to the grasping of spiritual truths is that they are indeed spiritual, while the worldly man remains stupidly carnal. As St Paul taught: 'a man who is unspiritual refuses what belongs to the Spirit of God: it is folly to him'. Such things can be judged only in the light of the Spirit.[3] As for the Old Testament, year in, year out, as the psalms are sung, the words of *Dixit insipiens* (psalm 14) come to mind: 'The fool hath said in his heart, "There is no God."' Not the wicked: the *nabal*, the empty fool.

An hour or two with biblical concordances, now as in the past, will suffice to open up a long series of texts where 'fool', 'folly' and so on are condemned in terms of sin.[4] Over and over again in Christian controversy the vocabulary of madness is applied to enemies and heretics.

Whenever laughter is permitted to Christians, laughter at anti-Christian worldly fools and heretics may find a place in it. The worldliness and the heresy are judged from the standpoint of the laughter. Two stray examples may suffice.[5]

First, Bishop Severianus – a mediocre thinker – writing on Genesis, 1:26, 'Let us make man in our own image'. His brief comments occur in his treatise *On the Creation of the World*. He states a standard interpretation: there are deep mysteries revealed in God's injunction, 'Let *us* make man in *our* own image.' To the initiate the grammar proves the truth of the doctrine of the Trinity; God did not say 'Let *me* make'; he said, 'Let *us* make'. That plural reveals the nature of the Trinity: one Person of the Trinity is addressing the other Two.

---

2. The principal Hebrew words translated as 'fool' in the Authorized Version are *halal* (boaster), *evil* (fool), *nabal* (an empty or vile person), *sakal* (a thick-head).

3. I Corinthians, 2:14; New English Bible version.

4. I owe a lifetime debt to an old edition of Cruden's *Concordance* (Berwick, 1818); to F. P. Dutripon's *Concordantiae Bibliorum Sacrorum*, Paris, 1840; and to R. Young's *Analytical Concordance of the Holy Bible*, London, 1879; eighth revised edition, London, 1939.

5. They were not sought for but stumbled across during one week's desultory reading. Literally thousands of examples could be cited.

But he also said, 'according to *our own image*'. Despite the plural *our*, the word *image* is in the singular. That reveals the unity of the Persons in the Godhead. Bishop Severianus is sure that his exegesis is right. Faced with such truth, we are told, 'heretics go mad'.[6] For the madness of those heretics the bishop uses the same Greek verb as Festus the judge applied to St Paul when he called him insane.[7]

Many centuries after Bishop Severianus, and in another tradition, the Reverend John Trapp writes on 'Who is wise, and he shall understand these things' (Hosea, 14:9). He comments thus:

Not many wise, wise I mean to Salvation, 2 *Tim. 3:15*, that make sure work of their souls, and draw their wisdom from God's holy word, from the mine of the mystery of Christ.

All others are foolish people, sottish children: they have no understanding, be they never so shrewd and of deep reach for the world, be they never so wise in this generation; the fox is so in his.

That exactly exemplifies 'Madman laughs at madman', since Trapp had already explained that notion in terms of good Christian madness apropos of Zechariah, 3:8, 'For they are men wondered at.' (The worldly laugh and wonder at God's followers whom they take to be idiots.) After citing Calvin he writes of the madness of true believers:

They were 'for signes and wonders in Israel'. Esay 8.18, hissed and hooted at, Psal. 71.7. as those that affected to be singular, and seraphicall. They think it strange, saith Saint *Peter* to his holy converts, '*that you run not with them the same excesse of riot*, speaking evil of you', as if you were no better than *mad-men*, Esay 59.15. robb'd of your right minds, as the word signifieth.

'There is,' he adds, 'a French proverb: *He that would have his neighbours' dog hang'd gives out that it is mad.*'

6. Such exegetical practices remained current during the Renaissance. The same contentions are found in Agostino Steucho.
7. αἱρετικοὶ μαίνονται (in Migne, *Patrologia Graeca*; John Chrysostom, *Opera*, vol. VI, Paris, 1869, col. 465, § [474]. Cf. Acts, 26:4.

In our wretched dayes (as the Turks count all fools to be saints, so) people account all saints to be fools.

Many moralists were mocked thus in their own 'wretched dayes'. Paul had armed us to expect as much. Does he not say:

We are made a *theatre* or are set upon the stage for a laughing-stock unto the world.[8]

8. I Corinthians, 4:9. John Trapp, *Commentary or Exposition upon the XII Minor Prophets*, London, 1654, p. 521.

21

Christ as Divine Madman

Jesus was a madman for his family, on one occasion at least. It is one of the great paradoxes of Christian laughter that it led Christians to emphasize the madness not only of Christians but of Christ.

The worldly-wise laugh at Christians; human beings laugh at real or perceived madness; what the worldly-wise laugh at in Jesus – not only as he hung on the Cross – is the sheer lunacy they see in him. The world admires money, power, self-interest, success: Christians, in so far as they turn their back on such values and hold them to be at best indifferent, are turning the world upside down and may indeed seem mad.

A learned theologian such as Johannes Viguerius brings that out well in the rather cramped but learned Latin of his *Institutions of Natural and Christian Philosophy*.[1] He saw that, in the eyes of the worldly-wise, the unworldly Jesus could appear to be a mere fool, a madman. So too, in better Latin, wrote Erasmus. But such unworldliness in Jesus is less than half the story. To the man who places his glory in his wealth and his power, the man of contemplation who despises riches and power and who cares for the poor and weak may certainly seem daft; but would he seem mad enough to be forced into chains as a raving lunatic? Yes. For Erasmus – and not only for Erasmus – that is biblical truth.[2]

Lopis Stunica believed that the Erasmus of the *Praise of Folly*

---

1. Antwerp, 1565.
2. Cf. M.A.S., *Erasmus: Ecstasy and the Praise of Folly*, Penguin Books, 1988, p. 71.

deserved to be constrained in 'Hippocratic fetters'. Erasmus, if he knew of those snarls against him, would have realized that he was in good company. Jesus too was believed to have been worthy of such restraint.

The starting event in the Gospels which led Erasmus – as well as some before him and many after him – to see Jesus acting as mad occurs in the third chapter of St Mark:

Then Jesus cometh home. And the multitude cometh together again, so that they could not even eat bread. And when his family heard it, they went out to lay hold of him: for they said, 'He is beside himself.'

The Greek is ambiguous here on one important point: not so much over the madness but over who made the accusations. The Authorized Version states that it was 'they' who said, 'He is beside himself.' The word *they* apparently refers to the members of Jesus's family. (His mother and brethren are mentioned elsewhere in the chapter.) But the Greek words translated as *they* can mean something else. It need not be *they* in the sense of his family, but simply *his friends*. Or it can be even vaguer: *they* in an unspecified gossiping sense – '*They* were saying' (as in the English; 'Whatever will they say!').

Any of those senses is possible. Following a tradition more completely at home in the Greek Church than in the Latin, Erasmus held that it was *they* in the sense of Christ's mother and brethren who came out to restrain Jesus. Indeed they 'came out with chains to bind him'. Those alleging that Jesus was mad were his earthly kith and kin. That makes the accusation more poignant. The words used in the Authorized Version, 'He is beside himself', may no longer convey the full seriousness of the accusation. 'He is mad', or, 'He is out of his mind', are clearer translations.

In his *System of True Theology* Erasmus wrote: 'the kinsfolk of Jesus are ready to cast him into chains, saying, as we read in Mark, 3: "He is raving mad".' For him, Jesus appeared to his brethren mad enough to tie up.

Whoever 'they' were, they were convinced that Jesus was at the very least out of his mind: others – the scribes who had come down from Jerusalem – believed that he was diabolically mad and in league with the Devil: 'He hath Beelzebub.' To them Jesus retorted, 'How can Satan cast out Satan?'

The atmosphere conveyed by Mark's Gospel at this point is one of unhealthy mass excitement, with diabolical influences at work in the foreground. The crowds following Jesus as he cured the sick were so great that he planned to slip away in a boat. But 'unclean spirits' fell at his feet shouting, 'You are the Son of God.' Jesus sharply ordered them not to disclose that truth. And he commissioned the twelve disciples with authority to drive out devils. When his family learned of all this, 'they set out to take charge of him. "He is out of his mind," they said.'

In his New Testament *Annotations*, Erasmus comments that Christ's relatives believed they were but doing their duty. They were convinced that Jesus, their kinsman, was insane.

The Latin word Erasmus used for those relatives is *agnati*. It helps us to grasp the disturbing truths which Erasmus found in this episode. Christ's mother and brethren, he holds, were doing what the law of the occupying Romans required. 'For it is the duty of the *agnati*,' he explained, to restrain a relation 'if he becomes mentally deranged'.

In law, *agnati* means kinsmen in a restricted sense. They are such kinsmen on the father's side as were under the authority of the paterfamilias, or would be if he were alive. Roman law had long placed important responsibilities on them. Some legal authorities such as Accursius placed that obligation to look after a mad relation on to both paternal and maternal relations. Many in the time of Erasmus would have followed him in that.[3]

When Erasmus came to the third chapter of Mark in his *Paraphrases*, he was even more explicit.

Moreover, since they were in *agnati*, they believed it was their duty, according to the laws of men, to restrain him with chains, as one who was out of his mind or possessed by a spirit.

---

3. Cf. the strictures of Guillaume Budé in his *Annotationes in Pandectas* (*Ex tit. De Verborum significatione, s.v. 'Nam cum dicitur apud veteres AGNATORVM GENTILIVMQVE'*) in *Opera Omnia*, Basle, 1557 (Gregg reprint, Farnborough, 1966), III, p. 390.

defence of his life in riches. The man who, for the Gospel, willingly exposes himself to exile, poverty, imprisonment, torturing and death, in hope of eternal blessedness, is a lunatic for the man who does not believe that, after this life, there is a more blessed one for the pious. He who spurns the honours of princes and of the people so as to obtain glory with God, is mad for those who really are mad.

But Jesus seemed more mad even than that.[9]

9. Erasmus, *Paraphrases on the New Testament*, LB, 7, 183DF; also, M.A.S., *Erasmus: Ecstasy and the Praise of Folly*, Penguin Books, 1988, p. 71.

22

Madness Providentially Feigned
by David: a Silenus

For a more developed meditation on Christ's madness Erasmus turns
to the psalms. Christian exegetes found Christ everywhere in the
Old Testament, not least in the psalms. In them, Erasmus uncovered,
half hidden, half revealed, the mad Christ of the Christians. In his
meditation on the psalms, Erasmus (who was never at ease with
Hebrew) allowed himself the freedom to range widely over the whole
field of his Christian convictions. He does so very movingly in his
reflections on the psalm *Benedicam Domino*.[1]

Benedicam Domino is indeed a very special psalm. Matthew Pole
in his *Synopsis Criticorum* stresses that it is 'full of doctrine and
consolation: the more it is read the sweeter it becomes, as Basil said
of all Scripture'. It was one of the most frequently cited texts of the
Old Testament.

Erasmus can readily link this psalm with the madness of Christ
because of its title in the Latin Vulgate. 'A psalm of David when
David changed his countenance before Abimelech'.[2] The force of
the expression 'changed his countenance' lies in the fact that it means
'he feigned madness'. Erasmus knew that. Modern versions often
emphasize it.

The allusion in the title of the psalm is to an episode in I Samuel
21. David, terrified, sought refuge by pretending to be mad: 'He feigned

1. The 33rd (34th) psalm: 'I will always give thanks unto the Lord'.
2. *Psalmus David quum David mutavit vultum suum coram Abimelech*. The Vulgate
does indeed refer here to Abimelech not Ahimelech. (Abimelech means 'Father of
the king', or 'My father is a king', while Ahimelech means 'Brother of the king',
or 'My brother is a king'.)

himself mad in their hands', scrabbling at the door and dripping saliva. Achish – here identified with Abimelech – angrily said to his servants, 'Lo, ye see the man is mad. Why have ye brought him to me. Have I need of madmen?' So David was allowed to go; and he escaped to the cave of Abdullam. Erasmus believed that this violent episode in the life of David bore hidden truths for Christians. David was a type, prefiguring Jesus himself. God in his providence wished it so.

Erasmus saw much of the Old Testament as a Silenus, an idea and a word later seized upon by Rabelais in the Prologue to *Gargantua*. Erasmus explains its meaning in his commentary on the adage 'the Sileni of Alcibiades'. The expression goes back to Plato's dialogue the *Symposium*. Socrates was divinely wise but very ugly; in the *Symposium*, Alcibiades compared him to little images of Silenus, the gross, wine-swigging follower of Bacchus. Those images were ugly on the outside, being covered with strange carvings; but they were hollow and could be opened up. Inside, was the figure of a god.

Such was Socrates. Penetrate into the man behind his ugly and absurd exterior and once you had, as it were, opened him up you would find a 'great, high, truly philosophical soul'. Sublime but beggarly-looking characters in Antiquity, such as Antisthenes and Diogenes, were all Sileni. 'But,' asks Erasmus, 'was Christ not the most extraordinary Silenus of all?' The prophet Isaiah (53:3) foresaw that truth when he wrote prophetically of the Messiah, 'He hath no beauty or comeliness: and there is no beauty that we should desire him.' Yet inside that Silenus who is Christ are untold riches: divine wisdom and life everlasting.

Erasmus judged that the very Scriptures have their own Sileni. The Old Testament is full of externally ugly stories which contain within them hidden God-given truths. The creation story in Genesis, taken literally, is no better than a ridiculous fable out of Homer. Yet within that 'ridiculous' tale lie everlasting verities. Even Christ's parables could seem the work of a simple, ignorant man: yet they too are Sileni: inside them is to be found boundless wisdom.[3]

3. There is a complete translation of the *Sileni Alcibiades* in Margaret Mann Phillips's excellent book, *The Adages of Erasmus*, Cambridge University Press, 1964, pp. 269ff.

Erasmus treated as such a Silenus David's feigned madness. Indeed, David's entire life was such a Silenus. It both prefigured and hid the glory of Christ. The value of both the psalm and the episode in I Samuel, 21, to which it refers, lies for Erasmus in their hidden correspondences with Christ's life on earth: if as Christians we read those texts in a spiritual way, we shall find revealed to our astonished eyes a sublime David. We shall find Christ himself. Within David, that 'fugitive, hungry man, *changing his countenance* and exposed to so many perils, we shall see him who is truly called King of Heaven and earth, the Lord Jesus Christ'.[4] Yet David who prefigured that King of Heaven and earth was rejected by Achish:[5]

'Lo, ye see the man is mad. . . . Have I need of madmen that ye have brought this fellow to play the madman in my presence!'

Those words applied to David: they apply to Jesus.

4. This psalm is treated in M.A.S., *Erasmus: Ecstasy and the Praise of Folly*, Penguin Books, 1988, ch. 6.
5. I Samuel, 21:14–15.

23

Theophylact and
a Lunatic's Chains

But where do those fetters and chains come from which the kinsmen of Jesus brought out with them? It is arresting – even troubling – that Erasmus should mention chains brought out to restrain Jesus. Those chains emphasize as nothing else the frenzied madness attributed to our Lord. Yet no chains are even hinted at by Mark, and by our standards Mark is our only source.

Erasmus found those chains in the Old Testament. Once more we can see how the Old Testament supplies details to complement the New. Those details were put there, he was sure, by the Holy Ghost. Erasmus was completing what is told by Mark. That vital detail was provided by the prophet Ezekiel. Erasmus was put on to him by one of his favourite guides to understanding the Scriptures, Theophylact. Behind Theophylact stood the tradition of John Chrysostom.

Theophylact tells how Jesus's family, believing him to be diabolically insane, 'came out to fetter him'.[1] The verb used by him is a powerful one, with a clear implication of physical restraint. But Theophylact did not invent the chains; he found them in Scripture. They are to be uncovered hidden in what Erasmus would no doubt have called the Silenus of Ezekiel, 3:25:

But thou, O Son of Man, behold, they shall put bonds upon thee, and shall bind thee with them, and thou shalt not go out among them.

Jesus is the Son of Man. Ezekiel had foretold what would happen to him as told in the Gospel according to St Mark.

1. In his exegesis of Mark, 3, 20–22.

93

Long after Erasmus, great and learned exegetes continued to explain that text of Ezekiel as Theophylact had done, linking it to the madness of Jesus. They further linked it to another apparently mad prefiguration of Christ.[2] That foreshadow of Christ was the obscure 'son of the prophet' sent by Elisha, without warning or explanation, to anoint as king the astonished Jehu in Ramoth-Gilead. As he carried out his mad-seeming task, the men about Jehu clamoured: 'Wherefore came this mad fellow to thee?'

That 'mad fellow' too was a 'figure' of Christ. And so we read in Matthew Pole's *Synopsis Criticorum*:

And they shall bind thee: that is, 'they', your friends and members of your family, thinking you foolish and insane when they saw you so attentive and as though amazed and keeping away from people. Cf. II Kings, 9:11, *Wherefore cometh this mad fellow to thee?* and Mark, 3:21: *For, they said, he is beside himself.*[3]

In the minds of those who scoured their Old Testament for prefigurations of Christ such texts interpenetrate and enrich each other. Many later commentators explained those texts exactly as Theophylact, Erasmus or, say, Grotius did. The words 'Wherefore came this mad fellow to thee?' lead to reflections on the fact that 'prophets were considered demented and insane'. Pagan prophets, as Cicero and Plato showed, were indeed possessed by *dæmons*: Jehovah's are not:

They were considered insane because of the chosen harshness of their lives and their garments and because of their contempt for the things of this world.[4]

For Erasmus Jesus really did seem insane – not only when he was mocked on the Cross by the titters of the mob which swell into

2. II Kings, 9:11.
3. The exegetes listed as supporting this interpretation are some of the greatest in their days: Tirinus, Cornelius à Lapide, Sanctius and Menochius.
4. Matthew Pole, *Synopsis Criticorum*, Utrecht, 1684–6, I, 637–8; III, 1069. A veritable galaxy of critics are listed who support that interpretation, including Piscator, Peter Martyr, Vatable, Menochius and Grotius; to whom we could add many of the direct followers of Erasmus.

guffaws in Handel's *Messiah*: he was (as the prophet foretold) mocked in a sense by his own family when they thought he needed fetters.

That is why Erasmus can write in complete confidence, in full assurance of faith, that 'Christ [*Christ*, not David] *changed his countenance* for us in Holy Writ'. That is, he was taken for yet another madman.

As such he would be good for a laugh.[5]

5. Cf. M.A.S., *Erasmus: Ecstasy and the Praise of Folly*, Penguin Books, 1988, pp. 225-6.

24

Laughing with the Great
Cardinal of Saint-Cher

In a very special way Erasmus associated his entire theology with the theme of the madness of Christianity; of the folly of the Gospel; of the madness of Christ. He had forerunners in this, and he is not always fair to them.

Every reader of the *Moria* and of his *Annotations on the New Testament* knows of his amused contempt for the scholarship of Hugo Carrensis – Hugh, the great Cardinal of Saint-Cher. It may come as a surprise to discover that some of the central preoccupations of Erasmus are firmly embedded in the exegesis of that medieval Cardinal, whose works he must have often had open before him.

Hugo's Latin lacks the elegance and clarity of Erasmus's subtle style. He himself lacks the vital injection into his theology of the knowledge of Greek and of the christianized platonism which revolutionized the thought of Erasmus: but Old and New Testament texts which mattered to Erasmus are linked together in similar ways. Erasmus had certainly read them in him. Hugo notes that when Mark alludes to those who came out to 'lay hold on' Jesus, St Bernard adds: 'as a madman'. Other comments, longer, are as challenging. In one, Hugo starts off with words from Mark, 3:21, 'And when they heard':

Would that his disciples had *laid hold on him* with prayers, lest his vengeance turn to fury. Isaiah, 64 [7]: *And there is none that called upon thy name that stirreth himself to lay hold of thee.* For that is the way that it pleased God 'to be laid hold on'.

We are a world away from 'gentle Jesus, meek and mild'.

Hugo evokes Ezekiel, 22, and Exodus, 32:10, 'Let me alone, that my wrath may wax hot against them.' He then turns to Mark, 3:21, 'He is beside himself.' His horizons are narrower than those of Erasmus, but the question of madness is there:

He is beside himself. Thus even to-day it happens that when parents see one of their family listening to lectures on theology they say he is insane or stupid: they would rather that he heard lectures on lucrative subjects, not worrying that he might lose his soul as long as he makes his parents rich.

Such folk, he asserts, are actually calling Jesus mad; elsewhere they call him a wine-bibber, an apparition (as when he walked on water), and so on.

And we too call him mad when we believe that one of his servants who does good and preaches well is a fool. Luke, 10: *He who despiseth you, despiseth me . . .*

Of this it is said *And he let his spittle fall down on his beard,* by which is signified the copiousness of preaching. *And Achis said to his servants, 'Lo, ye see the man is mad'* and II Kings, 9: *'Wherefore came this mad fellow to thee?'*[1]

Erasmus, in what is probably the only – very indirect – admission of indebtedness to the Cardinal whom he so regularly mocked, notes that 'some' strive to apply all the detail of David's assumed madness to Christ, including the spittle dribbling down into his beard: a pious enterprise, but scriptural allegories often contain irrelevant detail.[2]

But the convergence of Hugo Carrensis and Erasmus over the madness of Christ and its foreshadowing in David is revealing. The schools of Hugo and of Erasmus represent opposing strands within the Church. Both could conclude that worldly men would find Christ mad. Both find that those who follow him must expect to be laughed at.

---

1. *Postillae domini Hugonis Cardinalis super quattuor Evangelia,* Mark 3, ad loc. The fuller references are to Luke, 10:16; I Samuel (I Kings), 21:13; ibid., verse 14; II [IV] Kings, 9:11.
2. Cf. M.A.S., *Erasmus: Ecstasy and the Praise of Folly,* Penguin Books, 1988, p. 230 and context.

25

Jesus in Ecstatic Madness

Paintings of mystics rapt in ecstasy adorn many a baroque church and arrest us in many an art gallery. In them saints, half swooning, gazing heavenwards, are clearly 'not all there'. They are caught up outside themselves; enraptured. The apparent madness of Jesus in chapter three of Mark's Gospel was seen by some as just such an ecstasy. If that were so, then when the relatives of Jesus came out with their physical restraints, the Lord is his manhood was caught away to the Father. That is one of the possible meanings of 'He is beside himself'.

The madness of Christ was neither an invention of Erasmus nor of a relatively minor Western tradition. The Renaissance in Western Europe saw an influx of Greek-speaking Christians, including Orthodox monks, nuns and married priests. They came as refugees from Byzantium as the eastern Roman Empire was rolled back in the fifteenth century and finally destroyed by the Turks. They brought with them their knowledge of the Greek Fathers, and they had a comprehensive understanding of the New Testament in the original Greek. For them, the authoritative Old Testament was above all the Septuagint. They also brought with them a theology of the Christian life which encouraged the practising of a kind of inspired madness; it afforded an important place to saintly men and women who sought to appear and act insane, who (in the words of St Paul) made themselves 'fools for Christ's sake'.[1]

Another medieval theologian giggled at and devalued by Erasmus

---

1. I Corinthians, 4:10.

is Nicholas of Lyra.[2] Erasmus was unfair to him. Luther, and exegetes in general, held him in high regard. His knowledge of Hebrew far outshone Erasmus's. In matters of Christian folly he was already on the same track as Erasmus, who never acknowledged any debt to him. Despite his weaknesses and errors, which Erasmus delighted to throw into relief, he too wrote fascinating comments on the madness of Jesus in the third chapter of Mark.

He explained that the kindred of Jesus on his mother's side witnessed Christ's 'unwonted ferment'. That ferment caused Jesus to skip his meals. It manifested itself in his zealous preaching. 'His kindred also saw the unusual shine on his face: it arose from the power of his divinity.' With that 'shining face', Nicholas was assimilating what was happening to Jesus when his relatives came to lay hands on him with what was to happen at the Transfiguration. Then the countenance of Jesus became 'shining like the sun'.[3]

That assimilation could only displease Erasmus: he was persuaded that Jesus hid his divinity until, precisely at the Transfiguration, he partly revealed it to a few chosen disciples. Nicholas explains that the kindred of Jesus 'also heard him talking of difficult matters concerning things divine'; they were unusual matters, which they did not understand. 'So they thought Jesus was talking as a man who was raving, a man who was raging mad.'

The Latin words that Nicholas uses here are appropriate to extreme lunacy: *arrepticius* ('raving') and *furiosus* ('raging mad'). The first is essentially a Church-Latin word. It would bring to mind its sole appearance in the Vulgate, where it is rendered in English as 'man that raveth'.

... for every *man that raveth*, and maketh himself a prophet, thou shouldest put him in prison and in the stocks.[4]

The use of the word 'stocks' by Nicholas of Lyra would evoke a

---

2. Nicholas of Lyra's texts can be read in any edition of his *Postilla on the Four Gospels*, under Mark 3, or else in *Biblia Maxima*, The Hague, vol. XIIII, ad loc.
3. Matthew, 17, and the parallel accounts in the other Gospels.
4. Jeremiah, 29:26. For 'every man that raveth' the Latin Vulgate reads *omnem virum arrepticium*.

madman exposed to public ridicule. A man in the stocks is there for passers-by to laugh at. Nicholas implies that Jesus was taken to be a lunatic to be shackled and laughed at. Such a man was thought to be 'driven by demons not by the Spirit of God'.[5] It is not surprising then that Nicholas should conclude:

They therefore wished to lay hold on Jesus and to bind him, lest he should harm himself and others.

Nicholas's second word, *furiosus*, is as strong as you can get. It means here violently mad, raging as the Furies rage. Calvin explains that the man who is *arrepticius* – raving – would be restrained by 'manacles of iron'. Grotius and others take it to refer to a madman diabolically possessed – which is its implication in Nicholas of Lyra.[6] Calvin is of the same opinion, while insisting that the kinsfolk of Jesus were motivated throughout by a misplaced sense of duty and piety.

Since true Old Testament prophets were at times accused of being 'out of their minds' some theologians accepted that *arrepticius* could even refer to someone prophesying under the influence of the Holy Ghost.[7] Vatable and some Anglican critics support that contention. As Nicholas of Lyra could not fail to know – but Erasmus might have known – the Hebrew original translated in the Vulgate by *arrepticius* links together good, bad and feigned prophetic madness. It is used for the pretended madness of David but also of the true man of God whom the mob takes for an arrant fool.[8]

Nicholas of Lyra was the hero of the Franciscans; Hugo Carrensis, of the Dominicans; Erasmus, of the Humanists. They differed funda-

---

5. Calvin, Grotius and Vatable support that interpretation. See Matthew Pole, *Synopsis Criticorum*, Utrecht, 1684, ad loc.
6. Pole, *Synopsis Criticorum*, III, 878–9.
7. The word for 'out of their minds' is *amentes*.
8. The term is *shaga*. Cf. Jeremiah, 29:26 (cited above); Hosea, 9:7 (for the multitude, 'the spiritual man is mad'); and II Kings, 9:11 (for the feigned madness of David already mentioned). (Robert Young's *Analytical Concordance of the Bible* has an index-lexicon to the Old Testament, in which the Hebrew terms are conveniently transliterated and placed in alphabetical order.)

mentally on many things, but on one thing they did agree: all contributed to the certainty that the incarnate Son of God acted in ways which made even his earthly brethren believe he was mad. At best, Jesus was beside himself in ecstasy.

26

Lessons in Exegesis

LEFÈVRE D'ÉTAPLES

The Erasmian doctrine of the madness of Christ was so widely accepted by theologians of so many churches that it is wise to recall that there were a few dissenting voices. Erasmus's French rival for international esteem, Lefèvre d'Étaples, could not accept such bold ideas. Despite his very real Greek and Hebrew scholarship, he tended to slant his biblical texts towards traditional orthodoxy. In his own commentaries on the third chapter of Mark he concedes that those who came out to lay hold on Jesus were his mother and his kinsmen, but he insisted that the Blessed Virgin was already fully cognizant of her Son's true Godhead. She merely pretended to consider him mad. She did so to set an example of motherly care. Neither the Virgin nor the kinsmen said of Jesus, 'he is beside himself' and 'acting like a fool'. It was 'they', the pharisaic slanderers:

It was those who said of Jesus 'He hath Beelzebub.' Him whom Scripture calls the 'Wisdom of God' they alleged to be struck down by raving madness and insanity, or at least by delirium and mental agitation, and that as blasphemously as impiously.[1]

Lefèvre avoids the word *agnati*, indeed any term which could suggest that the brethren of Jesus had a duty to restrain him. But however much he exculpated the Virgin and the brethren, the

---

1. The references are to Mark, 3:22 and to St Paul, I Corinthians, 1:24.

accusation remained: Jesus was said by someone to be delirious and mad.[2]

MANY MEANS ONE

Erasmus could build on the foundations laid by Nicholas of Lyra, Hugo Carrensis and even Lefèvre d'Étaples, but he outstripped them all on the theme of Christ's madness. His were the ideas pillaged by Cornelius Jansen, Bishop of Ghent; his were the ideas which (once his name had been expunged) Gulielmus Estius, in his Commentaries on the New Testament, could take over without recognizing their source; his were the ideas which found their way into Robert Burton's *Anatomy of Melancholy* and into English religious pamphlets.

Johannes Maldonat, a Jesuit theologian who was an admired friend of Michel de Montaigne and one of the most learned men of his day, supported Erasmus's exegesis. He easily dismissed those who desperately tried to make the Greek of Mark mean not 'He is beside himself' but 'He is not here' or 'He has gone away'. Theoretically the words could just possibly mean that, but not here, not in context.[3]

He accepts that it was the kinsmen, *cognati* of Jesus, who came to restrain him; and he accepts that they thought they were performing their legal duty. But there is an important limitation. It could free the mother of Jesus from the suspicion that she had joined others in thinking her son to be mad. Maldonat raises a query.

2. Lefèvre d'Étaples in his *Commentarii in quatuor evangelia*, Paris, 1521 edition, fols. 219 verso; 221 verso; and 51 verso, § 125. On Matthew 12, Lefèvre is even more definite. Referring there to Mark, 3, he insists that it was other people's rumours which the Virgin and Christ's kinsmen heard; they themselves were 'full of pious solicitude'. The Mother of Jesus, fully aware of her Son's Godhead, was free from fear about him, knowing that nothing could happen to him but what he willed. Lefèvre completely avoids the crucial word *agnati* which is used by Erasmus for the relatives of Jesus. The term he employs for them is *necessarii*. That word certainly means 'relatives', but contains no hint of the duty of relatives under Roman law to restrain a mad relation.

3. The verb in Mark, 3:21 is ἐξέστη.

Several came out to bind Jesus, but may it not have been one of them – one only – who thought that he was mad?

Traditional methods do indeed maintain that biblical usage allows more than one person to be mentioned when only one is actually involved. The name given to that practice is syllepsis.[4] Maldonat cites two standard examples of it. In Matthew, 26, 'disciples' – in the plural – are said to object to the anointing of Jesus with a precious unguent; John, 12 makes it clear that it was one only: Judas. So too in Matthew, 27: there, both thieves who were crucified with Jesus blasphemed him; from Luke, 23 it is manifest that only one of them did so. Might syllepsis apply even here, when there is only one report of an event? If so, there is no need to assume that Mary and all Christ's kinsmen said he was mad; it could have been one person only, one of the kinsmen. Had there been a second account, it would have said so explicitly. But for Erasmus and those who directly followed him there is no tergiversating: even Mary on that occasion thought her son was mad.

Maldonat will not accept attempts to lessen the accusation of lunacy. Some do interpret the accusation in Mark less starkly: judging from the examples he gives, he could possibly be criticizing Erasmus. He admits that one of the expressions used tones down the idea of madness only marginally.[5] What he does condemn is the use, in the context of Mark's Gospel, of the term 'departure of the mind'.[6] That is a lesser and a different state. It will not fit the context. It was not to someone who was 'absent-minded' or 'distracted' that the Law of the Twelve Tables applied; it was to raving madmen. And that is the law which the kinsmen of Jesus were seeking to obey by going forth to restrain him.[7]

4. See, for example, the definition in *OED*.
5. The terms which Maldonat cites are certainly found at times in Erasmus. They are, *in excessu mentis incidebat* ('he has fallen into a loss of mind') and *alienatus est*. The latter he finds virtually no different from *in furorem versus est*. As for the former, it will not fit the context (of Mark, 3, of course; it can be used elsewhere).
6. The expression, which is good standard Latin, is *mentis excessus*.
7. As a *furiosus*, a raging lunatic.

That is interesting. Erasmus often uses of the Christian fool the expression which Maldonatus condemns as misplaced here.

There are, we are told by Maldonatus, exegetes who go even further, striving to lessen the accusation of madness levelled against Jesus by asserting that his kinsmen were only pretending. Their pretence was a ruse to get Jesus out of a tight corner and to look after him. That is possible but not probable:

Jerome, Bede, Theophylact, Euthymius, and all the venerable authors whom I remember having read think there was no dissimulation.

The relatives of Jesus gave their true opinion. Those great authorities all agree: Jesus was alleged, by his very kith and kin, to be mad.[8]

Maldonat clung to what the Vulgate says: 'He is become mad.'[9] Christ's kinsmen did not lay hold of him and bind him as one who had 'fallen into a loss of mind' as do prophets and other holy men while enraptured by the divine. They did so because they thought he was insane.

At least they did not laugh at him.

PURE SELF-DENIAL OR PURE MADNESS?

Erasmus realized that the unworldly would find the self-denying life of the Christian insane. By their standards, he would be.

Like Maldonat, Jansenius and many, many other theologians after him, he brought the subject back to the Greek original on which all depends: Jesus was 'beside himself'.[10]

The term used in Greek has many nuances even in the field of ecstasy. Its basic sense is 'to displace'. It can mean to be out of one's mind, beside oneself, or enraptured. For Christians it can mean being madly in love with God. It can apply to being in a daze from amazement or astonishment. The mind (or spirit, or soul) is thought

---

8. Johannes Maldonatus, *Commentarii in quattuor evangelia*, Venice, 1597, ad loc.
9. *In furorem versus est*, translated in the Douai version by 'He is become mad.'
10. That is, again, $\dot{\epsilon}\zeta\dot{\epsilon}\sigma\tau\eta$.

to be either succeeding in leaping out of its body or striving to do so. To an outsider it can look like madness. We still talk of mad bravery, being mad with anger, mad with desire, madly in love. Such mad states are forms of ecstasy.

In his rendering of the terms as used of Jesus in Mark, 3, Cornelius à Lapide, a Jesuit who professed theology in Louvain and Rome, gives the word its 'worst' meaning, exactly as Erasmus normally did:

The Greek is *ekseste*, that is, he is outside himself; he is mentally alienated; he has become *non compos mentis* from too much piety and zeal; he is delirious, insane.[11]

Erasmus accepted that meaning, which opened up such wide fields to the madness of Christ and his followers. But he also clung to the ambiguity which would make such madness a possible sign of prophetic ecstasy. Much later the Benedictine Augustin Calmet remarks:

The most gentle meaning that one can give to this word is that Jesus was outside himself, as prophets are during the moment of their actual inspiration; or as those persons who are in ecstasy are said to be outside themselves.[12]

That interpretation has a long history of acceptance, both on the Continent and in England. John Lacy was summing up a long and influential tradition when he linked the ecstasy of Christ in the third chapter of St Mark with the threat in Hosea, 'The Prophet is a fool; the spiritual man is mad'.[13]

11. Cornelius à Lapide, *Commentarii in IV Evangelia*. The edition cited is that published in Lyons, 1638, fol. 573.
12. Augustin Calmet, *Commentaire littéral sur tous les livres de l'ancien et du nouveau Testament*, vol. VII, Paris, 1722, p. 310.
13. *The General Delusion of Christians touching the ways of God's revealing himself to, and by, the Prophets, Evinc'd from Scripture and Primitive Antiquity*, London, 1713. (The words of Hosea are so frequently cited out of context that it is simply overlooked that, in context, they are minatory, a threat.)

27

Plato and Christian Madness

Erasmus linked biblical ecstasy with the ecstasies which Plato wrote about. He further insists that the madness of the Christian ecstatic is indistinguishable from a bout of medically attested insanity.

In the *Phaedrus* Socrates praised intelligence. It was then supposed that he would have held all forms of mania in horror.[1] It was not so. The greatest blessings come to man through manias, when, that is, they are sent to us as a divine gift.[2]

Socrates mentions four categories of good madness: the prophet's; the mystic's; the poet's; the lover's.[3] All of those manias are ecstasies. Each entails the soul leaving the body. When doing so she may come into contact with spiritual truths. The prophet strives after Truth and Beauty, but knows that such a goal can be fully attained only in death. In death the soul finally departs from the prison of its earthly body. Until then, the gifted philosopher will, in this life, 'practise dying'. That means what it says: he will practise separating his soul from his body. So in their own ways will the true mystic, poet and lover. To many who see them in their ecstasies, they will seem purely and simply mad.

The Greek word for such practising raises few problems when Socrates uses it.[4] But the classical Latin word used to translate it is

1. Mania in English is a borrowing from the Greek (of Plato and others). *Mania* was also borrowed in Latin.
2. Cf. the relevant passages of the *Phaedrus* here, particularly 244a–245a, 265a f.
3. They are respectively governed by Apollo, Dionysius, the Muses and Eros.
4. The word is μελήτη. It can apply to young orators who rehearse their speeches beforehand; to trainee barristers who practise before pleading in court; and to young soldiers practising the arts of war before being let loose on the battlefield.

normally *meditatio*. How many readers over the centuries have misunderstood it! Erasmus used it correctly, but even today it is still widely misinterpreted in his writings. It is taken to mean *meditation* (its most frequent sense in medieval Latin). But Seneca, Jerome, Erasmus, and indeed Rabelais and Humanists generally, use that term. When they do so they are not talking about *meditating on death* but about *the practising of dying*. That is something very different. There is an unbridgeable gulf between the true rendering and the error. In the *Moria* and in his straightforward theological works Erasmus uses it over and over again to refer to that 'practising of dying' which is philosophical ecstasy – and, for the enraptured Christian, true religious ecstasy.[5] The point is made clearly by Folly in the *Moria*. She does so on platonic grounds.

Clinical madness also results in the soul leaving, or striving to leave, the body. But both good (platonic) and bad (medical) madness produce similar dislocations of body and soul. Both have certain effects in common: similar causes producing similar effects. Both result in men and women being 'beside themselves': in such a state their souls, being temporarily outside their bodies, come in touch with spiritual realities. Both may acquire strange powers. As Folly says:

Thus, as long as the soul uses its bodily organs aright, a man is called sane; but, truly, when it bursts its chains and tries to be free, practising running away from its prison, then one calls it insanity. If this happens through disease or a defect of the organs, then by common consent it is, plainly, insanity. And yet men of this kind, too, we find foretelling things to come, knowing tongues and writings which they had never studied beforehand – altogether showing forth something divine. There is no doubt that this happens because the mind, a little freer from polluting contact with the body, begins to use its native powers. The same cause, I think, explains why something similar befalls those who travail close to death, so that they speak prophetically, as though inspired.[6]

5. The vital notion of 'practising dying' in ecstasy is obliterated by those current versions of Erasmus which wrongly translate *meditari* and *meditatio* by some such words as 'to meditate' and 'meditation'. Such an error falsifies an entire theology.
6. M.A.S., *Erasmus: Ecstasy and the Praise of Folly*, Penguin Books, 1988, p. 84.

No hyperbole there or foolish patter. Such a conviction permeated all fields of study, including medicine and law. With Erasmus we are in the world of platonizing Christianity. Many already knew of it, in rather different form, from, say, the writings of Ficino. Such a world had a place for theological, medical and legal convictions that the ecstatic and the clinically insane might share supernatural insights. Both might be able to speak languages which they had never learnt and know the contents of books which they could never have read. Many professional experts claimed to have experienced or witnessed such strange powers.

In the New Testament the great example of that phenomenon is the speaking in tongues of the disciples at Pentecost. That is often taken nowadays as an example of *glossolalia* – of ecstatic utterances which are close to gibberish. Not so then. Theologians emphasized that it was not a case of the disciples all speaking one and the same tongue, which was miraculously heard as their own by men from many different countries. That would have been a miracle of hearing. Pentecost saw a miracle of speaking. Under the inspiration of the Holy Ghost each apostle, simultaneously, spoke a variety of languages. They uttered truths in the multiplicity of tongues spoken amongst the Jewish Diaspora. Those languages they had never learnt: 'They began to speak with other tongues, as the Spirit gave them utterance.'[7]

It is quite moving to consult on such a topic the copy of the *Practica* of Dr Antonius Guainerius in the Bodleian Library, Oxford. It belonged to Robert Burton, the anxious author of the *Anatomy of Melancholy*. Guainerius devotes an entire chapter to the phenomenon of men and women speaking tongues they have not learnt. He cites examples which he had personally witnessed. Among his authorities is Socrates.[8]

Sebastian Barradus believed that the incarnate Lord possessed that same capacity of knowing languages he had never learnt and

7. Cf. Matthew Pole, *Synopsis Criticorum*, Utrecht, 1684, IV, 1404 (Acts, 2:4).
8. *Practica celeberrimi viri Antonii Guanerii Papiensi medicine doctoris clarissime*, Lyons, 1517, Tractatus XV, cap. iii, fol. XXXIX, verso f. (Burton's copy is at *Medical* 4° G.16.)

books he had never read. That is why his kinsfolk thought he was mad. (He cites Cardinal Cajetan on precisely this point.) The kinsfolk contrasted the Jesus they thought they knew and the one they now saw:

His kinsfolk, comparing his past life with such unexpected novelty, thought he was raving mad. For they knew that he had never studied books and therefore, on hearing what he was preaching, concluded that he had gone mad.[9]

In the *Anatomy of Melancholy*, Burton cites an example of what some believe to be diabolical and some, like Platerus, 'præternaturall' powers:

Stupend things are said of them, of their actions, gestures, contortions, fasting, prophesying, speaking languages they were never taught. &c. many strange stories are related of them . . .

The authorities mentioned were highly respected.[10]

Those who witnessed ecstatics possessed of special gifts of the Spirit were not necessarily overawed. Ecstatics look like fools. They often looked very funny.

---

9. Sebastian Barradus, *Commentaria in Concordiam et Historiam evangelicam*, Moguntiae, 1609, 55 1ii.B.
10. Part I, Section I, Memb. 1, Subs. 4. Burton limits his discussion, saying that since '*Deacon* and *Daurell* have written large volumes on this subject *pro & con.* I voluntarily omit it'.

28

Drunk with God and
Drunk with Wine

Not everyone who witnessed the babbling of the disciples at Pentecost was impressed. Some were indeed 'amazed' – driven into ecstasies. 'Others mocking said, "These men are full of new wine!"'

'Mocking' is the word. It enabled commentators to link the disciples at Pentecost to the moment when Jesus was mocked by the soldiers who dressed him up as a king. The disciples were taken to be madly drunk; Jesus was taken to be madly deluded.[1]

The drunkard, sometimes revolting, is often laughable. For Erasmus, there is a very close analogy between being drunk and being inspired by the Holy Ghost. He saw an allusion to the spiritual drunkenness of Jesus in the twenty-third psalm. Where we read 'My cup runneth over', the Vulgate reads, 'My cup that makes me drunk, how goodly it is.' The Apostles at Pentecost were laughed at: they too were flushed with 'new wine'. Erasmus linked together that Pentecostal new wine and the spiritual meaning of the psalmist's drunk-making cup. That cup prefigures the 'cup' that Jesus drank when he resigned himself to the Father's will:

Abba, Father. Take away this cup from me: nevertheless not what I will, but what thou wilt.[2]

For Erasmus that cup made 'many drunk to the point of despising

---

1. References to Acts, 2:13 and Matthew, 27:30. See also Matthew Pole, *Synopsis Criticorum*, Utrecht, 1684, ad loc.
2. Mark, 14:36; also, with variants, Matthew, 26:39; Luke, 22:42.

riches, family, stripes, stakes, racks and life itself'. It contained not
the water of the letter but the 'new wine' of the Spirit.[3]

To the worldlings who do not appreciate spiritual drunkenness,
Jesus, the disciples at Pentecost and all world-despising Christians
may seem tipsily funny. So do the worldlings to those whom they
find funny. It is the world which is grossly drunk, 'drunk with insane
pleasures'.

Erasmus is reviving the Greek patristic theme of 'sober drunkenness' – spiritual drunkenness. Gregory of Nyssa developed the theme
when explaining the wine-bibbing in the Song of Songs: drunkenness
always involves a displacement of the mind; spiritual drunkenness
even more so. David was beside himself and spiritually drunk when
he 'said in his ecstasy, "All men are liars"'. Paul was drunk
when, 'caught away outside himself to God, he would say, "When
we are raptured outside ourself, it is to God" (for it was to God that
he was caught away); "when we seem endowed with a sound mind,
it is to you"'.[4]

The theme of the apparent drunkenness which caused the Apostles
to be mocked at Pentecost mattered to Erasmus. Nine words in the
Vulgate turn into forty-four lines of text in his *Paraphrases*. Erasmus
explains that the world laughs at drunkards and that Christ's followers are indeed in a sense drunk when inspired by the Holy Ghost.
That is shown by the reaction of those in the crowd who 'mocking
said, "These men are full of new wine"'. They were apt pupils of
those Pharisees who, in the third chapter of St Mark, seeing Jesus
in ecstasy said, 'He hath a demon.' Erasmus tacitly recalled to those
who know the *Moria* what he had written there of the simply mad:
'It can happen then that someone may speak various languages he
has never learned.' But there is no *furor* which surpasses this one,
where so many could understand what was said.

3. LB, V, 315 A–D.
4. Gregory of Nyssa, *Opera*, Basle, 1571, fol. 400, lines 27ff. The reference to David
is to the Septuagint text of psalm 115 (116):11, which reads 'in my ecstasy' where
the Authorized Version reads 'in my haste'. The reference to St Paul is to a favourite
text of Erasmus's, explained as he explained it (following the Greek, not the
Vulgate): II Corinthians, 5:13.

Furor is a vital word for Erasmus. It was a standard term, regularly used by Cicero to translate the Greek word *mania*. It means both furious madness and inspired frenzy. It was used in that sense by poets, philosophers and medical experts as well as theologians. It was influential in law, where drunkenness was authoritatively defined as 'inducing a kind of ecstasy neighbouring on *furor*'.[5] That hostile crowd said what they said 'in order to laugh at the Apostles'.[6] Erasmus continues with a sound Humanist commonplace: 'Yet nothing stops truth sometimes being said in jest.' Mockers often say things truer than they ever guess.

He is invoking one of the best-known sayings of Horace: 'What is to prevent one telling the truth as he laughs?'[7] (Humanists do not keep their classical and Christian learning in discrete compartments.) Those Apostles were in very fact filled with new wine, that new wine which the Lord 'does not put into old wine-skins'.[8] The Apostles too had tasted of that cup of which the psalmist wrote, 'My cup that makes me drunk, how goodly it is.'[9]

Erasmus asks to be allowed to compare 'things in fact totally different in kind'. They are common intoxication and intoxication by the Spirit. Common intoxication produces four effects: it reveals things hidden in the heart; it leads to the forgetting of former ills; it exhilarates the mind with hope of joy and leads to life itself being despised; and it turns poor speakers into fluent ones.

But that is what happened to those Apostles! Full as they were of new wine, they forgot their old way of thinking and, like men born anew, forgot the very fears for which they deserted Christ; untaught by any human agency, they confronted kings and councils; torture and imminent death did not lessen their eager joy; foolish fishermen

---

5. Cf. I. Antonius and S. de Tournes, *Celeberrimorum Iuris Interpretum ad Titulum Digestorum de Verborum significatione*, Lyons, 1659, fol. 458, s.v. *Coram Titio, ad fin.*: 'Drunkenness induces as it were a banishment of the mind – *mentis exilium* – bordering on *furor*. One weighs it in the same scales as madness – *insania*.'
6. *Iudibrii causa.*
7. Horace, *Satires*, I, 1, 24–5: *Ridentem dicere verum Quid vetat?*
8. An echo of Matthew, 9:13 and cognate texts of Mark and Luke.
9. Again, psalm 23:5, Vulgate text.

though they once were, they withstood the pride of Pharisees, the enthymemes of philosophers and the skill of rhetoricians. 'Nothing is harder than to address a crowd.' They did, despite the fact that 'a crowd is always a many-headed monster, especially so when gathered out of many tongues and nations'.[10]

Those men who, inspired by the Holy Ghost, could do such great things, were laughed at. So was Jesus.

The deeper cause of that laughter and rejection was already revealed to the Greeks by that mythical cave of Plato's. Followers of Christ, like Plato's sage, live spiritual lives; they embody spiritual realities treated as unreal and absurd by carnal men.[11]

For Christians the highest form of ecstasy is when the soul, practising leaving the body, is vouchsafed a foretaste of heavenly bliss: a happy few are vouchsafed not a glimpse of God but a taste of God – 'O taste and see how sweet the Lord is!'[12] Such a privilege is rare. To the carnal majority imprisoned within the cave of this world, it is all but indistinguishable from madness, and in a sense rightly so. As wise Folly says:

Those who are allowed to experience such things – and it comes to very few – suffer something very like being out of their minds.

Such ecstatics speak disconnectedly and not at all as humans normally do; they utter (in Virgil's words) 'mindless sounds'; they laugh and they weep at the same time: 'in truth they are totally outside themselves'. They are spiritually demented.[13]

Such folk, being apparently mad, may be laughed at. They laugh at others in return; but, belonging as they do to the higher, privileged Christian madness, at times they do not laugh but weep.

The mockery is not limited to the ecstatics at the time of their

10. The comments of Erasmus on Pentecost can be read in LB, 7, 668.
11. See above, ch. 8.
12. Psalm 34:8, a central text for ecstasy, cited over and over again by mystical writers, including Erasmus. In the hierarchy of rapture, tasting God is an even greater privilege than seeing him.
13. The Latin words used include *dementia*; see M.A.S., *Erasmus: Ecstasy and the Praise of Folly*, Penguin Books, 1988, p. 182.

rapture. The spiritual truths which they reveal are laughed at too. Those whose thoughts, carnal and gross, remain riveted to this world, always laugh at spiritual things: for them they are madness. Such men would certainly have laughed at the madness of Jesus. How could they have done otherwise? Luther saw that. When commenting on the teachings of Jesus about eating his flesh and drinking his blood, he wrote:

Of course those words must have appeared laughable and mad, just as if you yourself were to say, 'If you want to live forever, you must eat my body and drink my blood.'

At that point would not you yourself have been moved to exclaim: 'Ha! Whatever has happened to him! Bind him with chains!'[14]

What applies to Christ applies to his followers. Supposing that he, Luther, possessing riches which nobody suspected, were to promise the Holy Roman Emperor a fortune:

Would the Emperor not laugh at me, saying, 'Restrain that good fellow. He is mad. He has somehow gone out of his mind.' That is the reaction of the crowd to, 'I am the Bread of Life.' They exclaim, 'Are you, now!'[15]

14. *Luthers Werke. Weimarer Ausgabe*, XXIII, pp. 15–16, referring to John, 6:27.
15. ibid., 56–7; on John, 6:35.

29

Christ's Mad Disciples:
Erotic Madness

'The disciple is not above his Master.' Men laughed at Jesus as a lunatic: they laughed at his followers, starting with one of the greatest of them.

'Paul! Thou art mad; thy much learning doth turn thee to madness!'

The words which Mr Justice Festus addressed to Paul as he stood before him in chains ring out over the centuries: '*Paule! mainetai*' – 'Paul you are a maniac', 'Paul! you are insane', 'Paul! you are mad.'

It is far easier for the notion of Christian madness to attach itself to Christ's followers than to their Master. Piety sees to that. Moreover Paul was not called insane only by others: he admits that he is a fool. He glories in the fact.

What made Justice Festus break across Paul's passionate defence of his religious certainties was the doctrine of the Resurrection.[1] Something similar occurred in Athens, when Paul preached to the philosophers idling in the market-place:

And when they heard of the resurrection of the dead, some mocked; others said, 'We will hear thee again on this matter some other time!'[2]

In other words, 'Tell it to the marines.'

The accusation against Paul was one of *mania*. Paul used the same verb himself when he warned charismatics that they risked the same accusation: to outsiders their wild, ecstatic utterances must sound like gibberish. If a whole congregation went in for it and were

1. Acts, 26:25.   2. Acts, 17:32.

surprised by uninstructed unbelievers, 'Would they not say that ye
are mad?'[3] In Paul's case he was at least uttering words which Festus
could recognize. In the case of Paul's gibbering congregation, the
full implications of his constrictions apply: the learned exegete
Estius, when explaining Paul's meaning here, emphasizes that those
enthusiastic churchfolk were taken to be insane, fanatics and raving
madmen. Grotius adds: 'The insane say things which nobody under-
stands.'

Paul felt forced to boast of his sufferings for the Gospel in order
to defend his place amongst the apostles. To boast thus was 'foolish',
but it had to be done. Paul is more of an apostle even than the others.
Are they apostles? Undoubtedly, but 'I speak as a fool, I am more.'[4]
His flock can call him mad, but, mad or not, they must not exclude
him:

'I say again: Let no man think me a fool: if otherwise, yet as a fool receive
me.'[5]

Boasting may well be foolish; but in a deeper sense Paul believes
that Christians are fools – to this world.[6] As he says of himself with
sarcasm, using the royal *we*: 'We are fools for Christ's sake, but ye
are wise'.[7]

For many, the episode in Paul's life which would have seemed the
most mad was his privileged rapture to the third heaven.[8] He was
caught away to witness ineffable truth. Paul's was the kind of rare
and sublime rapture which enabled him to make Isaiah's teaching
his own: 'What God hath prepared for them that love him' cannot
be conceived or uttered. But it was known to Paul.[9]

Christian rapture, interpreted with the help of the teachings of
Socrates, furnished the *Moria* with its climactic end. Folly describes
such an ecstasy as 'very, very like dementia';[10] it is akin to being 'out
of one's mind'. The joy of such an ecstasy, combined in one man,
surpasses the natural joys that all human beings put together have
ever known in this wide world:

3. I Corinthians, 14:23. 4. II Corinthians, 11:23. 5. II Corinthians, 11:16.
6. I Corinthians, 1:26. 7. I Corinthians, 4:10. 8. II Corinthians, 12.
9. I Corinthians, 2:9, Isaiah, 64:4. 10. *dementiae simillimum.*

That is the extent to which the spiritual surpasses the corporeal, the invisible the visible. This is most certainly what the prophet promises: 'Eye hath not seen, neither hath there entered into the heart of men, what God hath prepared for them that love him.' Those who are allowed to experience such things – and it comes to very few – suffer something very like being out of their minds.[11]

Pious minds looking for madness in Paul did not have far to look, once ecstasy was classed as a mad-seeming rapture. If Paul's rapture was 'in the spirit', then he was literally beside himself.

The vital importance of 'mad' rapture for Paul is clearer in the Greek original than in the Vulgate. On one occasion the Vulgate deliberately hides the notion of madness. If we trust the Vulgate, Paul wrote:

For if we be transported in mind, it is to God: if we be sober, it is to you.[12]

'Sober' is a possible rendering but not the probable one here in context. As Erasmus emphasized, the Greek contains a more striking contrast, one between sanity and insanity:

If we are beside ourselves, it is for God: if we are in our right mind, it is for you.

Paul is prepared to sacrifice at times the joys of a 'mad' ecstatic union with God in order to attend to the needs of his churches. This meaning mattered so much to Erasmus that, in his own translation, he chose to emphasize the full force of the insanity and sanity. He did so by his choice of words and by repetition:

If we are insane, we are insane to God: if we are sane, we are sane to you.[13]

That is clearer even than the apostle himself.

11. M.A.S., *Erasmus: Ecstasy and the Praise of Folly*, Penguin Books, 1988, pp. 174f.; 181–2, citing Isaiah, 64:4 and I Corinthians, 2:9.
12. II Corinthians 5:13: *Sive enim mente excedimus, Deo: sive sobrii sumus vobis.*
13. *Nam sive insanimus, Deo insanimus: sive sani sumus, vobis sani sumus.* Cf. the annotation on this verse, which expresses the same idea in different words: *Sive enim mente excidimus, deo excidimus: sive sanae mentis sumus, vobis sani sumus.*

Paul's Greek would recall to the minds of many a Humanist that similar contrasts between the 'man of sound mind' and the man given over to a divine *mania* can be found in Plato.[14] The verb used for the madness of Paul is the same as that used by Mark for the madness of Christ.[15] The fusion of Christian ecstasy with platonic *mania* became almost complete. That privileged rapture of St Paul's, those rare raptures which, for Erasmus and so many others, are 'very, very like dementia', were seen as the Christian expression of the highest form of the four *manias* recognized by Socrates.[16] As Erasmus notes, Theophylact, Bishop of Ochrida, 'attributes insanity here to St Paul, but an insanity which is amatory, *erōtikē*'.[17] St Paul's passionate love of God is just such an erotic love. It was not *agapē*. It is a spiritual Eros: the adoring response to the revealed goodness of God.[18] Being a form of madness it can and does seem laughable. Socrates already knew that.

Such intense love for God is not confined to the more obvious places. If divine madness provokes laughter from the worldlings, then there are numerous places in Scripture where laughter is unexpectedly called forth. For Agostino Steucho, a contemporary of Erasmus, what happened to Adam might do so. In his *Cosmopœia on Genesis*, he was one of many theologians who (like Bishop Severianus, met in chapter 10) explained that when God said, 'Let us make man in our own image', God as Trinity used the royal plural. But then God

14. II Corinthians, 5:13 reads: 'If we are beside ourselves' (ἐξέστημεν): 'if we are in our right mind' (σωφρονοῦμεν). Cf. Plato, *Phaedrus*, 244B; *Republic*, I, 331C; *Protagoras*, 323B, *Phaedo*, 68C.
15. Mark, 3:21. (The vital verb is ἐξίστημι, with the sense of to be out of one's mind, beside one's self, insane.)
16. *Phaedrus*, 265B.
17. *Erasmus' Annotations*, ed. Reeve, Duckworth, 1986, II, p. 538; M.A.S., *Erasmus: Ecstasy and the Praise of Folly*, Penguin Books, 1988, p. 144. In 1527 Erasmus quotes Theophylact in his explanation of II Corinthians, 5:13, and places the whole matter firmly in the context of the madnesses of the *Phaedrus*.
18. Paul in his ecstasies was madly in love with God. That fact proves of great importance to Christian theology and to Christian imagery. It allows the passion of the lovers in the Song of Songs to be interpreted as the mad *eros* of Christ for his Church, of his Church for him, and of the individual soul for God.

as Unity linked that plural *us* to a singular noun: 'our own *image*'. Under a veil, God was hinting at plurality-in-unity, at the unity of the Trinity.[19] Adam was in fact created after the image and in the likeness of the Son. As soon as Adam was thus created he glimpsed the beauty of his Prototype, who exceeded in beauty the finite beauty of any creature whatsoever.[20] With such beauty he fell ecstatically in love. For love of his Prototype, Adam was driven mad.[21]

That Prototype is that same Son whose glory Peter and the chosen disciples glimpsed though a cloud at the Transfiguration. By that unique foretaste of Christ's glory those disciples too were caught away, falling into ecstasies of amazement. It was a mad ecstasy. Peter babbled he knew not what. Origen thought it probable that Peter at that time was diabolically possessed.[22] Erasmus wove that mad ecstasy of Peter and the chosen disciples into the fabric of the *Moria* at its climax, with its fine and subtle laughter.

Moses, too, saw God in a rapture: in that sense being like Paul.[23] Paul's rapture was altogether exceptional. Peter's was an extraordinary privilege.[24] Such privileges make those who receive them abstracted, beside themselves, incoherent.

To the world, which laughs, they seem mad. There is madness in plenty on the surface of Scripture: much more was ingeniously to be found divinely hidden within it. As Cornelius Jansenius reminded

19. Similarly, the word for God in Genesis, 1:1 is *elohim*. It is plural in form even when it means God (and evidently plural when it means angels).

20. It is the Son of whom the psalmist (45:2) wrote, 'Thou art fairer than the children of men'.

21. The words used of Genesis, 1:26 are *amore insanisse*.

22. Augustino Steucho, *Cosmopœia*, cap. I *Genesis* (in his *Opera*, Paris, 1578, p. 45E). Origen's *Commentary on Matthew*, which survives only in Latin, in Migne's *Patrologia Graeca*, XIII, 1074Aff. See also Erasmus's paraphrases of Mark and Luke (LB, 7, 224ff. and 371ff.).

23. Cf. *Formalitates juxta doctrinam Angelici Doctoris D. Thomae Aquinatis*, compiled by the R. P. Aquarius and edited by the R. P. Alphonsus de Marcho, Naples, 1605, p. 102. The relevant part of the *Summa Theologica* of Thomas Aquinas is II^a II^{ae} q. 157 *ad.* 4, etc., and, on *extasis*, II^a II^{ae} q. 175.

24. Acts, 2:5. Cf. Cornelius à Lapide, *In Omnes Divi Pauli epistolas commentaria*. Lyons, 1660: *Proemium in Praerogativis S. Pauli*, cap. vii; see him also on Acts, 2:5.

his readers, the very verb 'to prophesy' can also mean 'to be deranged':

Now those who were inspired by the Holy Spirit and uttered very unusual things – for which they were taken for insane and beside themselves by carnal men (since the flesh calls insane whatever exceeds its grasp) – were said to prophesy, therefore *to prophesy* is sometimes used in Scripture for *to be deranged*, or *to be insane* and *to utter unusual things under the influence of an evil spirit*.[25]

Jesus was thought to be prophesying in that mad sense in the third chapter of St Mark. And when he was flogged and laughed at before the Crucifixion, he was urged to prophesy.

25. Cornelius Jansenius, Bishop of Ghent, *Commentarii in suam Concordiam*, 1613, Antwerp edition, p. 355, with reference to Old Testament prophets.

30

The Philosophy
of Christ

Madness was also inextricably interwoven into Erasmus's concept of what Christianity is. The way of the Christian he called the philosophy of Christ.

Philosophy implies no weakening of Christianity into an admirable ethical system. On the contrary: it emphasizes the erotic mystic rapture to which it gives access. It retains and exceeds its full Socratic sense. Infinitely more than even Socrates managed to achieve, the philosophy of Christ is a way of 'practising dying'.

In death the soul quits her body. Then at last she will be at home, no longer *in via* but *in patria*, where she will be in the realm of the spiritual. There at last she may be at one with God, having knowledge unattainable in this world, knowledge unbounded by time.

Philosophers are 'lovers of wisdom'. A lover of Christian wisdom anticipates such joy and splendour: he practises dying. As far as it is right and proper – an Aristotelian reservation – he detaches his soul from his body. His migrant soul glimpses things spiritual, throwing herself about as she experiences something of the joys to come.

In his hope-filled treatise *On Preparing for Death*, Erasmus reminds his readers that when a Christian practises dying he is 'practising' the life immortal, the true life.[1] But true life or no, practising dying will seem folly to carnal men who laugh at the madcap antics of those who practise the philosophy of Christ. By the world's standards they are right to do so.

1. LB, 5, 1295D – 1296B.

The soul who enters for a while into the realm of the spirit shares some privileges with prophetic souls on their deathbeds: they may (like John of Gaunt in Shakespeare or the Seigneur de Langey in Rabelais) speak deep truths and foretell the future. In a platonic image, souls when partly detached from their bodies are like men on a ship edging home into harbour: they can already interpret the signs of friends waving from the jetty. But Christian ecstatics share prophetic gifts with the medically insane. They too have souls which are ill-attached to their bodies from which they strive to escape. They too hover about the fringes of the spiritual world. That explains why fools may know things unknown to the wise.[2]

That led to a further emphasis on the foolishness of Christian philosophy practised in the Christian life, and so to its being for some even more risible. If prophet, Christian lover of God and clinical madman all show similar symptoms of insanity, they will be similarly laughed at.

2. For Guillaume Du Bellay, the Seigneur de Langey, who died in the presence of Rabelais and other named doctors, see the *Tiers Livre*, TLF, XXI, 39-55; and the *Quart Livre*, TLF, XXVII, 49-67.

31

The Foolishness
of God

The world's mocking hostility to spiritual truth led Paul to contrast not the wisdom of God and the wisdom of man – that would be too easy – but the madness of God and the wisdom of men. Even God's madness (or foolishness) is wiser than men – not of any men but of the wisest of men. God has made 'foolish the wisdom of this world'. The preaching of the cross is 'foolishness' to those that perish.

Renaissance partisans of Christian folly were heirs to a long tradition, anchored in St Paul. It was associated with many great names, including Origen and Anselm. Erasmus gave the theme of Christian folly a fresh and durable force.

Cornelius à Lapide was aware of that long tradition when he explained St Paul. His starting-point is Paul's injunction,

If any man amongst you seemeth to be wise in the world, let him become a fool that he might be wise.[1]

He wrote:

A *fool*: certainly the foolishness of humility, of faith, and of the Cross of Christ.

That 'foolishness', as Anselm says, 'is for God the only true wisdom'.

Since the wisdom of this world is foolishness to God, and vice versa, it follows that we cannot be truly wise unless, to the world, we are fools.

Even though we may be great men and wise in the eyes of the world,

1. I Corinthians, 3:18.

yet let us subject ourselves to the faith, discipline, Cross and obedience of Christ, as children, indeed as fools.

The Magi did so, as St Bernard teaches. Wise, they bowed before the infant Jesus. Jesus taught that those who are blessed are the poor, the meek, those who weep, those who are thirsty, those who suffer persecution:

The world teaches that the blessed are the rich, the elated, the laughers, the feasters and the powerful.

St Ambrose and St Anselm taught that it was the foolishness of God which conquered Satan and overcame the entire world:

The wondrous wisdom and power of God are manifest from his overcoming all the world's wisdom and power by something foolish and weak: the Cross.[2]

God is pleased to save the world by the 'foolishness of preaching'. It is striking that Erasmus and others refer not merely to the 'foolishness' of preaching the Cross (that is straight out of St Paul) but, arrestingly, to the 'foolish Cross of Christ'.[3]

The very Cross is madness . . .

Such an expression goes beyond the strict warrant of Scripture; but when Paul writes of the 'foolishness of God' he does not merely mean that God's truth seems foolish to the worldly-wise but that all the wisdom that God reveals to Man is in a sense his own foolishness, his baby-talk. That very foolishness infinitely surpasses the wisdom of even the greatest apostle. That is what Origen taught. Hence the *stulta crux Christi*, the 'foolish Cross of Christ'.[4]

Those who heeded the incarnate Son were fools too. For Erasmus, the Son prays:

2. Cornelius à Lapide, *In Omnes divi Pauli Commentaria. editio ultima, aucta et recognita*, in the edition published in Lyons, 1660, p. 105, on I Corinthians, 3:18f. and 1:21f. (to which he refers the reader).

3. For example, in LB, 5, 1295D – 1296B.

4. I Corinthians, 1:18; cf. 1:25 and 1:21. The connections between the conception of divine folly in Origen and Erasmus are a theme of my study, *Erasmus and the Praise of Folly*.

LAUGHTER AT THE FOOT OF THE CROSS

I thank thee Father that thou hast hid these things from the wise and hast revealed them unto fools.[5]

Not babes. Fools.

---

5. See Matthew, 11:25 in Erasmus's edition of the New Testament, where he gave that rendering of Christ's famous saying; he then took it over into his *Praise of Folly*. He defended it, but gave way under pressure. Towards the end of the century Cornelius Jansenius, Bishop of Ghent, adopted it in his *Commentarii in suam Concordiam* (ad loc.: see Matthew, 11:25 and Luke, 10:21). Thereafter; it became even more widely known.

32

Socrates

Socrates was not only a teacher of wisdom: he was for many a paragon who helped prepare the way for the Gospel. Yet Socrates enjoyed a laugh. Socrates enjoyed a drink. Socrates had a sense of fun. He was laughed at too. He showed by his example that worldly fools kill what is spiritual and good. They also laugh at it.

In September 1524 Erasmus wrote a long and full letter to Humanist circles in Strasbourg. In it he joked about the stone which was restricting him to his bed. That stone helped him to avoid distractions which would have kept him away from his books.[1] The pain of the stone was recognized as suicidal, yet Erasmus jests about it. Anticipating surprise on the part of Wimpfeling, he added: 'You ask how I can make a joke out of something so full of anguish. But why me any less than Socrates? He joked as he drank the hemlock and died with a jest on his lips.'

The example of Socrates justified laughter, banter, friendly drinking and jesting. That mattered. For Humanists he was not merely one of the intellectual, moral and spiritual heroes: he was *the* hero. But there was a paradox. Platonism venerates beauty: Socrates ('Philosophy's master and ours', as Montaigne calls him) was spectacularly ugly; he was the original Silenus of Alcibiades, gross outside; divine within. That divine exemplar was treated during his lifetime as a fool. It was Zeno the Epicurean, the teacher of Cicero, who referred to him as a *scurra atticus*, an Attic buffoon. Zopyrus the

---

1. Or rather he wrote it to Jacob Wimpfeling, sure that its contents would soon be known to the great and not-so-great scholars and writers who lived there.

physiognomist, studying the face of Socrates, pronounced him to be *stupidus et bardus*, 'stupid and dull-of-wit'. Both judgements are known from Cicero, and so roll down the ages, shocking or amusing generation upon generation.[2] That anyone should cite Zopyrus apropos of Socrates would surprise nobody: he was remembered exclusively for that remark. On the other hand it tells us a lot when Erasmus applied those same terms to the true followers of Christ: they it is who are 'stupid and dull-of-wit'. Like Socrates! In the eyes of the world, that is.[3]

There was also the Socrates of legend and tradition. It took some decades for scholars to come to terms with the difference between him and the Socrates of Plato and Xenophon. The late medieval *Nuremberg Chronicle* pulls him towards all the traditional Christian virtues:

although he was the wisest of men, he reckoned that he knew nothing. Hence he often said, as Jerome told Paulinus, 'This alone I know: that I know not.' Socrates was moreover of marvellous chastity, justice and other virtues.[4]

The school of Ficino brought to light a more learned Socrates, but he was even more a precursor of Christian truth and values. One theologian saw him as a model for bishops.[5]

---

2. *De natura deorum*, I, xxxiv, 93 (for Zeno); *De fato*, V, 10 (for the *stupidus et bardus* of Zopyrus).

3. The extent to which Socrates can be absorbed into Christianity by Erasmus can be seen by the use that he makes of *stupidus et bardus*. Folly tells how Christ preferred simple, guileless men and simple, guileless beasts. The Holy Ghost came down as a dove, not as a hawk. Jesus, who could have ridden astride a lion, chose to ride an ass. His own, he calls sheep: 'No animal is so silly – witness the Aristotelian saying, *Sheepish ways.*' Because of the obtuseness of sheep, Aristotle's saying was applied as an insult to the *stupidi et bardi*. But in the *Praise of Folly* that infamous tag is applied not to Socrates but to the followers of Christ. That is equivalent to saying that, when Christ chose 'sheep' to be his own, he was choosing simple men and women who, like Socrates before them, could expect to be laughed at as 'stupid and dull-of-wit'.

4. *Cronica nurembergensis*, 1493, fol. CXVII, verso.

5. When Ludovicus Miræus wrote a dedicatory letter for a fresh text of Erasmus's

The parallels between Socrates and Christians go back at least to
Justin Martyr, who pointed out that Socrates 'was accused of the
very crimes imputed to us' and that – an amazing privilege – he had
some independent knowledge of Christ.[6] Even when Socrates was
brought down a peg, he was judged against the very highest standards
of Christian revelation.[7]

Socrates was on the right side. Sayings in his favour from the lips
of his pupil Plato were repeated from generation to generation. In
The Preparation for the Gospel, Eusebius called Plato an Attic Moses.
Guillaume Budé cites that judgement and defends it. Whoever praises
Plato praises Socrates, his master.[8] From the twelfth century Plato
was increasingly seen in the West, as he had long been in the East,
as a prophet of Christianity.[9] Dating from about 1290, Plato appears
with Habakkuk on the façade of the Cathedral of Siena; both are
prophets of Christ.[10]

Socrates and Plato were widely held to have learnt truths about
God from Hebrew books left in Egypt by Moses. (They included
lost scrolls, otherwise unknown to Jew and Christian alike.) They

---

critical edition of the *Opera* of Hilary of Poitou (Paris 1544), he presented Socrates
as such a model: bishops, as Paul wrote to Timothy, should be given to hospitality;
Socrates, with his kindness to foreigners and his open welcome to those seeking
his instruction, was the example to follow.

6. Justin Martyr, *Apologia II*.

7. As Guillaume Budé wrote in his book *On Crossing over from Hellenism to
Christianity*, Socrates said he knew nothing: Paul, wiser, said he knew nothing,
save Christ crucified. Socrates brought philosophy down to earth: Christ took it
from earth to Heaven.

8. Guillaume Budé, *Commentarii linguae graecae*, in *Opera Omnia*, Basle, 1557
(Gregg reprint, Farnborough, 1966), IV, col. 1370.

9. It was once accepted that a brass table had been found in his mausoleum stating,
'I, Plato, believe in the Christ who is to come, to be born of a Virgin.' Cf. M.-T.
D'Alverney, 'Humbortus of Balesma', in *Archives d'Histoire doctrinale et littéraire
du moyen âge, Année 1984*, 1985, pp. 128ff.

10. That really does give Plato, and Socrates his teacher, a very special place indeed.
They were truly inspired. To reach even a hazy knowledge of the Trinity and other
specifically Christian truths required not intelligence but divine inspiration. Cf.
Raymond Klibansky, *The Continuity of the Platonic Tradition*, Warburg Institute,
London, 1930, plate no. 2.

were vouchsafed knowledge of some truths yet to be revealed, such as the nature of the Trinity.

Many Renaissance Humanists replaced naïve legends by more complex ones. Long accustomed to read foreshadowings of the life, death and teachings of Jesus into the figures of the Old Testament, they did much the same with their classical 'prophets'. Socrates, the forerunner of Christianity who taught 'practising dying', played a role analogous to that of Moses or of David. He prepared the way for the Lord. Yet that divine man was put on the stage by Aristophanes and laughed at. Plato, the Attic Moses, was taught by Socrates, the Attic buffoon.

In the *Colloquies* of Erasmus, a character in the *Religious Banquet* was not speaking for himself alone when he reacted with awe to the teachings of Socrates and Cicero:

The first place must indeed be given to the authority of the Scriptures, yet I sometimes find – even in pagans and the very poets – things written by the Ancient authors so chastely, so piously and so religiously, that I cannot convince myself that they were not divinely inspired when they composed them; and perhaps the Spirit of Christ is more widely diffused than we imagine; and that there are more saints than we have in our kalendars.

That is a character in a book speaking. Erasmus never put in doubt the uniqueness of Christ, God and Man. But he did write those words. And while it is wrong to claim that Erasmus could personally evoke Socrates in prayer he made one of his characters able to do so – almost:

Indeed one wonders at such a mind in a man who knew not Christ nor Holy Writ. Whenever I read such things of such men, I can scarcely refrain from saying: *Sancte Socrate, ora pro nobis.*

That good man was not only laughed at: he was a good laugher himself; all sorts of apocryphal philosophical jests became attached to his name, not least because of the way he bore the tantrums of his wife Xantippe: Socrates was sitting calmly on his doorstep. Xantippe's stormy temper had driven him out. She rushed upstairs and emptied her chamber-pot down on his head. He quietly remarked that rain often follows hard upon a storm.[11]

His wit was added to over the ages. In an apocryphal saying he asks, 'How can I govern others, who cannot govern myself?' Rabelais put those wise words into the mouth of the reluctant Frère Jean when, in *Gargantua*, he was offered a very special Renaissance 'monastery', the Abbey of Thelema, as a reward for his heroism. That rollicking monk unexpectedly cites them to explain why he intends never to rule over a monastery.[12]

Socrates was seen as an inspired man of great but smiling virtue. He had much to teach Christians. Wherever Humanists smile and laugh, Socrates holds a privileged place. He dominates Erasmus's adage, the Sileni of Alcibiades. He contributes to the final pages of three major Renaissance books: to the climax of the *Moria*; to the climax of the last book Rabelais published not long before he died; to the climax of the last chapter of the *Essays* of Montaigne.[13]

Socrates had that jesting wit which Aristotle admired in the gentleman – which did not save him from being mocked.

11. It can be found, for example, in Johann Peter Lange's jolly little work, *Democritus ridens, sive campus recreationum honestarum, cum exorcismo Melancholiae*, Amsterdam, 1655, p. 29.

12. Rabelais, *Gargantua*, TLF, Geneva, 1970, ch. 50, p. 280.

13. *Le Quart Livre de Pantagruel*, and *De l'Expérience*. (In the judgement of Montaigne, philosophical ecstasies such as those of Socrates are best not sought after; they are dangerous, degrading in practice and to be ranged infinitely below that true foretaste of heavenly bliss which is granted to a few privileged saints.)

33

Christian Laughter
all but Nipped in the Bud:
Eutrapely Condemned

'Neither filthiness, nor foolish talking, nor jesting, which are not befitting.' St Paul was instructing the church at Ephesus.[1] Christians, it seems, may not, as the prophets did, jest even at the madness of their enemies and the worldly-wise. Can that be right?

With his vast authority, Paul risked killing Christian laughter stone dead. Low and obscene speech (filthiness) and rash and stupid prattling (foolish talking) are likely to be condemned by many kinds of moralist. But what of jesting? The question had to be posed. The term St Paul used for jesting is *eutrapelia*. What did he mean by it? Aristotle used the same word. For him it is a virtue. For Aristotelians, eutrapely (as it may be called in English) is not a bad quality at all; it is good. It is the conversation of the civilized man with a fine turn of wit. In Latin the Greek term *eutrapelia* was translated as *urbanitas* ('urbane' humour). Must that quality really to be denied to Christians? Can a Christian not be a witty and urbane gentleman?

If he cannot be, that leads to a head-on clash with the Philosopher. That clash would become unavoidable once Christianity moved outwards and upwards into the world of the scholars and gentlefolk of the Roman Empire. In those circles eutrapely was appreciated as one of the seven moral virtues of the Peripatetics. Some glum Christians accepted that clash. Meditating on what St Paul meant here, Christians who were overwhelmed by the wickedness and the suffering rampant in this world did not even wish to jest, to laugh or be merry. For them, eutrapely was indeed wrong.

1. Ephesians, 5:34.

Others clung to another meaning of *eutrapelia*. It is well attested. *Eutrapelia* can mean not only the virtue it is for Aristotle but also a humour which is lewd, vulgar, bad or evil. Many seized upon that meaning to explain what Paul intended. Paul was not opposing urbane jesting, but lewd talk. Others thought otherwise; those church Fathers and their classical authorities who frowned on all civilized banter, all virtuous *eutrapelia*, were cited down the centuries by theologian and exegete. To avoid a long and tedious list of authorities known and unknown, I quote here from the once famous scriptural commentary of John Trapp, a seventeenth-century divine:

'What have we to do with tales and jests?' saith Bernard. Tertullian saith he was 'born for nothing else but repentance'. . . . Saith Seneca, 'True mirth is a severe business.'

Bernard is cited as particularly scathing:

What have we to do with tales and laughter? I judge that not only extravagant jesting is to be condemned but all jesting.[2]

Bernard's choice of adjective is revealing. The word translated 'extravagant' is, in his Latin, *profusus*. By using that word in such a context, Bernard shows that he was adapting to his monastic version of Christian morality two judgements of Cicero in which that word appears. Cicero, who liked a jest and had a most urbane wit, was known to have condemned 'extravagant' hilarity (hilarity

2. John Trapp, *A Commentary or Exposition upon all the Books of the New Testament*, London, 1656, p. 766. St Bernard is cited thus:

Quid nobis cum fabulis, cum risu? non solùm profusos sed etiam omnes jocos arbitror declinandos.

While agreeing that for Aristotle *eutrapelia* meant 'urbanity, facility and facetiousness of speech', Trapp insists that 'Jason in Pindar stated that he had never known Chiron his tutor to say or do anything *scurrilous* – using the word *eutrapelia* for scurrilous or abusive'. All eutrapely is tainted for Trapp. He has no patience with jesting among serious men. He was too much aware of the tragic elements in life for merriment to find a place. That Thomas More 'never thought any thing well spoken, except he had ministered some mock in the communication', leads to doubts whether to call him a foolish sage or a sage fool.

when *profusa*). He also condemned extravagant delight – 'that *profusum* and immoderate kind of jesting' which results from an emotional disturbance'.[3] St Bernard went well beyond Cicero, rejecting even the civilized laughter which he allowed and which Thomas Aquinas equally allowed precisely because of those same passages of Cicero.

Cicero's word *immodestus* could also be a snare. Lesser latinists could take it to mean not immoderate (which it does) but immodest. Such an error cuts out a great deal of what human beings find funny. A lot of merry humour is moderate but immodest.

The non-laughers did not have it all their own way. Many saw to that. They insisted on the two sorts of *eutrapelia*. It was admitted that *eutrapelia* can be employed in a bad sense by authors of the greatest importance. There are places even in Plato where it is identified with *bōmolochia*, with mere ribaldry, the low buffoonery to be expected from the type of thief who would steal meat-offerings from an altar.[4] But there is the other kind. St Paul doubtless outlawed not Aristotle's virtue but that other base eutrapely. Nevertheless the ambiguity persists. The non-laughers might well have won; fortunately for religion and for laughter, the problem was resolved, for those who wished it to be so, before the Latin world drifted apart from the Greek. For that we owe a major debt to St Augustine.

The general history of the problem is traced by several Renaissance commentators. Paul's *eutrapelia* is translated in the Vulgate as *scurrilitas*. It is a good translation, though somewhat restrictive. It has one great drawback: for those who had no Greek there was no means whatever of knowing that it is in fact a rendering of *eutrapelia*, a word well known to them from their Latin Aristotles.

---

3. In the *Tusculan Disputations*, IV, vii, 15, Cicero refers to *profusa hilaritas*, 'extravagant or immoderate hilarity', which he sees as a perturbation, a symptom of an unbalanced delight. Again, in *De Officiis*. I, xxix, 103, he condemns *genus jocandi profusum et immodestum*, 'an extravagant and immoderate kind of jesting'.
4. For good *eutrapelia*, cf. Aristotle, *Rhetoric*, II, ii, 16, and *Nicomachæan Ethics*, IV, viii, 1–12; for *bōmolochia*, cf. Plato, *Republic*, 606C; for the *bōmolochos*, cf. Aristotle, *Nicomachæan Ethics*, IV, viii, 3, and *Rhetoric*, III, xviii, 7.

We could turn for enlightenment to Cornelius à Lapide, who knew both his Aristotle and Aquinas well. He treats the problem when explaining the relevant part of St Paul. He refers to the standard sections in Aristotle, to St Augustine and to Thomas Aquinas, all of whom defend that virtuous, urbane wit which is eutrapely. They show how such wit can stimulate physical and mental health by tempering moroseness and providing relaxation from mental rigor and vigour. Wit does so by means of jokes and jesting.[5] Chrysostom, it is true, denied that there was any place for eutrapely among Christians, for whom not jesting but grief and tears are befitting. He was not alone. Yet the context shows that Paul – and hence Chrysostom – are really condemning *bōmolochia*: scurrilous buffoonery. Jerome, we are told, condemned all jocularity as unbecoming to a saint, who should ever be grieving. Jerome cites a saying of Jesus from a Hebrew Gospel: 'Never be joyful until you see your brother in charity.' Cornelius is prepared to accept that judgement when restricted to jocularity for its own sake. When one's brother is not 'in charity' there can be no justification for laughing in his presence. But jocularity can lead to things beyond itself: to happiness, to mental agility, to healthy Christian minds and bodies:

It makes a man more lively, more animated, more suited to his tasks and to obedience to God. Then *eutrapely* is honourable and becoming to a Christian. Thus did Paul, Anthony, Hilarion and other hermits have their jests – Christian jests seasoned with salt.

'Salt' has the Horatian sense of wit, of intellectual acuteness; it has a wide field of meaning, including facetiousness, shrewdness and even sarcasm.

Cornelius is cited here as a sound and important compiler of a standard view. What enabled him and others to distance themselves even from the great Jerome in his severer mood was the combined authority of Augustine and Aquinas. Since Aquinas quotes Augustine, the two authorities are often cited in tandem. Echoing St Paul,

---

5. He cites, ad loc., the *Nicomachæan Ethics*, IV, viii; Augustine (with no definite reference), and Thomas Aquinas, *Summa Theologica*, II, II[ae], 168, AD 2.

Augustine wrote in his *Musica*, 'I wish to spare you.' It is appropriate that a wise man should relax tensions.[6] In his *Summa Theologica* Aquinas comments on that 'sparing'. For him, 'such relaxing of the mind from business-in-hand is achieved through ludicrous words and deeds'.[7] He allows jesting, sporting and playing games.

Aquinas leaves the Christian with a wide field for his fun. He does so on the authority of the Philosopher, who, we are reminded, 'posits the virtue of *eutrapelia*, which in Latin we call *jucunditas*, enjoyment'. His conclusion rejoices smiling Christians: 'To sporting and jesting, which are occasionally employed to relieve the mind, that virtue applies which is called *eutrapelia*.'[8] A man cannot do physical work all the time: he needs recreation for the body. So too for the mind. Mental fatigue is worse still than physical, since it can affect the body as well as the mind. Just as bodily fatigue must be cured by physical relaxation, mental fatigue needs mental relaxation.

Such relaxation of the mind is called *delectatio* – that is, delight, pleasure, amusement. Aquinas supports his case with a tale taken from the celebrated *Collations of the Fathers* by John Cassian. John the Evangelist scandalized some folk who saw him jesting with his disciples. John showed them an archer's bow. He asked whether it was right to keep it continually bent. 'No,' they said, 'it would break.' John applied that lesson to the mind: Man needs to unbend. Man's mind requires for its delectation *ludicra* (things which are sporting, ludicrous or jesting) and *jocosa* (things which are humorous, jocose or facetious). Of course Aquinas places limits to such joy and jesting. No filthy gestures or words (Cicero supports that). Gravity must be retained (Cicero and St Ambrose support that). We should adapt what we say to time, place and person (Cicero supports that too). Chrysostom rightly condemned those who, in the words of Solomon, 'accounted our very life to be a plaything'.[9] Nevertheless, Christians can rightly enjoy the Philosopher's virtue of *eutrapelia*.

The last words are given to Cicero, in *De Officiis*:

---

6. Cf. I Corinthians, 7:28.   7. *per ludicra verba et facta.*
8. Thomas Aquinas, *Summa Theologica*, II[a] II[ae] qu. CLXVIII, art. 2, *Utrum in ludis possit esse aliquid virtus.*   9. Wisdom of Solomon, 15:12.

We have not been brought into the world by Nature to act as though we were made for playing and jesting, but rather for earnestness, as well as for certain greater and most serious activities. We may indeed resort to sporting and jesting, but in the same way as we enjoy sleep or other relaxations: that is, only after we have satisfactorily completed what is weighty and serious.[10]

Whatever he intended, Thomas Aquinas opened wide the stable door. Cicero was thinking in the context of literary jokes, of stage comedy. There are, Cicero reminded his readers, two main sorts of jesting: one is coarse, rude, depraved, obscene; the other is elegant, urbane, witty, discriminating. In the superior category he placed Plautus and the Old Comedy of Athens; it is also found in the writings of the Socratic philosophers and in apophthegms such as those Cato collected.

The reference to Socrates and to collections of proverbs and pithy sayings constitute a major finger-post pointing to the fun and laughter which Renaissance readers would find in books where we might be less inclined to seek it or to find it. The collections of *Apophthegmata* and *Adagia* of Erasmus could be read for fun. As indeed they still can: there are many witty sayings and tales in them.

Praise of dialogue, apophthegms and adages could be nothing but music to the ear of Erasmus, who excelled in all three; but laugh-raisers by the thousands put their limits elsewhere than did Cicero. Who is to say where they should be put? Cicero's criteria are subjective. One person's limits are well inside another person's excesses. Such criteria inevitably differ greatly for the senator in the Roman forum, the noble about the court of Renaissance princes, the monk in his cloister, the crowd at a village feast in Brueghel, and the equivalent, at any period, of the man – or woman – on the Clapham omnibus.

Amongst theorists at any rate, Aristotle and Cicero became an essential counterweight to a restrictive reading of St Paul. But open the stable door and the horse will bolt.

---

10. Cicero, *De Officiis*, I, xxix, 103.

Aquinas does not mention Paul in the particular passage where he praises *eutrapelia*, though he does so very fully elsewhere.[11] Since he knew no Greek it never occurred to him that the *scurrilitas* of his Latin Bible was a kind of *eutrapelia*. Had he realized it, Paul might indeed seem to condemn the very *eutrapelia* which he favoured. When Greek became more widely known editors discreetly put that right, noting that there are distinctions to be made: Paul condemned *eutrapelia* only in the sense of something immoderate. Aquinas is favouring something moderate: *eutrapelia* as an Aristotelian virtue, which consists in mental relaxation and honourable fun. As such it is not merely permitted to Christians: it is positively laudable. It is indeed a means of avoiding mental and physical exhaustion.[12]

St Paul's letter to the Ephesians is the foundation of Christian worries about eutrapely. It is interesting to see what Erasmus makes of it all in his *Annotations*. He finds it a good place to condemn his constant *bêtes noires*, the monks. *Eutrapelia* recalls for him too, though he does not explicitly say so, the teachings of Aquinas. His opening words are an echo of what we read in the *Summa Theologica*.[13] Noting Jerome's objections, Erasmus counters them and states his own limits:

While I am in favour of jokes anywhere, provided they be seasoned with

---

11. *Summa Theologica*, II^a II^{ae}, qu. CLXVIII, art. VI. Aquinas makes *eutrapelia* the virtue of moderation in relation to jesting (I^a II^{ae}, qu. LX, art. 5, and II^a II^{ae}, qu. CLX, conclusion).

12. Thomas Aquinas, *Summa Theologica*, Editio Taurinensis, London and Turin, 1895, vol. II, on I^a II^{ae}, qu. LX, art. 5, citing in note 3 Nicolai and Parmeus.

13. For the comments on the relevant text, Ephesians, 5:4, see *Erasmus' Annotations, Galatians to the Apocalypse*, ed. Anne Reeve, Duckworth, 1986, p. 611, s.v. *Aut scurrilitas*:

Eutrapelia: witticisms (*facetia*) or pleasantry (*lepos*); for it is taken in a good sense by philosophers. Here it means however a scurrilous jesting, unworthy of a serious man. Notwithstanding the fact that Jerome believes jests which are made merely to provoke laughter are unworthy of Christians, citing the Gospel according to the Hebrews, *Never rejoice, until you see your brother in Charity*: I, whilst I am in favour . . .

And so on, as in the text about to be cited.

salt, I equally cannot stand those who, whenever they want to be amusing, twist words of Holy Writ for use in their absurdities.

Which brings him to the religious:

Unpleasant pleasantries of that kind are, I find, agreeable to certain monks and to some priests; if they wish to rail against a person, they take the song of Mary, *Magnificat*, or the canticle *Te Deum*, change a word here and there and pervert them to their venom.

Such ignorant monks have never got beyond the long-disgraced textbooks which Humanists – including Rabelais – found barbarous and laughable.[14] The more seriously you study such books the more ridiculous you become – it is, as in the Greek adage, like 'a camel dancing'.

In the light of what Thomas Aquinas and Erasmus wrote it is amusing to find that Thomas himself became the butt of a jest which embodied what they both loathed. Thomas was silently composing a hymn in his mind while eating a lamprey. He finished hymn and lamprey together. To give thanks to God for his hymn he muttered one of Christ's seven last words on the Cross, *Consummatum est!* – 'It is finished!' Bystanders were shocked. They thought he was lightly referring to the lamprey he had just consumed.[15]

There were bonuses when Christian exegetes turned increasingly to the Ancients for guidance on laughter. One was that it brought back into Christendom the idea of laughter as fun. When Bartholomew of Medina wrote his explanations of Thomas Aquinas he emphasized the role of laughter in producing delight and joy.[16] Laughter's warm and humid nature (within the system of humours) makes it come easier to boys, youths and to those in good health. There are kinds of laughter the causes of which are entirely physical;

14. They include the *Catholicon* and *Mammaetrechtus*, mocked by Rabelais in the bad education of Gargantua.
15. Cf. Rabelais, who briefly and effectively alludes to the event (*Tiers Livre*, TLF, II, 149–53). The Latin *Consummatum est* makes the ambiguity more comic than 'It is finished.'
16. *delectatio* and *laetitia*.

for example, laughter from tickling. There is a bastard laughter which arises from anger and grief: the face may grin but no laughter lies behind that grimace. True laughter is born of the emotions: innocent, moral laughter comes from joy or fresh delight.[17] Such contentions strengthened the right of joyful laughter to warm the hearts of Christian folk.

17. *Risus quid ex affectu nascitur, de laetitia est, aut delectatione nova.*

34

The Gospel according to Lucian: Christianity is once again Stupid and Mad

The Bible, explained and codified by scholars who knew their Aristotle and, increasingly, their Plato made it possible for Christians to provoke laughter with a good conscience. But what models, especially literary models, could they follow? Must Christian laughter forever hover around imitations of the mocking taunts of Elijah and indignation at the same kind of taunting laughter directed at Jesus in his trial and agony?

Renaissance authors were heirs to many forms of vibrant laughter which delighted their contemporaries and forebears. By no means all those forms of laughter were welcome. Many were indeed literary in either origin or expression. Laughter was encouraged during the liturgical year, mainly at Shrovetide and Twelfth-Night. Laughter found its way into the pulpit, at times encouraged by the liturgy, at times because of the style of the preacher: the Franciscans especially were renowned for their amusing preaching. Laughter came into meetings of the guilds. There were student romps, satirical sketches put on by budding lawyers or medics. A particular kind of coarse humour was associated with friars and monks in refectory or common-room.

The presses also produced comic or lighter books both for the less learned or unlearned readers who were to be found in all classes of society, and also for Humanist readers in lighter mood. We know that Calvin had a copy of *Pantagruel*. The first reference we have to that first laughter-filled book of Rabelais comes in a learned Italian doctor's account of medical charlatanism in Nantes.[1]

1. M.A.S., 'The earliest reference to a *Gargantua* and *Pantagruel*', in Michael Heath (ed.), *Some Renaissance Studies*, THR, CCLXII, Droz, Geneva, 1992,

For Humanist writers such as Erasmus most of that kind of laughter and laugh-raising meant nothing good. They preferred to turn mainly to the laughter-raisers of classical literature; Greek authors in particular had an exciting freshness. The richest model for Erasmus, and for Rabelais too, was Lucian of Samosata. Although living at the time of the early Church he wrote in good classical Greek. Some still think of him primarily as an anti-Christian scoffer.

Both Erasmus and Rabelais, having abandoned their convents, remained secular priests. Both were men of wide experience of life outside convent and cloister; both left their orders with the eventual connivance of the Vatican. Papal approval was in both cases a lateish recognition of a *fait accompli*.[2]

When Erasmus first discovered Lucian is not certain: probably as soon as he began seriously to study Greek. Rabelais knew him well when he was still a Franciscan. What those two priests discovered in Lucian was a stimulus, a challenge and a laughing support for their evangelical faith. They met opposition from some quarters. At the time, and as the years went by, the devotion of Humanists to Lucian was deeply suspect in the eyes of some. Was not Lucian's very name a byword for anti-Christian irreverence? Lucian was the only extant author writing in classical Greek who was late enough to know Christianity and irresistibly to laugh at it. The uses of 'Lucianist' or 'Lucianic' cited in the *Oxford English Dictionary* all bear out the dangerous reputation of Lucian and his scoffing:

– Their most light, and wanton Lucianicall wittes (Bullinger); – My betters need not take it grievously, to be taunted, . . . when Saint Peter and Christ himself are Lucianically and scoffingly alleged (Gabriel Harvey) . . .

---

pp. 215–16. The reference comes in Dr Petrus Baptista's *Epistolæ tres.* (Sebastian Gryphius? Lyons? 1535?).

2. Erasmus obtained the permission of Leo X. Rabelais had moved up from the Franciscans to the Benedictines with the support of his patron Bishop Geoffroy d'Estissac; he was fully and successfully supported by the ingenious manoeuvres of Cardinal Jean Du Bellay, which left him, like Erasmus, a secular priest, absolved of his 'apostasy'.

Of his own contemporaries Calvin wrote:

– The Epicures and Lucianists doe profess that they believe, whereas notwithstanding they laugh inwardly.[3]

Erasmus was suspect from the start. In the case of Calvin in his maturity, the allegation that Lucianic scoffers were secret unbelievers dangerously embraced Rabelais.

What gave Lucian his unjust reputation as a scoffer at all things Christian is not far to seek. It lies in a shocked exaggeration of a real characteristic. Lucian scoffs mainly at the gods of the pagan pantheon, but he does incidentally scoff also at the early Christians and their crucified Lord.

In one of his most widely read works he turned his laughing attention on to the wilful self-immolation of a certain Peregrinus. Peregrinus had abandoned the philosophy of the Cynics so as to join the Christians and exploit their gullibility. Far from being impressed by the showy suicide of Peregrinus and the hint of his reappearance or resurrection, Lucian found it all very laughable:

This 'Dear Sir' has burnt himself to a cinder, like Empedocles. But when Empedocles cast himself into Ætna he managed to avoid turning it into a spectacle. This fellow waited for one of the most crowded of the Greek festivals; he then built up a huge pyre and, in front of that great audience, jumped into it. Only a few days before his silly action he even prated to the Greeks about it! I think I can hear you laughing at that old man's senile stupidity.

The tale of that self-immolator is told in a dialogue entitled *The Passing of Peregrinus*. Laughing at a silly, vain old confidence-trickster and his spectacular suicide might seem insensitive and cruel. Nobody seemed to find it so. It is no more cruel than Elijah's mocking of the priests of Baal. The Renaissance witnessed cases where stubborn victims of persecution were seen by their ecclesiastical opponents not as martyrs but as laughing-stocks. Martyrs are witnesses.

3. *OED*, s.v. *Lucian* and *Lucianist* (1). Bullinger was translated by Dans and Calvin by Fetherstone.

If such were martyrs, they were martyrs to the Devil. Rival Christians may burn each other with laughs or smirks of satisfaction on their lips.

Inevitably *The Passing of Peregrinus* attracted the attention of the censors. What apparently disturbed the ecclesiastical compilers of the *Index librorum prohibitorium* of the Council of Trent (1564) was not Lucian's scoffing as such but some of its implications and butts. They could not ignore the explicit mockery of the simple-mindedness of the gullible Christians of sub-apostolic times.

But the hostility of some guardians of Christian purity was often ill-founded: Lucian was delighted in by generations of impeccable believers. Even the assembled Fathers at Trent condemned only two works of Lucian, one of them of doubtful authorship. They are listed by their titles: 'Dialogues of Lucian, namely *The Passing of Peregrinus* and *Philopatris*.'[4]

All the other works of that scoffing Greek went unscathed, and so in practice did those two also. They continued to be available in print.

Peregrinus was a real man, not a character in a skit. He was surnamed Proteus since he was as changeable as that legendary figure in Antiquity. Lucian refused to believe that Peregrinus had ever been a genuine philosopher (a genuine 'lover of wisdom'). He was a quack. After his conversion he became a leader amongst the Christians, and was soon interpreting Scripture for his childlike disciples; he then forged Scriptures of his own. Those generous Christian simpletons who followed him virtually worshipped him, though not, of course, as they worshipped the 'great man' who, on the charge of introducing 'that new mystery into men's lives, was crucified in Palestine'.[5]

---

4. Rome: Church of Rome, Council of Trent, *Index Tridentinus* [the *Index Librorum prohibitorum*]; § *Certorum auctorum libri prohibiti*, under the letter L:

Luciani Samosatensis Dialogi, videlicet *Mors Peregrini* and *Philopatris*.

5. The Greek text of Lucian is unclear at this crucial point and is often emended. To stay close to the interpretation dominant in the Renaissance I have re-translated the standard Latin version of Vincentius Obsoponeus in *Luciani Opera*, Venice, 1503, p. 294 verso. (It was often reprinted.)

When Peregrinus is thrown into gaol, the simpletons who follow him pour out money to help him. Those wretched Christians despise death; they even court imprisonment, persuaded that they are to become immortal. 'Their original Law-giver convinced them that they are all brothers to each other.' Rejecting the Greek gods, they worship the Crucified – their 'Sophist, impaled by a pole'.

Quitting the Christians to become a Cynic again, Peregrinus found his criminal – indeed parricidal – past was catching up on him. He was, we are assured, a murderer, a cheat and an impostor. He conceived the idea of convincing the mob of his integrity as a philosopher: he would announce that he was about to cast himself into a specially constructed pyre. Many were taken in. Not Lucian! At each turn and twist he finds Peregrinus laughable. Peregrinus had hoped to be held back at the last minute by his followers, but they failed to save him. Lucian's narrator, who was witnessing the event, guffawed: 'How I laughed, I expect you know! It was not appropriate to pity a man so besotted with vainglory.'

Peregrinus had caused incense to be sprinkled on to his pyre. He had evoked the spirits of his mother and of the father he had secretly murdered. (Again the narrator laughs.) He then throws himself headlong into the flames, which immediately engulf him.

'Once more I can see you laughing.' Lucian's narrator cannot produce on his own all the laughter the event requires. He evokes Democritus, the fabled laugher of Antiquity: even he could not supply enough. The narrator's friend has to contribute his share of laughter too.[6]

Lucian ought not to have been condemned for scoffing at the simplicity of those early Christians: Christians must expect their fellow believers to be taken for idiots by the worldly-wise. A fake Christian such as Peregrinus deserved to be scoffed at; such are the rules of

---

Itaque etiamnum magnum illum hominem colunt, qui in Palestina crucifixus est, quoniam primus novum illud mysterium in hominum vitam invexerat.

The Greek original uses a verb which means impaling rather than crucifying, but in practice the sense was much the same.

6. *The Passing of Peregrinus*, 11, 13, 34, 37.

comedy. But, to timorous souls, Peregrinus and his death can read at times like a parody of the death and resurrection of Jesus himself. Peregrinus yearned for altars at which he himself would be worshipped. After his death a venerable old man claimed to have seen him alive, clad in white raiment. Peregrinus had dispatched to great cities 'epistles' containing his testament. (The word employed by Lucian for that testament is used by Christians for the New Testament.)[7]

Another Christian parallel: before his death Peregrinus had sent out 'ambassadors' to spread his teachings. The word Lucian uses for such an ambassador in *presbeutēs*. Now St Paul used a very similar word to refer to himself: *presbutēs*,[8] which means 'an old man'. But *presbutēs* is so similar to *presbeutēs* – meaning 'ambassador' or 'apostle' – that, in Paul, the first is often taken to be a substitute for the second; Lucian could have been laughing indirectly at the likes of Paul, old men who were apostles of their Master. St Jerome may have thought so.[9]

Particularly worrying to Humanists was Lucian's assertion that Peregrinus had forged ancient Christian writings. Scholars were studying the writings of Christian antiquity as never before: some of the very earliest could be forgeries of the man whom Lucian mocked.

Lucian's chilling amusement chimes well with the widespread conviction that laughter is incompatible with pity. His own ideas on laughter conform to what was found in Plato.

What provoked amusement was the stupidity of Peregrinus, his *abelteria* – the uncontroversial term which Socrates used for clownish stupidity in the *Philebus*. When Lucian's narrator evoked his correspondent's laughter at that old man's snotty stupidity, he added: 'I

7. *Diathēkē.*   8. Philemon, 9.

9. For the relevant text (Philemon, 9), the translation 'ambassador' rather than 'old man' is to be read in the margin of the Revised Version. It appears there as a modern conjecture by Bentley, but Erasmus already cites St Jerome as referring to Paul as 'an apostle, and an old man, and a man bound in chains'. By using both *apostolus* and *senex*, Jerome (who, as Erasmus notes, was following the Greek) may have recognized the possible substitution of 'old man' for 'apostle'. Cf. *Erasmus' Annotations, Galatians to the Apocalypse*, ed. Anne Reeve, Brill, Leyden, 1993, p. 703, under *Cum sis talis ut Paulus*.

can indeed hear you mouthing – as you naturally would – "Oh, the *abelteria*! Oh, the vainglory! Oh, the this! Oh, the that." '[10]

Obsoponeus was the first to translate *Peregrinus* into Latin. His brief introduction was normally reprinted with his version. In it, he notes that Peregrinus was driven on not by mere ambition but by *insane* ambition. Peregrinus displayed therefore that combination of stupidity and madness, of *abelteria* and *anoia*, which provokes Socratic laughter. Lucian would further confirm, by his worldly scoffing, that Christianity is a form of folly.

Did Lucian laugh at St Paul also? Yes – but only if you can still persuade yourself that he wrote the other work attributed to him by the Tridentine censors: the *Philopatris*. The anti-Christian edge of that work is much less clear-cut. Since the early nineteenth century at least it has been thought to be the work of an imitator of Lucian who lived in tenth-century Byzantium. If so, he wrote some eight hundred years after Lucian himself. When taken as authentic, the *Philopatris* assumes a leering satirical quality; yet its anti-Christian savour is by no means always evident. It ends in fact with a contrast made by a certain Triepho between the good 'unknown God' evoked by St Paul in Athens and the nonsense of classical paganism.[11] The speakers in the dialogue now claim to have found that 'unknown God'. It can, I suppose, all be taken as ironical . . . yet as irony it is not always compelling.

Earlier in *Philopatris*, Triepho alludes light-heartedly to St Paul's rapture to the Third Heaven.[12] An arresting allusion. So much Christian mysticism depends upon that rapture. The subject turns then to what the Greeks called *To Pan*, the ALL. Triepho is well informed on the subject:

I shall teach you who is that ALL; who it is who existed before that ALL, and about the regular governance of that ALL.

Triepho can do so since he has recently met 'a Galilæan, with a bald

---

10. *Luciani Opera*, Venice, 1503, introduction to the *Mors Peregrini* by Vincent Obsoponeus. For laughter at arrogance, cf. ibid., p. 290.

11. Acts, 17:23.   12. II Corinthians, 12.

forehead and a long nose, who had walked on air to the Third Heaven'. The Latin version of those words gives Paul an 'aquiline nose' and does not have him walking on air; he is less irreverently shown as 'entering the Third Heaven through the air'. (There is a little less cause for laughter in the Latin.) Lucian's Paul, who had heard wondrous things during his rapture, baptized Triepho and 'redeemed him from the regions of impiety'.

The *Philopatris* contains echoes of the New Testament, of the psalms, and of the Creeds. It borrows the detail of the balding forehead of Paul from an early apocryphal treatise.[13] It light-heartedly mentions God as 'Three in One, and One in Three' and, even more light-heartedly, treats God the Father as an old man in the sky, keeping records of everyone's naughty doings. There was clearly enough for the censors of Trent to place *Philopatris* on their *Index*.

Lucian's authentic satire of simple Christians, as well as passages of doubtful authenticity such as that which treats Paul disrespectfully, were often cited out of context. Some appear for example in Cornelius à Lapide's *Proemium on the Prerogatives of St Paul*. He emphasizes the mockery and sees the mention of Paul's receding hairline as intended to raise laughter:

Chrysostom says Paul was no more than three cubits yet transcended the heavens. Yet Lucian in the *Philopatris* laughs at Paul for his balding forehead.[14]

Such laughing might recall the punishment of those wicked boys who yelled 'Baldy' after Elisha.

And so, for the censors of Trent, *Peregrinus* and *Philopatris* had to go, though in practice they did not. Throughout the sixteenth century 'Lucianesque' or 'Lucianical' were used by frightened sobersides as a term of random religious abuse. Both Erasmus and Rabelais were condemned as vile imitators of that scoffing Greek. Those who wrote of them in such terms often meant that they had ceased to be

13. *Acts of Paul and Thecla*, 1:9.
14. Cornelius à Lapide, in *Omnes Divi Pauli Commentaria*, Lyons, 1660, *Proemium De Praerogativis S. Pauli*, p. 8, col. 2, and p. 362, col. 2.

Christians and were probably atheists, mocking the very religion of which they were priests.

As the years rolled by, the extent to which some zealous writers would go in their hostility to Lucian almost beggars belief. One example. In 1619 Garasse published a pamphlet against a treatise *On the Vocation of Pastors* from the pen of Pierre Du Moulin, a celebrated minister of the *Église réformée*. Garasse called his tract *Rabelais Reformed by the Ministers*.[15] He makes great play on the fact that 'Caluin' is an anagram of 'Lucian' – as indeed it is, as Calvin was then spelt with a *u*, not a *v*. In his tirade all religious nuances, all religious differences amongst his numerous opponents, are effaced: Rabelais, Calvin, Erasmus, are all Lucianic atheists. So too are Aretino, Plautus and Socrates! Du Moulin must have been aware, we are told, that Lucian strove to destroy Christianity by his scoffing and impiety; and 'recently we have witnessed what excesses have ravaged minds from the reading of Rabelais'.

One of the very few contemporaries whom Rabelais mocked by name in his writings was Calvin; that does not prevent Garasse from lumping them both together. Lucian and Rabelais were false prophets:

Soon afterwards came Caluin with the double mind of those two false prophets: as poisonous as Lucian (whose name he bore as a fated and inauspicious anagram) and as much of a buffoon as Rabelais.

(Garasse could not forgo the pleasure of repeating that anagram yet again.) Calvin had read Rabelais; he had drunk in his libertine quality, causing great harm to the Church,

as much by the poison of his raving pen as by his juggler's tricks, which can be seen on every page of his works; by the report of Baudouin in his *Apologie*, Calvin gloried in it, congratulating himself on having, he said, the humour of Socrates – that is buffoon-like and ironical.

15. *Le Rabelais réformé par les Ministres, et nommément par Pierre Du Moulin, ministre de Charenton, pour réponse aux bouffonneries insérées dans son livre de la Vocation des Pasteurs*, Christophe Girard, Brussels, 1619.

Resorting to doggerel, Garasse asserts that Rabelais was spurred on by 'reading the tales of Erasmus'. He loved them above all else: they were his inspiration – his *'entousiasme'*. And then came Calvin, who being of a 'maniacal humour' wrote 'a fat book in which he talks like a demoniac'.[16]

For some, the gospel according to Lucian is a gospel for atheists. For many – whom admirers of Lucian readily laughed at – Lucianical laughter was bad laughter.

In the seventeenth century, when Erasmus was widely appreciated in England, Thomas Fuller still remained ill at ease with the Lucianism in his writings. He found that in his *Colloquies* Erasmus 'doth Lucian-it too much'. But he fairly adds, 'yet truth may be discovered under the varnish of his scoffing wit'.[17]

Judgements were often more generous.

For many, Erasmus was the very model of reborn Lucianic laughter; for others, it was Rabelais. Both used their laughter to illuminate abuses in the teaching and structures of the Church. Both turned to Lucian for guidance. In the light of that a certain kind of critic assumed the worst: they were both mocking atheists, masquerading as priests!

16. ibid., pp. 6f.; p. 12:

> De plus on dit qu'il s'animoit,
> En lisant les contes d'Erasme;
> Car sur tous livres il l'aymoit
> Et s'en servoit d'entousiasme.
>
> . . .

and p. 13:

> Et Calvin de près me suivit
> Car estant d'humeur maniaque
> Un gros livre il escrivit
> Où il parle en démoniaque.

17. Thomas Fuller, *The Church History of Britain*, London, 1655, VI, 1, 34. (Cited also in *OED*, s.v. *Lucian*.)

35

Lucian in the Pulpit

But there was another view of Lucian. Others knew they would find in him refined moral laughter. In more recent times J. A. Froude was following a long tradition when he maintained that Lucian was 'doing the Church's business when he seemed most distant from it': his laughter condemned liars, charlatans and 'the impious theology of the established pagan religion'. Most Humanists would have said Amen to that.[1]

Generalized attacks on Lucian were effectively fended off. The Renaissance reader showed that he enjoyed the happy marriage between Christian zeal and Lucianical laughter. Lucian was not by any means entirely tainted. Trent did not seek to stifle Lucian's laughter; how could the authorities of any Church proscribe a great classical author on whom towering Christian scholars had bestowed their accolade? The long list of Humanists who translated works of Lucian into Latin testify to a wide appreciation of his sense of fun and to their delight in it. Erasmus translated him. Thomas More did. So did Melanchthon. So did Rabelais while a Franciscan, though his version is lost. So did Billibald Pirkheimer, Gilbert Cognatus and other fine scholars now far less widely known. The translators came from various Christian traditions: whatever else separated them, their enjoyment of Lucian brought them together. Lucian meant laughter. The very title chosen by Erasmus and More in 1506 emphasizes the amusement to be found in their shared volume:

1. James Anthony Froude, 'A Cagliostro of the second century', in *Short Studies on Great Subjects*, vol. IV, London and Bombay, 1901, pp. 438–9.

Compulurima opuscula festivissima, 'Several very humorous little works'. They promised wit, pleasure and gaiety.

Erasmus held that an ideal theologian should know 'the three languages', Latin, Greek and Hebrew – especially the first two. For their Greek texts, schoolboys should study Homer and Lucian – which must have been a treat. When the theologian James Latomus of Louvain criticized such ideas as dangerous to religion, Erasmus defended them. He would not accept that the fictions of Homer and Lucian are 'impious, impure and superstitious'. Latomus calls their fables unworthy of their gods; but, Erasmus pointed out, that ought to make them dear to us Christians! They are exposing to ridicule gods we know to be false:

'Lucian constantly laughs at the gods. Hence he is called an atheist; and there is the risk that a boy might imbibe pagan superstition from his fables!' On such grounds there is more reason to be wary of Aristotle, who not infrequently mentions the gods, and in earnest, too.

Plato would have to go as well. So would many Ancient historians.

Why Latomus should call Homer obscene I cannot see; nor Lucian either – certainly not in the dialogues that I have translated.

The modesty of youth is more easily corrupted by Catullus, the poet of sensual love, or by the Roman satirists, Juvenal and Martial. Then there are the priapic poems; the Arabic philosopher Averroes, who blasphemes Christ; Pliny, 'who openly laughs at the immortality of the soul, the very basis of our religion'. Suetonius and Tacitus are both anti-Christian. Yet only Homer and Lucian are to be picked out for blame. Nobody teaching them to boys presents their gods as true. You might just as well fear that a lad reading Æsop would believe that foxes or lions can talk!

That last point was a strong one. Æsop was unique amongst the 'seven moral authors' of medieval schooling. The other six were rejected with scorn, whereas Æsop remained a darling for Humanists seeking texts to give moral guidance to young and old.

Erasmus points out that a good teacher always tiptoes carefully over anything obscene or lascivious in any of the books he is teaching – including the Bible, where there is much to be careful about.[2]

So far so good. But Erasmus did far more than read Lucian for the quality of his Greek. He took him as a model. His *Colloquies*, parts of the *Moria*, and even some of the comments in his *Annotations on the New Testament*, are marked by the influence of Lucian. Either the slant of his mind was inherently Lucianic or else the writings of Lucian had helped to make it so. Thanks to Erasmus and, later, to Rabelais, there really was born in the Renaissance a committed 'Gospel according to Lucian'. Lucian helped many to distinguish between material symbol and the spiritual or moral reality it signifies. How can holiness be found in a Franciscan's cloak, if you do not love God and live like St Francis? Some religious avoided touching money: they handled it with gloves. Where is the spirituality to be found in that? If the eurcharist means no more than hanging about altars, listening with a carnal mind to monkish bellowing from the choir-stalls, and swallowing the host with one's thoughts full of malice, where is Christ to be found there? The laughter that Lucian directed at the classical gods, pedants or charlatans readily lends itself to be adapted to mock popes, scholastic theologians, and monks, as well as the superstitious cult of saints and other accretions to evangelical doctrine. With the help of Lucian, heretics, false prophets, and theologians ignorant of Greek could be treated as idiots or nincompoops, their ideas compounded of stupidity and madness.

2. See Erasmus, *Apologia quorundam suspiciones ac rumores natos ex dialogo qui eximio viro D. Iacobo Latomo sacræ theologiæ licentiato inscribitur*, in the edition published by Froben, Basle, 1518; text in Erasmus, LB, 9, 79–106.

36

A Taste of Lucianic Laughter
in the *Colloquies*

Generations of schoolboys, not least in England, used to study the *Colloquies* of Erasmus when learning their Latin. They are presented by Erasmus as a textbook. They begin with simple lists of useful and elegant phrases – greetings and suchlike. Swiftly they move on to those witty dialogues which expound a subtle humanist Christianity and expose superstition and doltishness to ridicule. They propagate a laughing religion, as effectively then as now. Many interested in Christian laughter may not yet have read any of them. That can be put right: a taste of a mere passage or two from them will go a long way towards giving anyone who needs it an idea of how far a priest can go in laughing at error within the Church and what is meant by the gospel according to Lucian.

Could Lucian himself have done better than Erasmus in, say, his colloquy *The Religious Pilgrimage*? Two men, Menedemus and Ogygius, are discussing the subject of gadding about after shrines and relics. Ogygius, riddled with superstition, has just returned from St James's shrine at Compostela. Clearly henpecked, he had undertaken his pilgrimage at the behest of a bossy wife and mother-in-law. Ogygius had discovered to his dismay that newfangled evangelical humanist teachings had led to a decline in the popularity of saints, relics and shrines. The dialogue has a lightness of wit which must have made its Latin a joy to study in the schoolroom. (Erasmus abbreviates the names of Menedemus and Ogygius to *Men.* and *Ogy.*):

Men. Tell me, I pray, how does the good man St James fare? and what was he doing? *Ogy.* Why truly, not so well by far as he used to be. *Men.* What's the matter? Has he grown old? *Ogy.* Trifler! You know saints never grow old. No, but it is this new opinion that has been spread abroad through the world which results in his having fewer visits made to him than he used to have; and those who do come give him a bare salute, contributing either nothing else at all or only a tiny sum; they say they can bestow their money to better purpose upon those that lack it.

It was a constant complaint of evangelical Christians – not all of whom were by any means schismatics – that money lavished on shrines, church buildings and the like would be better spent on the poor. So we know where Menedemus stands amongst the self-condemned when he retorts: 'An impious opinion.' Ogygius continues, undeterred:

Ogy. And this is the cause, that this great apostle that used to glitter with gold and jewels is now reduced to the very block that he is made of, and has scarce a tallow candle. *Men.* If this be true the rest of the saints are in danger of coming to the same pass. *Ogy.* Nay, I can assure you, that there is a letter handed about which the Virgin Mary herself has written on this matter. *Men.* What, Mary! *Ogy.* She that is called Maria à Lapide. *Men.* That is up towards Basle, if I am not mistaken. *Ogy.* The very same. *Men.* You talk of a very stony saint.[1] But to whom did she write it? *Ogy.* The letter tells you the name. *Men.* Whom did she send it by? *Ogy.* An angel, no doubt, who laid it down in the pulpit, where the preacher to whom it was sent took it up. And to put the matter out of all doubt, you shall see the original letter.

The scholarly Menedemus, who plainly was used to the problems of dating inscriptions, asks all the right questions:

Men. Do you know the hand of the angel that is secretary to the Virgin Mary? *Ogy.* Well enough. *Men.* By what token? *Ogy.* I have read St Bede's epitaph, that was engraven by the same angel, and the shape of the letters is exactly the same; and I have read the discharge sent to St Ægidius, and they agree exactly. Do not these prove the matter plain enough? *Men.* May

---

1. *Lapis* (of which *lapide* is the ablative case) means a stone.

a body see it? *Ogy.* You may, but you will damn your soul to the pit of hell if ever you speak of it. *Men.* It is as safe as if you spoke it to a stone. *Ogy.* But there are some stones that are infamous for not being able to keep a secret. *Men.* If you cannot trust to a stone, speak to a mute then. *Ogy.* Upon that condition I'll recite it to you; but prick up your ears. *Men.* I have done so.

Ogygius then quotes at length the very letter written by the Virgin and dispatched directly from Heaven to her shrine near Basle:

'Mary the Mother of Jesus to Glaucoplutus sendeth greeting. This is to let you know, that I take it in good part, and you have much obliged me, in that you have so strenuously followed Luther and convinced the world that it is altogether needless to invoke saints. For before this time I was wearied out of my life with the wicked importunities of mortals. Everything was asked of me, as if my Son – because he is painted so – was still a child and at my breast; they therefore take it for granted that I have him still at my beck and call, and that he dares not deny me anything I ask of him, for fear I should deny him the bubby when he is thirsty. Nay, and they ask such things from me, a Virgin, that a modest young man would scarce dare to ask of a bawd, and which I am ashamed to commit to writing. A merchant that is going on a voyage to Spain to get pelf recommends to me the chastity of his kept mistress; and a professed nun, having thrown away her veil in order to make her escape, recommends to me the care of her reputation, which she at the same time intends to prostitute. The wicked mercenary who butchers men for money bawls out to me, "O Blessed Virgin, send me rich plunder!" The gamester calls out to me to give him good luck, and promises I shall go snips with him in what he shall win; and if the dice do not favour him, I am railed at and cursed because I would not be a confederate in his wickedness. The usurer prays, "Help me to get large interest for my money!" If I deny them anything, they cry out that I am no Mother of Mercy.'

Such superstition is not the preserve of the criminal and the sleazy. There are also the simple and gullible:

'And there is another sort of people, whose prayers are not properly so much wicked as foolish: the maid prays, "Mary, give me a handsome, rich husband!" The wife cries, "Give me fine children"; and the woman with child, "Give me a good delivery." The old woman prays to live long without a cough and thirst; and the doting old man prays, "Send that I may grow young again." The philosopher says, "Give me the faculty of starting difficult problems never to be resolved!" The priest says, "Give me a fat benefice." The bishop cries out for the keeping of his diocese; and the mariner for a prosperous voyage; the magistrate cries out, "Show me your Son before I die!" The courtier, that he may make an effectual confession when at the point of death; the husbandman calls on me for seasonable rain; and a farmer's wife, to preserve her sheep and cattle. If I refuse them any thing, then at once I am hard-hearted. If I refer them to my Son, they cry, "If you will but say the word, I am sure he will do it."

'How is it possible for me, a lone body, a widow and a virgin, to assist sailors, soldiers, merchants, gamesters, brides and bridegrooms, women in travail, princes, kings and peasants? And what I have mentioned is the least part of what I suffer.'

The cult of the Virgin and her shrines have taken a knock along with other superstitions. So laughter is aroused by Mary's taking a different satirical tack:

'I have indeed more leisure, but also less honour and less money. Before, I was saluted as Queen of Heaven and Lady of the World; but now there are very few from whom I hear an *Ave-Mary*. Formerly I was adorned with jewels and gold, and had an abundance of changes of apparel; I had presents made me of gold and jewels; but now I have scarce half a vest to cover me, and that is mouse-eaten too. And my yearly revenue is scarce enough to keep alive my poor sexton who lights me up a little wax or tallow candle.'

Those are but the signs of the times. (One would be hard put to it to tell Erasmus's ideas from Luther's on this particular topic.)

'But all these things might be borne with, if you did not tell us that there were still greater things going forward. They say you aim to strip the altars and temples of the saints everywhere. I advise you again and again to have a care what you do: for other saints do not lack power to avenge themselves for the wrong done to them. Peter, being turned out of his church, can shut the gate of the kingdom of Heaven against you. Paul has a sword, and St Bartholomew a knife. The Monk William has a coat of mail under his habit, and a heavy lance too. And how will you face St George on horseback, in his cuirassier's arms, his sword and his whinyard? Nor is Anthony without his weapon: he has his sacred fire; and the rest of them have either their arms or their mischiefs that they can send out against whom they please.

'And as for myself, although I wear no weapons, you shall not turn me out unless you turn my Son out too, whom I hold in my arms. I will not be pulled away from him: you shall either throw us both out or leave us both, unless you have a mind to have a Church without a Christ. These things I would have you know, and consider what answer to give me; for I have the matter much at heart.

> 'From our Stone House, the kalends of August,
>   the year of my son's Passion 1524.
> I the Stony Virgin have subscribed this
>   with my own hand.'

Erasmus, a priest, was stirring up a hornet's nest.

Men. In truth this is a very terrible threatening letter, and I believe Glauco-plutus will take care what he does. *Ogy.* He will if he is wise. *Men.* But why did not honest James write to him about this matter? *Ogy.* Truly I cannot tell, except it is because he is a great way off, and nowadays all letters are intercepted.[2]

The Virgin comes to the fore again later in the same colloquy. With Dean Colet, Erasmus had visited the shrine of Our Lady at Walsingham. He found it all laughable, scoffing at the replica of the Holy House of Nazareth. Ogygius in his turn went there and innocently remarked that the house did not actually look very old.

---

2. N. Bailey, *All the Familiar Colloquies of Desiderius Erasmus of Roterdam Concerning Men, Manners and Things, translated into English*, second edition, London, 1733, pp. 320–24. (Colloquy after colloquy could be considered for its Lucianic tone.) To keep the period savour which Bailey succeeded so well in creating, instead of translating Erasmus afresh I have adapted Bailey, changing a word or phrase here and there.

The wily verger gets out of that somehow. And then we return to the relics of the Virgin:

Therefore seeming to be satisfied, and excusing our dullness of apprehension, we turned ourselves to the heavenly milk of the blessed Virgin. *Men.* O Mother like her Son! for just as he has left us so much of his blood upon earth, so she has left us so much of her milk that it is scarce credible that a woman who never bore but one child should have so much, even if her child had never sucked a drop of it.

   Ogy. And they tell us the same stories about our Lord's Cross, which is shown up and down, both publicly and privately, in so many places that if all the fragments were gathered together they would seem to be sufficient cargo for a good large ship; and yet our Lord himself carried the whole Cross upon his shoulders. *Men.* And do you not think that this is curious? *Ogy.* It may be said to be extraordinary but it is not curious, since the Lord who increases these things according to his own pleasure is omnipotent. *Men.* You put a very pious construction upon it, but I am afraid that a great many such things are forged for the sake of getting money.

To which Ogygius has a quick and would-be pious answer ready:

Ogy. I cannot think God would suffer anyone to put these mockeries upon him. *Men.* Nay, when both the Mother and Son, Father and Spirit are robbed by sacrilegious persons, they do not seem to be moved in the least to deter wicked persons so much as by a nod or a stamp; so great is the levity of the divine Being. *Ogy.* That is true, but hear me out: that milk is kept upon the high altar, on which Christ is in the middle and his Mother, for respect's sake, at his right hand; for the milk represents the Mother. *Men.* Why! Is it plain to be seen? *Ogy.* It is preserved in a crystal glass. *Men.* Is it liquid then? *Ogy.* Why do you talk of it being liquid, when it was put in above 1,500 years ago! It is so concreted, you would take it for beaten chalk, tempered with the white of an egg. *Men.* But why do they not show it open? *Ogy.* Lest the milk of the Virgin should be defiled by the kisses of men. *Men.* Well said, for I believe there are some who put lips to it that are neither pure nor virgin ones. *Ogy.* As soon as the officer sees us, he straightway runs and puts on a surplice, and a stole about his neck, and falls down very devoutly and worships and, by and by, gives us the holy milk to kiss.[3]

Similar laughter accompanies a visit to the shrine of Thomas Becket at Canterbury. Ogygius's attempts to persuade Menedemus to set off on such a pilgrimage fall on sceptical ears. Menedemus, a true evangelical, is more concerned to stay at home and look after his household, his daughter's chastity, his business and the due employment of everyone in his charge. Ogygius attempts to counter his arguments:

Ogy. But St James would take care of such things for you. *Men.* The Holy Scriptures enjoin me to look after them myself, and I do not find any text telling me to leave them to the saints.

With that markedly Lutheranizing quip the colloquy ends.[4]

It is worth reading Erasmus's *Colloquies* closely; apart from the pleasure they afford, they provide a yardstick against which to judge the boldness of others.

---

3. ibid. (adapted), pp. 328–9.
4. Menedemus made a very revealing assertion. Erasmus, Luther, Rabelais and others read precisely such a message into St Paul's Epistle to the Galatians, 6:10: 'As we have therefore opportunity, let us do good to all men, especially unto those who are of the household of faith.' There is no scriptural text which actually condemns pilgrimages and instructs men to stay at home for the reasons which Menedemus states. Evangelicals, sure that there must be such a text, read a meaning favourable to themselves into the words 'household of faith'. The phrase was taken to mean that men should remain at home and care for their families.

37

Laughter in
the *Annotations*

The *Colloquies* were soon famous and infamous for their Lucianism. On picking up a copy, all but the ill-informed must have known what to expect. Those subtle dialogues laugh at ignorance, superstition and pomposity of all kinds. Among the many which remain highly enjoyable are *The Abbot and the Learned Woman* and *The Lying-in Woman* (in which the man has the highly significative name of Eutrapelus). The Latin in which they are written is light, elegant and clear: a joy to read. Laughter or smiles mark page after page. But nothing prepared readers of that time to find satire or laughter at ignorance and madness in Erasmus's *Annotations on the New Testament*. He had invented a new genre.

How many voluminous commentaries on Scripture there are! From the earliest to those of Erasmus they already form an imposing array. Does anyone read them for fun?

Few scriptural commentators have ever encouraged scoffing and laughter in their glosses and explanations. Erasmus constantly does. The ever-expanding annotations are peppered with occasional laughter at the ignorance and folly of monks, pompous clerical asses, scholastic theologians, would-be authorities who had inadequate Latin and no Greek, as well as at opaque theological jargon and stupidity of all sorts.

'Madman laughs at madman' certainly applies here.

Erasmus was ruthless in provoking laughter at the gaffes of guides who knew no Greek. (How could they avoid errors when daring to expound texts written in that pliant tongue?) He was bitterly laughed at in return. A laugher at others, he never got used to being laughed at himself. He bridled at the laughter of opponents who preferred Aristotle's teaching on war to Christ's. They included many bishops, theologians and monks:

Some who strongly believe themselves to be Christian wrinkle their noses in mockery at precepts which, if we are truly Christians, should be venerated by us. I have heard them.[1]

Laughter was returned in kind. With the years the scoffing increased.[2] Each new edition contained some fresh nodes of sneering and laughter. Theologians long venerated, who were studied in the universities and treated with awe as saints or pinnacles of learning, were dismissed: not refuted, but held up to ridicule. Greekless, they had feet of clay. Honoured scholars from the past who were laughed at included Peter Lombard, the twelfth-century Master of the Sentences; Nicholas of Lyra (1270–1340), the best-equipped biblical scholar of his day, a theologian admired by Luther as well as by traditionalists: he had no Greek but good Hebrew. Then there was Hugo Carrensis, the great Cardinal of Saint-Cher, and Thomas Aquinas himself. Each had his following in college and convent; each was subjected to giggles or laughter. Where one might expect nothing but quiet philology or, at worst, *odium theologicum*, we find laughter at ignorance, much of it concerning an often faulty Vulgate and its Latin commentators.

Impatient mockery of those without Greek can be found near the beginning of Erasmus's *Annotations*. Joseph, in Matthew's Gospel, was unwilling to 'make a public example' of Mary, whom he then held to be unfaithful. The Greek verb meaning 'to make a public example' is precise, and is elegantly translated in the Vulgate – so elegantly that it requires a sound knowledge of classical Latin to grasp what the verb means. The verb is *traducere*. Medieval commentators were foxed by it. Peter Lombard, 'in his almost boundless sea of questions', thought

1. *Erasmus' Annotations*, ed. Anne Reeve, Duckworth, 1986, I, p. 26, s.v. *omne malum*.
2. The first edition was 1516. Erasmus published revised and expanded editions in 1519, 1522, 1527 and 1535. All the variants are given by Anne Reeve.

that it means 'to have sexual intercourse'. According to him, Joseph, believing Mary to be unfaithful, was unwilling to lie with her. Erasmus scoffs at such a shameful lapse, especially on the part of one of those 'who set themselves up as instructors to the whole world'. Some exegetes try to wriggle out of their ignorance with a quibble. They opine that that difficult verb means, not as Peter Lombard wrongly taught, to *have* sexual intercourse, but rather to *consent* to it:

That is as if someone who was correcting a man who maintained that *gourd* meant the rump of an ass were to deny that it meant the rump itself, but rather a pack-saddle fixed on to the rump.

Good Latin was all but unknown in those far-off days! What on earth, Erasmus wondered, was Nicholas of Lyra up to when he explained that tricky verb by another one meaning, 'to exhibit'?[3] The *Glossa Ordinaria* makes things worse still: its author Wilifrid Strabo thought that Nicholas's verb was not Latin but Greek. As for the Cardinal of Saint-Cher, he guessed – wrongly – that the disputed verb meant 'to marry to his disadvantage'. At each of such gaffes we are invited to make dismissive giggles or guffaws.

Some medieval exegetes do seem to have had access to Greek commentators – indifferently translated, it is true. Erasmus is suspicious: why had they been suppressed? Anyway, some were not up to much. That justifies a passing blow at Thomas Aquinas, whose towering reputation was based on his marriage of Christian theology and the philosophy of Aristotle:

But how could Thomas even guess at what Aristotle meant on the basis of a Latin version which Aristotle in person could not have understood, even if he had been hot on Latin!

Accusations of madness levelled against medieval authorities are sometimes quite specific. Peter Lombard misunderstood Jerome: 'He seems to have been wandering in his mind' when he explained that tricky part of St Matthew.[4]

3. *propalare.*
4. *Erasmus' Annotations*, ed. Anne Reeve,
I, pp. 6–7, s.v. *Nollet eam traducere.*

In Matthew, 9:16 Jesus warns that 'no man putteth a piece of undressed cloth upon an old garment'. Erasmus correctly explains an obscure word in the Greek, and then has a swipe at Cardinal Hugo of Saint-Cher. The Cardinal, too ignorant to understand the Greek behind the Latin, had recourse to 'higher' meanings.[5]

It is worth looking and laughing at Cardinal Hugo as he rages about, wondering if it can be gathered from this text whether fasting is to be required from novices. He thinks that it applies rather to certain monks who entice some men or other to be ensnared in their nets. Finally it is applied to those who wear parti-coloured robes.

O copious author! Thus are huge volumes born![6]

Erasmus had a particular delight in laughing at some of the fanciful etymologies accepted by his pet aversions as they strove to explain Scripture with their aid.[7] Having mocked one, he comments:

In this manner it is not hard to produce huge tomes, provided it be permitted to pollute wretched paper with such trivialities.

After learnedly correcting another false etymology (which seems nowadays to be of startling silliness), Erasmus further exposed that venerated Cardinal to our mocking laughter, adding:

It amazes me to find men so lacking in shame that they are not afraid to teach so authoritatively things they know nothing about.

Repeated remarks like that set the tone for much of the laughter in the *Annotations*. It is the tone of mockery, railing, ridicule. And that tone is seldom a gentle one. With more than a little self-deception and self-righteousness, Erasmus claims to be moderate in his criticism: 'I have heard that Hugo Carrensis was numbered amongst the Cardinals. I have never heard that he has been numbered amongst

5. The matter concerns the word for a piece of cloth, *rhakos*.
6. *Erasmus' Annotations*, ed. Anne Reeve, I, pp. 44–5, s.v. *Panni rudis*.
7. The Cardinal thinks *piscina* ('a pond'), derives from 'fish' (*pisces*) by antiphrasis and means 'no-fish'. He believes *sycomore* comes from *sicut morum*, 'like a mulberry tree'. Even by the standards of the unscientific etymology of the time that was odd enough.

the saints.' And even if he were, saints can err, and 'we can defend the truth without abusing the person'.[8] With that asseveration Erasmus was following the advice of Martial, the Roman satirical poet who guided so many modern satirists.[9]

Erasmus's laughter at ignorance is inexhaustible. A difficult crux for the exegete was the reference in Luke to 'the second-first sabbath'.[10] What on earth can it mean? St Ambrose ignores the literal meaning and resorts to allegory. So does the Venerable Bede. The Cardinal of Saint-Cher thinks that a 'second-first Sabbath' is a sabbath which follows upon its predecessor: 'At that rate,' laughs Erasmus, 'every sabbath save the first is a second-first sabbath!'

In contrast with the pitiful wrigglings of Peter Lombard, Erasmus prefers the irony of the Gregory Nazianzenus. St Jerome tells how he asked that learned Greek Father what the term meant. He really had nothing to say, but promised to tell him later 'before the congregation where, with everyone cheering and clapping, you will be forced to agree with me whether you want to or not'.[11] In 1527 Erasmus added the comment that 'it would be easier to say, I do not know'. In 1519 he was reminded of a donnish quarrel during a college feast:

Recently, during a gaudy, a monk, who was a doctor of theology, was asked by another doctor, learned in a different field, what Luke meant by a *second-first sabbath*. That monk denied that any such phrase could be found anywhere in the Gospels – and he knew them well! When that other doctor earnestly maintained that it was in Luke, our most steadfast theologian challenged him to put it to a duel: 'I will cast away this cope of mine,' he said, 'if Luke ever wrote any such thing!'

When Erasmus wrote and expanded the *Annotations*, he used the same desk as he used for writing and expanding the *Moria* and the

---

8. *Erasmus' Annotations*, ed. Anne Reeve, I, p. 237, s.v. *Quod cognominatur Hebraice Bethsaida*; p. 251, s.v. *Facta post encaenia*.
9. Martial, *Epigrams*, X, xxxiii, 10: *Parcere personis, dicere de vitiis* ('to spare the persons: to sing of the vices').
10. Luke, 6:1. The Greek word is *deuteroprōtos*. It may mean the second sabbath after the first.   11. In his *Epistle to the Monk Rusticus*.

Colloquies, with their sustained and elegant laughter.[12] The same jokes can be found in more than one of his works. In the colloquy *The Religious Pilgrimage*, Erasmus was seen laughing at relics such as the Virgin's milk and chunks of the Cross. We find the same laughter, in virtually the same words, in the *Annotations*. It occurs in the comment on Matthew's phrase, 'For to be seen of men'.[13] Partly following St Jerome, Erasmus criticizes ostentatious hypocrisy which, in church as formerly in the synagogue, takes in 'little women'. (Erasmus had a liking for diminutives.) Jerome had condemned the kind of superstition 'which strained at gnats but swallowed camels':[14]

What would he say if he saw to-day, exhibited for cash: the milk of Mary, which they venerate with almost as much honour as the consecrated body of Christ; miraculous oil; fragments of the wood of the Cross so numerous, that if you heaped them up in a pile, a merchant-galleon would be scarcely able to transport them all. They display the cowl of St Francis here; an intimate undergarment of the Virgin Mary there; elsewhere, the comb of St Anne; elsewhere, the clog of St Joseph; elsewhere the sandal of Thomas of Canterbury; and elsewhere again, the foreskin of Christ, which, dubious though it be, they worship more than they do the whole person of Christ.

It is not as though such nonsense were tolerated as a concession to the simplicity of the common folk. It is presented as the height of religion. Behind it stands the 'greed of priests and the hypocrisy of certain monks. That is fed by the people's folly.'

Folly! There's the rub.[15] Bishops *in partibus infidelium* play a dishonest role in it all. Such shrines and their hypocritical guardians of false relics are 'worthy of comedy':

A major role in such comedies is played by bishops with fictitious sees. To avoid appearing useless, they show their support for such relics in letters

---

12. *Erasmus' Annotations*, ed. Anne Reeve, I, p. 178, s.v. *In sabbato secundo-primo*, which begins on p. 177.

13. Matthew, 23:5. See ibid., I, p. 91, s.v. *Vt videantur hominibus*. The note was added in 1519, which makes the writing of it contemporary with Erasmus's major expansion of the *Moria*.   14. Matthew, 23:24.

15. Erasmus uses here the word *stultitia*, which he used for Folly throughout the *Moria*.

of commendation, embellishing them so solemnly with attributes that whenever I read of their approval my belief dwindles even further.

But Christ is gentle to sinners. When little harm is done to true piety, such practices may be tolerated. Nevertheless those practices are farcical, comic. 'Comedy' is the pregnant word. In comedies we laugh – laugh at madness, at folly.

In the *Moria* Folly laughs at monks with their jealous and quarrelsome attachment to mere objects and to petty human traditions. Contrast that with Christ's unique commandment: 'That ye love one another'. The satire in the *Moria* is effective, yet no more so than comments in the *Annotations on the New Testament*.[16] The monks, who are seldom far from Erasmus's satirical gaze, come into prominence in an addition made in 1519 to the note on the warning of Jesus in Matthew's Gospel: 'Then if any man say unto you, Lo, Christ is here, believe it not.'[17] There are false, hypocritical Christs – not least the professed religious who narrow loyalty down to the rules of their own order; as Christ goes on to warn the faithful, they may deceive the very elect.[18]

That warning of Christ's, as Jerome saw, applies not to enemies threatening the Church from outside, but to schisms within. 'Everywhere we can hear monks yelling, "Christ is here!"' They never agree amongst themselves:

The Observantines say that Christ is not with Coletans or the Conventuals: *He is here!* with them. The Jacobites cry, *Christ is here!*, not with the Augustinians. Again, the Benedictines cry, *Christ is here!*, not with the Mendicants. Finally the whole tribe of them yell, *Christ is here!*, not with secular priests who wear no cowl.

Everywhere there is the din of voices clamouring, *Christ is here!* But what does Christ say? '*Do not believe them*.'[19]

---

16. *Moriæ encomium*, ed. I. B. Kan, p. 130.
17. Matthew, 24:23.   18. Matthew, 24:24.
19. In 1527 Erasmus added phrases claiming to limit his criticism to superstitious monks only. He is opposed, he claims, to ceremonies which encourage disunity, not piety.

Christ is not divided. Christ is not in material objects. His religion is of the spirit. He is found wherever there are affections worthy of him.[20] In the *Annotations* those scathing criticisms have something of the tone of the satirical banter of Folly in the *Moria*. But in neither case is the laughter gay and joyful: it is laughter to scorn.

When Erasmus is less sure of carrying his readers with him, the laughter may turn rather desperately into scorn itself. In the *Moria* of 1519 Folly mockingly contrasted the gentle religion of Christ with what some popes and others make of it. The bone of contention is the arresting admonition of Jesus to his disciples:

'But now, he that hath a purse let him take it, and likewise a wallet; and he that hath none, let him sell his cloak and buy a sword.'[21]

At first Erasmus took literal interpretations of that injunction to be self-evidently laughable. Such literalism forms the basis for renewed mockery of Nicholas of Lyra, and – after his death – of the warrior pope Julius II, who actually led his armies in the field. For Erasmus it is manifest that Jesus was talking not of a soldier's sword but of the sword of the spirit.

In Folly's oration in the *Moria* an element of banter lightens the whole of the satire of the likes of Julius II and Nicholas of Lyra. At the outset, the deeper implications of Erasmus's pacifism were not clear even to him. Folly speaks as though the case had already been won. It could be laughed out of court. Sustained play in the *Moria* between the name of Nicholas of Lyra and the Greek saying 'an ass at the lyre' had already reduced that great Franciscan exegete to an ignorant figure of fun. And how can that 'sword' justify Julius's field-pieces?

Some theologians, it is suggested, will try to get away with anything. Nicholas – again that 'ass at the lyre' – drew conclusions from Christ's words which are as compatible with Christ's mind as fire is with water. Nicholas wrote that Jesus in Luke was correcting

20. Erasmus toned down his criticism a little in 1527, emphasizing the risk of disunity and superstition; *Erasmus' Annotations*, ed. Anne Reeve, I, p. 26.
21. Luke, 22:36.

himself, going back on what he had once taught his disciples; times had changed: now was the time to find money for their travels and a sword to protect them on their way. For Erasmus that is sheer lunacy: Jesus was not arming but disarming his apostles. Jesus meant that they should now get rid of every material possession, 'bringing with them nothing but a sword: not that sword with which thieves and parricides lurk in wait, but the sword of the spirit'. Such a sword penetrates into the innermost recesses of men's breasts, 'so lopping off all their affections, once and for all, that nothing remains in their hearts but piety'.[22] Any other interpretation is laughed away – in the *Moria*, that is. And on the whole the laughs and smiles predominate.

Erasmus attempted the same technique in his *Annotations on the New Testament* when commenting at ever-increasing length on this very passage of St Luke. From the original edition onwards the laughter is present in the very first words:

Christian reader, I ask you! Who can be so glum as to refrain from laughing when he considers the ridiculous things written on this subject by men who are not so much modern theologians as modern theologasters?

But the laughter is a bastard one; it co-exists with deep indignation:

Yet can anyone be so fond of laughing as not to feel displeasure that such heavenly teachings should be corrupted by that sort of exegesis?

The fault is Nicholas of Lyra's, 'a sound teacher (it seems to many)'. Erasmus accused him of twisting Christ's words. Nicholas makes Christ tell his disciples to obtain provisions and a means of protection, 'lest they should lack things to eat or be overwhelmed by oppressors'. Concern for food is just what you would expect from a monk!

But even the bastard laughter does not last. By the time of his death, Erasmus had expanded this note several times. In the fifth and last edition of 1535 it spreads over six folio pages.[23] The laughter cannot be kept up. Some theologians do remain apparently easy targets. As in the *Moria*, they include Hugo Carrensis: he can be

22. *Moriæ encomium*, ed. I. B. Kan, pp. 168–9 (ch. LXIV).
23. It occupies the equivalent of five full pages at fifty-three lines per page.

laughed at for misunderstanding Chrysostom – laughed at too with a vague play on his name which suggests that *Carrensis* would be better employed as a carter.[24] (Erasmus had a sporadic fancy for mocking play on men's names: Schwenckfeld, say, might become Stinkfield, and a cantankerous Carmelite a Camel-ite.)

But some ancient theologians who were normally allies of Erasmus were now, when read more closely, apparently ranged against him. Chrysostom is cited as explaining Jesus's meaning by an analogy: Jesus, with his command to sell cloaks and buy swords, 'was turning his chicks out of their nests, teaching them to use their own wings'.[25] Erasmus counters that contention with the bastard laughter of sarcasm. In 1527 he adds, after 'to use their own wings', 'and to prepare lances, helmets, bronze shields and field-pieces'.

In fact he was hard put to find any theologian, ancient or modern, who fits snugly into his own pacifist exegesis of Christ's injunction to buy a sword. Even Origen, 'without controversy the most learned of early theologians', partly let him down: Origen declared that it was pernicious to interpret this verse literally; he promised to return to it elsewhere, but failed to do so.[26]

In this long annotation Erasmus divides the world into the sane (his side) and the insane (the side of his opponents – potentially to be laughed at). Marginal notes refer to the 'insane' wars. But the laughter fails to take off. Some said Christians should carry swords but never use them: but to be ordered to bear a sword one is never to use is 'laughable'. Perhaps; but Erasmus does not succeed in arousing even an anaemic laugh.

24. The word-play is between *Carrensis* and *carrucae*. It was cut out in 1527.
25. The Chrysostom here is Pseudo-Chrysostom.
26. Origen is cited from his *Homily on Matthew*, 7:

So if anyone, intending to respect the letter but not understanding the intention of those words, were to sell his bodily raiment in order to buy a sword, seizing upon those words of Christ against the intention of Christ, he will perish, and perhaps perish by that sword. But this is not the place to expound the nature of the sword which he was proclaiming.

Origen seems not to have returned to this subject anywhere else; but then, so many of his works were destroyed by his enemies in the Church (*Erasmus' Annotations*, ed. Anne Reeve, I, p. 211).

Again, 'as though princes were not insane enough on their own', preachers and counsellors egg them on to war. In the *Moria* such madness does indeed evoke some wry amusement and perhaps a laugh or two; not so in this note as it finally appears, dense and over-long. Laughter is sought but never found. Rhetoric alone lends its dubious force to the final contention; what Christ tells us to obtain is a spiritual wallet and a spiritual sword:

Accept the sword of the Gospel. Accept the wallet and tunic of the Gospel.

Christian laughter demands certainty and conviction. A long and ever-expanding note such as this one betrays a nagging unacknowledged doubt, not unshakeable conviction that the text actually bears the meaning you would like it to. The Lucianic scoffing – in so far as there is any – slides to the level of Elijah's mockery without Elijah's certainty.

Erasmian mutual laughter of sane against insane cannot work effectively without firm convictions on both sides. Folly in the *Moria*, with her banter and her laughter, does makes a convincing case. We laugh where she wants us to. But when that case was exposed in the *Annotations* to serious theological opposition over many years, the laughter withered on the vine.

Plenty of assured and uncomplicated laughter is found elsewhere in the *Annotations*: an English clerical buffoon (who also appears in the *Moria*) thought in his crass ignorance of Latin that *Devita!* ('Avoid!') meant *Devitalise!* (that is, 'Kill!'). That bloodthirsty idiot thought St Paul was telling his followers not to avoid heretics but to kill them! Behind such laughable ignorance lay the weighty matter of life and death. Yet – especially as the story is true – the laughter at that buffoon can be effective and spontaneous. The ignorance is preposterous; it is madness to hold such views as his.[27]

Time obscures many a jest, and weakens many more. There are

---

27. To those who doubted the reality of such crass ignorance from so egregious an ass, Erasmus replied that he heard of the gaffe directly from John Colet himself. That Dean of St Paul's was presiding at a synod when he heard the bloodthirsty booby make this remark.

plenty of jests in Erasmus which now fall flat.[28] It would be nice to be able always to join in the joke, but at least some of them show laughter taking the place of hatred or coercion. Sometimes a story may never rise above the level of an anecdote from modest tellers of tales. A rustic priest was baptizing a child; he thought that the rubric *Salta per ter* ('Jump three pages') meant 'Jump thrice over the stone in the apse.' Which he did.[29]

The laughter of Erasmus is more effective when it succeeds in deflating the obstacles to Christian truth by making the ignorance or wickedness of the authoritative or the powerful comic. His mockery of would-be theological Atlases – silly arrogant men, complacently convinced that, like Atlas of old, they bear the world on their shoulders – is still amusing. Orthodoxy, they believe, depends on them! The Atlas repeatedly mocked in the *Annotations* is Noël Béda, the syndic of the Sorbonne, a college often jeered at by Humanists as a swamp of error, intolerance and laziness.

Erasmus pointed out that, in the Greek of Luke's Gospel, *Magnificat* portrayed Mary aware of her 'low estate'. Her lowliness was social, not moral. For that Greekless Atlas, Mary was rejoicing in her modesty: she was proclaiming her humility. Only the Latin can lead to such a misunderstanding. In the original, Mary was not drawing attention to any virtue she might have: she was acknowledging that she was the lowly handmaid of the Lord. The demolition of error is done with humour and lightness of touch, but with never a sign of charity. Humanists, proud of their linguistic achievements, mercilessly mocked wretched donnish critics hampered by their ignorance of Greek and their doggy Latin. Erasmus's laughter at Béda would find its natural audience in Thomas More's book-room and round the common-tables of progressive scholars.

---

28. Augustine sought a mystical meaning for the name of Adam in Greek numerology. But Adam is a Hebrew name. Augustine was looking in the wrong place. How funny! Jerome – and Erasmus – also laughed at those who found Greek allegories in Hebrew letters: see *Erasmus' Annotations*, ed. Anne Reeve, I, p. 233, on John, 2, s.v. *Quadraginta sexannis*.
29. ibid., II, p. 197, s.v. *Per ter*.

But the laughter worked both ways. Philologists like Erasmus trespassing into theological territory might be treated as piddling pedants. Erasmus expected to be laughed at for his pains:

Let anyone who wishes mock these grammatical annotations – but let him acknowledge that theologians have fallen into error a time or two.

That Parisian Atlas insisted that Mary was proclaiming her modesty, and so her fitness to be the mother of her Lord. Erasmus will have none of it. She was his mother by God's grace, not by any merit of hers:

How much better it would be for Theology if those who profess it in perfection would kindly accept whatever contributions linguists and gram-marians might make to the common cause; and should, in return, fraternally communicate to them their more sublime mysteries – doing so all the more modestly the more deeply they have penetrated into the innermost recesses of that Philosophy which unteaches arrogance and haughtiness and teaches the highest patience towards imbeciles.

The humour is fine. Erasmus has just crushed ignorant theological arrogance with a knowledge of Greek beyond the wit of his Parisian Atlas; but he affects to place himself with his mere linguistic skills amongst the weak, the 'imbeciles'.[30]

Erasmus and Lefèvre d'Étaples were 'clandestine Lutherans' for Béda. He dubbed them so in the very title of a book infamous for its invective. Erasmus was well aware of the dangers represented by so highly placed an enemy. He answered Béda in works of detailed scholarship. But he knew that mockery can be more effective than counter-arguments. By repeated ridicule he turned Béda into a figure of fun: if the King of France is looking for a court fool, Béda is just the man! If the Church has no better Atlas than such a nincompoop, then it is time to write her epitaph! Béda is a coarse quibbler, who trusts in works, not the grace of God. His malice can turn anything whatsoever into heresy. No one, nothing, is safe from him. Take the central prayer of Christendom: 'What is more to be venerated

---

30. ibid., I, p. 158, s.v. (p. 157) *Humilitatem ancillae.*

or more sacred than the Lord's Prayer? Allow me to play the Béda with it.' Béda the censor's condemnations of it would read like this:

Our Father, etc. Those words are redolent of Arianism, as though the Father alone should be addressed as the one true God; no mention is made here of the Son or of the Holy Ghost;

Our Father: such words are misleading, since they could lead Christians to imagine that they, like Christ, are sons of God by nature; the words should read, *Our Father, not by nature but by adoption*;

Which art in heaven: that is well nigh blasphemy, as if God, who is not in one place more than another, could be in any one place, definitively and circumscriptively . . .

Humanists would have enjoyed the gentle mockery of the adverbs taken from scholastic Latin: 'definitively' and 'circumscriptively'; they are barbarous – no classical author would have understood them – they introduce concepts incomprehensible to the simple 'foolish' men whom Christ chose to be his Apostles. Better laugh them out of court.[31]

Erasmus could always get quiet amusement from pretentious error in tiny matters, especially when Greek was involved. The Greek *ek* (from) is sometimes translated into Latin by *ex* (from) and sometimes by *de* (of). Latin is like that. Greekless theologians find deep mysteries in those *froms* and *ofs*. A generation before Erasmus, Laurentius Valla had already found that silly. He had laughed at those who found mysteries in the grammatical variations of the words of the creed in Latin: 'Conceived *of* the Holy Ghost; born *from* the Virgin Mary.'[32]

Erasmus's *New Testament* was primarily read by those who had good Latin and who at least respected Greek erudition. The laughter

---

31. *Definitivè* is a technical adverb alluding to something which has a definite position but does not occupy space; it might apply to an angel, say, or to the soul, or to Christ's presence in the eucharistic elements; it is often contrasted with *circumscriptivè*, which alludes to something which is totally confined – as is matter – to definite spatial limits. (Definitions and examples are given in Nuntio Signorelli's *Lexicon peripateticum philosophico-theologicum*, Rome, 1931, p. 70.)
32. *Erasmus' Annotations*, ed. Anne Reeve, I, p. 2, s.v. *De Thamar*.

is such as one would expect in such circles: laughter by no means free from pride of knowledge.

Bernard Shaw set out to reform our world and ended by trying to reform our spelling. There is something of that in Erasmus. As time went on it pained him to hear consonants or vowels elided or skimped in Greek or Latin. For him there really is an *h* in *Christus*. That topic takes up quite a lot of space in his annotation on *Who is called Christ*.[33] The Lord is not offended by the barbarisms of simple folk, but from the learned things are different. People who would object to being addressed as *Pheter* or *Pilip* scoff at Erasmus when he tells them to pronounce that *h* in *Christ*. It is no laughing matter. God himself is involved in the anger. Simplicity is of course forgiven,

but if anyone is given advice and then still persists in error, laughing at the one who gave it and even attacking him instead of showing gratitude, [. . .] who can fail to see how far that is from that Christian simplicity to which pardon is due? God hates learning when it is haughty: how much more must we believe him opposed to arrogant and intractable ignorance.[34]

33. Matthew, 1:18.
34. *Erasmus' Annotations*, ed. Anne Reeve, I, pp. 3f., s.v. *Qui vocatur Christus*.

175

38

He who Calleth his
Brother a Fool

The butts of Erasmus's laughter are his brothers and sisters, his fellow Christians. He sets out to show them to be fools. He must tread with care; any Christian raising laughter would do well to linger over a warning from Jesus:

Whoever shall say to his brother *Raca* shall be in danger of the council: but whoever shall say, *Thou Fool!* shall be in danger of hell fire.[1]

How does that square with Erasmus's reflections on Folly, the Socratic spur to laughter? *Raca* or *Racha* is a term corresponding to 'brainy' – used sarcastically, as 'hare-brained', or 'empty-headed', or 'brainless'.[2] That may appear quite straightforward, but is it? What Hebrew term, what concept, was Jesus condemning? It will not suffice to avoid that one Greek word. Jesus spoke in a Hebrew dialect. We are all at sea. May we not say 'Thou fool!' in Greek? Matters of eternal reprobation are involved.[3]

Erasmus had written an entire book in praise of Folly. Folly permeates his entire conception of Christianity. In his writings many a brother Christian is called a fool. Distinctions simply had to be made.

1. *Erasmus' Annotations*, ed. Anne Reeve, Duckworth, 1986, I, pp. 27–8, s.v. *Qui dixerit fratri suo, racha*.
2. ibid., I, pp. 27f; the words translated above are in the Latin *cerebrosus, cerebro carens* and *vacuus*.
3. ibid., loc. cit.: 'If the Chaldæans say *rocho* for *racha*, is it surprising if Jesus said *rocha* for *recha*?' It does not follow that Jesus pronounced that forbidden word as it is found in the Old Testament.

The forbidden term 'Thou fool!' is, in the Greek, the vocative of *mōros*. What Matthew or his source originally had in Hebrew is irrecoverable, but, without absurdity or appalling injustice, Christ's words cannot apply to each and every use of *mōros* in Greek, or its equivalent, *stultitia*, in Latin. (And it certainly cannot be allowed to apply to Erasmus's widespread use of it to laugh at his brethren.)

Paul uses *mōros* of the Lord's disciples: 'God chose the *foolish things* of the world', meaning by *mōroi* not the impious but the humble and those unskilled in the ways of the world. Paul too accepted the name of fool.

That is from the *Annotations* on Matthew. But that last sentence is also to be found word for word in the *Moria*. Erasmus continues:

Not that Paul really was a fool, but because fools boast about themselves, which is not impious but at most inept. If anyone rebukes a slow-witted man by calling him slow-witted, that is not a matter of railing; nor is it railing to correct an impious man by calling him a fool.

'Thou fool!' It is not a question of what you say. It is in a question of your emotions and intentions when you say it. There must be no anger or wickedness of intention. Erasmus turns the text on its head:

But whilst the Lord bids us to bless the impious who curse us, he conceded that we could say *Thou fool!* – but only in the sense which we have shown.

Despite its air of special pleading, what Erasmus asserts here conforms to his sustained practice of seeking the spiritual truths behind 'Jewish literalness'. That was his sheet-anchor; it sustained his laughing at wayward brothers. We can be grateful for that. Some of the liveliest of the *Annotations* could figure in the *Moria* with only a modicum of changes.[4]

In 1516 his annotation on 1 Timothy, 1:6 occupies barely half-a-dozen lines, commenting upon the phrase, 'unto vain talking'. By 1535 it has grown into two and a half folio pages. 'Vain talking' is,

4. One thinks of those denizens of St Donatian's of Bruges who, typical monks, 'caring as they do more about money than books, throw themselves into carousing rather than reading' (On Matthew, 3:16).

in Greek, *mataiologia*.[5] That led (especially in Latin) to puns between *theologia* and *mateologia*, between theology and babble. In 1516 Erasmus sees that play on words as containing a warning 'to us' (including himself):

We must be also beware lest we so pursue theology that we fall into mateology, disputing endlessly over frivolous trifles. Let us rather treat matters which transform us into Christ and which render us worthy of Heaven. What end is served by earnestly fighting over the means by which sin is received? whether sin be a deprivation or a stain inherent in the soul? A theologian so acts that all are horrified by sin and loathe it.

And that was all. Was Erasmus treating Original Sin in too cavalier a fashion? Some thought so. By 1535 one of his longest notes is devoted to lowering the tension over that subject. At all events, by 1535 that trickle of words on *mateologia* had swollen into a torrent – the year in which the text was first printed is given here in square brackets:

[1516] We have been disputing for centuries whether that grace by which God loves us and draws us to him is the same as that grace by which we love him in return, [1527] and whether it is created or uncreated. [1519] Let us rather so act, with pure prayers, innocency of life and pious deeds, that God may deem us worthy of that gift.

We endlessly quarrel over what distinguishes the Father from the Son, and both from the Holy Ghost; whether it is an entity or a relationship; how it is consistent to say *Three*, when none exists without the others, since all are of one essence.

We should not scan the Trinity but mirror such ineffable concord by concord of our own. Instead,

we quarrel about how the fire by which the souls of the wicked are tormented can, being material, act upon the soul, something incorporeal.

The idle questions grow and grow. They were both amusing and shocking to those who, preferring the Greek Fathers, had first studied

---

5. It was latinized as *mateologia*.

scholastic theology and found it barren. The warning of vain-talking is no longer 'to us' but to others:

[1519] . . . If such matters were treated as a means of mental relaxation or without wrangling, it could be borne with; nowadays the whole life [1535] of some people [1519] is swallowed up by such questions, and matters get as far as shouting, real dissension, loud altercations and even occasional fighting. What swarms of questions are raised about baptism, the communion and the sacrament of penance, many of which are of such a kind that it does not much matter whether we know the answers or not: they can be stated but neither refuted nor proven.

(In 1535 Erasmus changed 'many of which' to 'a few of which': a slight concession in fact, since the list of nonsense remained spread over two and a third folio pages.)[6]

It would be better to exhort each other to live lives worthy of our baptism 'and to approach the Supper so often, and in such purity, that there would be little in our lives requiring to be cauterized'.

[1527] . . . What shall I say now about those trivial little questions – which are not only utterly vain but, dare I say, impious – which we raise about the power of God and of the Roman pontiff? Whether God can do anything evil, requiring hatred even to himself, and forbidding all goodness and even the love and worship of himself. Whether he can extend infinity in every direction. Whether, from all eternity, he could have made this world better than he did. Whether he could produce a man who never once even wanted to sin. Whether he can reveal to any man a future state or his damnation. Whether he can understand anything as distinct, if there are no distinct relations of reason towards it . . .

The mere listing of these topics would have produced laughter from those who preferred the simplicity of the Gospel to the logic which men like Erasmus had been drilled in as children and young men. Their studies had been anchored in the writings of the 'Schoolmen', the great masters of thought and controversy in the universities of medieval and early Renaissance times. Once Erasmus and others

6. Erasmus changed *pleraque* to *nonnulla*.

like him had discovered the New Testament in Greek, and also the Greek theologians, many rebelled, rejecting all the subtleties of the Schoolmen and seeking a religion which fishermen such as Peter could have understood, and which a philosopher such as Socrates could adumbrate. Erasmus eventually countered his mockery with a generous tribute to the goodness of his patron and defender, the reigning pope, Leo X.[7] So the list grows and grows. Many of the items are not understandable nowadays except by experts, but many are:

[1527] . . . Whether God can produce universal nature and conserve it without singulars. Whether he can be constrained by any predicament. Whether he can communicate the capacity to create to a creature. Whether he can undo what has been done, thus making a virgin out of a harlot. Whether any Person of the Trinity can take any nature upon him, as the Word took upon him our human nature. Whether all three Persons could take the same nature upon them at the same time. Whether one created supposition can assume a different created nature.

And then we meet the terms and tone of the *Moria*, in which it is asked 'whether God could take upon him the nature of a devil, an ass, a gourd or a flint':

Whether the proposition *God is a beetle* or *God is a gourd* is as possible as the proposition *God is a man*.

The word 'gourd' was particularly arresting: in Latin it is applied to a dolt. The list expands, with more and more Scholastic subtleties dismissed as laughable yet dangerous nonsense:

Whether God assumed an individual humanity or the species of humanity. Whether the assertion *God cannot do the impossible* is more appropriate

---

7. *Erasmus' Annotations*, ed. Anne Reeve, loc. cit., p. 664:

Such questions are not without clear marks of flattery, nor without injury to Christ, in comparison to whom princes, however great, are but as grubs. Do people think that they are pleasing to a real and true Vicar of Christ like Leo, who, as a true pastor, holds nothing to be more important than the well-being of Christ's flock and who, as Vicar of Christ, holds nothing more dear than the glory of Christ his King?

to God than the assertion that *The impossible cannot be done by God.*
Whether it is more appropriate to God to be able to produce, or to the
creature to be able to be produced. Whether the Ideas of all things are in
the divine mind, and whether practically or speculatively . . .

Some seemed striking examples of blasphemy as well as futility:

Whether this is a possible proposition: *God the Father hates God the Son.*
Whether the soul of Christ could be deceived, could deceive, or tell lies.

And then it is the turn of the popes:

The power of the popes is almost as busily discussed as that of God,
whenever we inquire into a pope's twin powers. [Whether he is really the
universal head of the entire Church, and whether he is really superior to a
General Council.] Whether he can abrogate what is decreed in the apostolic
Scriptures; whether he can decree anything which clashes with the teachings
of the Gospel; whether he can insert a new item into the Creed; whether
he has greater power than Peter, or equal power; whether he can give
orders to angels; whether he can cancel the whole of purgatory; [and
whether he can, by his own wishes, exclude even the innocent from Heaven];
whether he is simply a man or a *quasi-God*; and whether he partakes of
both natures as does Christ.

The last question might seem outrageous, but papist lawyers had
given ample scope for raising it.
    There is more to come:

[1527] Whether the pope is more merciful than Christ, since we do not
read that Christ ever released anyone from the pains of purgatory; [1522]
whether he alone is infallible. [1527] Many hundreds of such questions are
debated in huge printed volumes, and that by great Theologians, especially
ones marked by the insignia of the monastic profession.

The technical jargon of the Schoolmen was an unquenchable
source of humanist laughter. Simply to cite it produced smirks or
guffaws. No attempt was made to assess its value. Having suffered
from it in classroom and amphitheatre, they had no desire to do so
again once they thought, spoke and wrote in elegant Latin.

One term picked out for mockery by Erasmus is 'circumincession'. A definition of it in barbarous and incomprehensible Latin in attributed to Duns Scotus.[8] For all his subtlety Duns became the *bête noire* of the Humanists, his very name giving the Renaissance a new term, 'dunce'. Applied first to hair-splitters, it became a teacher's word for dolt or booby: it is no longer applied to an over-subtle boy but to a stupid one.

I once knew a theologian who maintained that nine years were not enough to understand what Scotus wrote merely in his preface to Peter Lombard. I heard another preach that it is impossible for any man to understand one single proposition anywhere in Scotus, unless he keep in mind the whole of metaphysics.[9]

The mockery of Erasmus echoed through the places where Latin was read and enjoyed. Others saw that similar laughter echoed through royal Courts and any place when intelligent and knowledgeable men and women enjoyed jests in their vulgar tongue. A similar send-up of scholastic language has remained one of the best-known jests of the Reverend Doctor Rabelais. Later, he too found comic the jargon of the Schoolmen which he had once had to study. There was never any attempt to sympathize with the need for it in certain discussions. The very type of theology they exemplified was to be laughed off the stage. It was enough to guy the barbarous latinity. In *Gargantua* the Dean of the Faculty of Theology wanted to get back the bells of Notre Dame borrowed for Gargantua's mule. He pleaded for them on the grounds of 'the substantificient quality of the elementary complexion, enthronificated in the terrestreity of their quiddity.'[10]

8. 'Circumincession' means the existence of the three Persons of the Trinity in each other. The definition attributed to Scotus as given in the *Annotations*, III, p. 664:

Circumincessio est subsistentis in subsistente realiter distincto mutua præsentialitatis assistentia in eadem essentia.

Other definitions follow, equally mind-bending.
9. The whole expanded note with datings can be found in Anne Reeve's edition of the *Annotations*, II, 1993, pp. 662–5. It makes an enjoyable humanist read.
10. Rabelais, *Gargantua*, p. 116.

For Erasmus, pedantry so opaque would be meaningless to the 'foolish' fishermen whom Jesus chose to follow him. It is as bad as 'cabbalistic and talmudistic smoke' (Jewish mysticism and orally transmitted learning). 'What can be pleasing in such a waste of time?' Did not Paul warn that 'time is short' (or 'foreshortened')?[11] Contrasted with the simplicity of Christ's teachings addressed to 'foolish' disciples, such scholastic jargon is really simple-minded.

Erasmus has been likened to Voltaire. Both might well have been surprised. Yet they do have in common an apparently inborn sense of mockery. In the case of Erasmus his native bent was informed by the folly of the Gospel and the art of Lucian. That his laughter should find an outlet in the *Moria* is natural; the very genre of that declamation required it. What never ceases to surprise is to find so much of the same laughter where traditionally one expected to find none of it. Such unexpectedly placed laughter produced powerful reactions. In the *Moria*, Folly mocks most amusingly idle or scandalous theological problems robed in scholastic jargon. Terms held up to our laughter include, in their technical senses, *relations*, *substances* and *filiations* (the third meaning the processes of becoming the Son). By 1522, when treating the same theme in the *Annotations*, Erasmus makes an interpolation which suggests he had at last learnt to show some little discretion. He first wrote:

Chrysostom is always vexed by quarrelsomeness, yet he had never even heard of our arguments about *filiations*, *relations* and *instances* . . .

In 1522 Erasmus added, prudently, even fearfully:

. . . let alone other things I could say more rightly, but more perilously.[12]

'More perilously'. . . . Laughter-raisers need protection. Leo X gave him his; papal approval notably embraced the *Annotations*. Leo's letter to Erasmus of 10 September 1518, beginning 'Greetings, dear son', is proudly prefixed to all the subsequent editions of his *New*

---

11. I Corinthians, 7:29.
12. Cf. *Erasmus' Annotations*, ed. Anne Reeve, III, pp. 687–8, s.v. *Devita*; and the *Moriæ Encomium*, ed. I. B. Kan ('Chapter LIII'), pp. 115–16.

Testament. Leo praised not only the texts of Erasmus but, quite specifically, his 'many annotations'. Such papal approval did afford some real protection. But Erasmus continued to add, yet he cut little out. So even papal approval could not stop the censors of the Sorbonne from criticizing and censoring the scriptural works of Erasmus. Erasmus was a scoffer, and censors the world over have a nose for laughter.

But so had Erasmus. He uncovered insanity in the enemies of true Christianity as he saw it. He uncovered it too in his own enemies. When under personal attack he became even more inclined to see insanity – and hence a kind of bitter laughableness – in all his opponents. His harsh Spanish critic Lopis Stunica died, only to be succeeded by a member of the same anti-Erasmian school. Thoughts of Stunica's death did not blunt the edge of his resentment, not least when Steucho, an Italian critic, grew more aggressive:

Stunica had died, to be succeeded it seems by Sepulveda, an alumnus of Albert Pius, an intimate of Stunica and the most boastful of all the Spaniards, whose book against me I expect you have seen; it is notably stupid and abusive.

When Italians go mad, they go richly mad: Agostino Steucho has replied to a letter of mine, but madly and unlearnedly.[13]

As at the end of the *Moria*, the Christian life is centred on *meditatio*, 'practising'. Why do we not practise such things as transforms us – changing our form as man into the spiritual form achieved for us by Christ?

We shall do that if we practise his innocence with all our might; if, abstaining from all that is shameful, we emulate as far as we can his love, deserving well of all men; if we imitate his forbearance, being so far from returning an injury that we repay evil with good.

Those who fail to do that can be made the butt of Christian laughter.

13. *Erasmi Epistolae*, ed. P. S. and H. M. Allen, X, p. 357 ('. . . *insigniter stultum & contumeliosum. Itali quum insaniunt, insaniunt luculenter: Augustinus Steucho respondet epistolæ meæ, sed furiose & indocte*' – madly, *furiose*, implies raving or raging).

Erasmus is an adept at doing that quite briefly. But as time went on enemies became more dangerous and Erasmus himself more provocative, in straight criticism and in mockery.

Nevertheless the satire of the *Moria* prepares us for the happy climax: that happy climax throws into relief the mocking laughter of Christians at errant fools.

39

Fools in Cap-and-Bells?

'Fools' for many meant Sebastian Brant. Erasmus called him 'incomparable'. He was famous far and wide for his *Narrenschiff*, his *Ship of Fools*, which proved a publisher's dream ever since it first appeared in 1494. He composed a Latin poem to print after the first Schürer edition of the *Moria*, which was published in Strasbourg in 1511. Brant was a distinguished man-of-law and a power in Strasbourg. His support counted. But was it support that he gave?

> Content to have carried vulgar fools in our *Narrenschiff*, we allowed the toga to go untouched. *Moria* now comes forth, who, censuring the *bryyha*, the *syrmata* and the *fasces*, conveys as well philosophers and druids. Alas, what smears of blood she will call forth, arousing anger with wrath.

Brant tellingly emphasized the wide scope of Folly's laughter, which had taken on groups Brant never touched: the professions (the *toga*), the cardinals with their red cloaks (the *byrrha*), the lawyers with their long robes (the *syrmata*), and even the state (the *fasces*). Not least, Erasmus had taken on the 'druids': the clergy. Brant foresaw trouble, 'bloodshed'. Erasmus was not amused. Never again were Brant's verses to be published with the *Moria*.[1]

About his *Ship of Fools*, Brant was right. It is an accessible work, making few demands on its readers. It is conservative in religion and morality; it has few literary pretensions. It is above all a picture-

---

1. Cf. *Erasmi Epistolae*, no. 305; II, p. 24 for Erasmus on Brant, 21 September 1514. For the poem, see M.A.S., *Erasmus: Ecstasy and the Praise of Folly*, Penguin Books, 1988, p. 7.

book. It consists of 114 woodblock prints, accompanying poems of various length, all straightforwardly moralizing. No great person or influential corporation is mocked. The satire is straightforward, plain and sober, taking on bad manners and vices: gluttony, chatterers in church, usurers, the ungrateful and the proud, grasping peasants who seek undemanding jobs for their sons in the Church. Perhaps the only satire which might have raised a smile on the lips of a Humanist is the first one, condemning those who display in their shelves books they cannot read or understand. The Evangelical could sympathize with the condemnation of blasphemous mockers of God, and pluralist clerics. The good have the standard virtues of piety, courtesy and prudence.[2] The popularity of the *Ship of Fools* owes much to its woodcuts; they were copied, pirated and reproduced for decades in several countries.

The literary and social antecedents of the *Ship of Fools* are not those of the *Moria*. Brant's work is much more at home in a long medieval tradition of fools and foolery. Erasmus, writing in elegant Christian Latin and seeking to adapt to his uses the humour and paradoxes of classical literature must have found it irritating to have Brant complacently putting his book beside his own.

Despite all those woodcuts of fools, there is very little laughter in Brant's *Ship*. Yet there are similarities. The less philosophical pages of the *Moria* pass in review groups of men and women laughed at as foolish for their vices, or for their self-love and self-deception. Brant was correct in saying such pages were – with their well-aimed laughter – hard-hitting and destined to provoke hostility and wrath from those who were attacked. All who are criticized by Folly are classified as fools; but there is never the slightest suggestion that Folly and her fools were fools in cap-and-bells. Their folly is internal, mental, spiritual. It is their standards that are wrong. They have no baubles or any of those insignia typical of fools that are sported by the fools who appear in every single one of Brant's woodcuts.

2. An approach to the *Ship of Fools* for readers of English is E. H. Zeydel's *The Ship of Fools by Sebastian Brant. Translated into rhyming couplets with an introduction and commentary, with reproductions of the original woodcuts*, Dover, New York, 1962 (first published in 1944). In England it is published by Constable.

Folly mocking fools in the *Moria* has closer analogies with Socrates and St Paul than with court jesters. That is what made the *Praise of Folly* confusing for many. In the *Moria*, Folly intertwines eulogies of good Christian madness and satires of multiform bad or merely silly madness. Far from toning down his laughing satires in later editions because of Brant's warnings, Erasmus increased them. The *Moria* as we read it nowadays is far more bold and far-reaching than it was when it first appeared.

For example, Folly had at first been content to laugh at the punctilious attachment of the religious to the rules of their Orders. From 1514 she added, far more woundingly: 'Their concern is not to be Christ-like but different from each other.' After listing their various partisan names – Benedictines, Bernardines, Augustinians, and so on – Folly adds, 'as though it were not enough to be called Christians!' From 1514 it is the very ideal of monasticism which is held up to ridicule: many monks so rely on their rituals and human traditions that they believe a single heaven will not suffice for their multifarious merits, 'scarcely considering that Christ, despising all such things, will demand his own Rule: love'.

If laughter remains, it is close to Elijah's diasyrm. One monk will rely on so-called fasting, his ample guts stuffed with fish. Another will cite his hundred peck of chanted psalms. Another will enumerate his countless periods of fasting – 'frequently attributing his all-but-bursting stomach to one single dinner a day'. Another will cite such a heap of ritualistic observances that they would fill seven cargo-ships. Another will not touch money at all – except through double gloves. Another will never wash his filthy cowl. Another will claim merit from remaining rooted like a sponge to one spot for fifty years.

Such scrupulosity is for Erasmus akin to a neo-Judaic concern for law over Christian freedom. One religious will adduce his voice made hoarse by chanting; another will cite his acedia brought on by solitude; another will point to his tongue made useless by a vow of silence.

The list might be never-ending, but Christ puts an end to it, saying through Folly, his mouthpiece:

'One commandment only do I recognize as truly mine. That is the only one I never hear mentioned. Once, openly, without wrapping anything up in a parable, I promised my Father's inheritance not to cowls, silly little entreaties or fasting, but to the offices of love.'

Christ, with scathing irony, dispatches those religious who would be holier than he is, to the gnostic Abraxians with their three hundred and sixty-five hierarchically arranged spheres. Christ simply will not accept as his those who profess their own merits:

Those who would appear holier than I am may invade if they please the Abraxian heavens or command a new heaven to be built for them by such as rank their own silly little traditions above my commandments.

That is diasyrm indeed. Banter or no, it is Christ who is speaking, Christ who is dispatching the religious – or most of them – to any heaven but his own. Folly's Christ is basing his judgement on a definite text of Scripture.[3]

Then shall the king say unto them on his right hand, 'Come ye blessed of my Father: inherit the kingdom prepared for you.'

Those who enter the Father's inheritance are those – and it seems only those – who devote themselves to works of love, doing good to those in need, and so doing them to Christ:

For I was an hungered, and ye gave me meat: I was thirsty, and ye gave me drink: I was a stranger, and ye took me in . . . I was sick, and ye visited me: I was in prison, and ye came unto me.

At one vital point Erasmus does slacken the tension and so leaves an entry for easier laughter. In Scripture Jesus curses the justly disinherited and consigns them 'into everlasting fire, prepared for the devil and his angels'. Erasmus softens that into a monkish scramble for places in a hierarchical series of imaginary heavens reserved for an elite of those-in-the-know. Erasmus's diasyrm does not extend to laughing at the tortures of the damned: better to turn damnation into a jest about gnostic heavens.

3. Matthew, 25:34ff.

But are those satires really funny? Do they provoke laughter? Yes, if madness does. What can be madder than to claim to be holier than Christ!

There is little published laughter in Erasmus before the *Moria*. After it, laughter may appear anywhere. In widely different works Erasmus often has recourse not only to the same themes but to the very same words. One example: Folly's laughter at the religious orders, so obvious in the mature *Moria*, bursts out afresh in the annotation of the claim of the false Christs and false prophets in Matthew: 'Lo, here is Christ':[4]

Everywhere I can hear monks clamouring (the superstitious ones, I mean, not the pious) *Lo, here is Christ*: yet they do not agree amongst themselves. The Observatines say, *Christ is here*, not with the Coletines or the Conventuals. The Jacobines say, *Here is Christ*, not with the Augustinians. Again, the Benedictines clamour, *Here is Christ*, not with the Mendicants. Finally the whole tribe clamour, *Here is Christ*: Christ is not with the secular clergy who wear no cowl!

Erasmus is paying off a score. He had been an Augustinian and attempts had been made to force him back to the cloister.

The religious are so copiously mocked elsewhere in the *Annotations* that Erasmus is devastatingly brief in his note on 'The least of my brothers'. For some reason the Vulgate translates the same word in the same context in two different ways: 'to the least' (*minimis*) and 'to the lesser' (*minoribus*). That is simply an error.

And yet I think it from that text that some members of the Franciscan family have adopted the name of *Minorites*.

An entire movement trumpeting abroad its ignorance.[5]

From the *Moria* onwards, the many fools of Erasmus – those who figure in his New Testament writings as well as those we meet in lighter works like the *Colloquies* – all share in the same madness.

4. Matthew, 24:23 and context.
5. *Erasmus' Annotations*, ed. Anne Reeve, Duckworth, 1986, I, p. 96, for '*Hic est Christus*'; p. 100 for '*Fratribus meis minimis*'.

The good fools are good and the bad fools are bad for the same reasons judged against the same standards.

Erasmus based both his theology and his ethics on the tripartite division of Man into spirit, soul and body. The authority for that division is St Paul. Writing to the faithful in Thessalonika he said: 'May your spirit, soul and body be preserved blameless in the Lord.'[6] That tripartite division was dominant amongst the Greek Fathers. Erasmus particularly associated it with Origen. (He also accepts, of course, the simpler division into soul and body, but the tripartite division proves richer and more fundamental.)

The basic idea owes much to Plato as well as Paul. It is in essence quite simple. If it was not always immediately grasped in his own times, it was partly because the classical world had bequeathed to scholars a different order for the same trilogy. That confused some people.[7]

The spirit is destined to worship God and to seek union with him. Its values are the eternal absolute values. Towards those values tends the whole life of the spiritual man. Seeing that, the carnal man, the worldly man, will judge him mad, laughable.

Below the spirit the soul occupies the middle ground. Its domain is the physical, the senses, the 'natural', the 'animal'. ('Animal' is the adjective from *anima*, the Latin term for soul.) St Paul refers in this sense to the 'natural man' who is not open to the Spirit of God.[8] The man who rises no higher than his soul – in the tripartite sense of soul – is Paul's 'natural' man. It is right that the soul should exercise its powers in its domain, but in the good man or woman it should also strive upwards. The spirit should also reach downwards

6. Thessalonians, 5:23. The Greek terms are *pneuma*, psyche and *sōma*. The equivalent Latin terms are *spiritus*, *anima* and *corpus*.

7. The Pauline hierarchy has *spirit* at the top, then the *soul*, then the *body*. The hierarchy found in Plato and in classical culture generally is not *spirit*, *soul*, *body*, but *soul*, *spirit*, *body*. (Where Man is thought of by Christians as simply soul plus body, then plainly the soul is used for all that is highest in Man. When the Pauline tripartite system is used, the soul abandons that role to the spirit and becomes an intermediary between spirit and body.) The spirit in Man is by nature akin to the Holy Spirit.   8. I Corinthians, 2:14.

in order to spiritualize the concerns of the soul for those things 'animal' and 'natural' which belong to the domain of the soul.

The body is the lowest in the hierarchy. It is very much to be respected. It is, or should be, the temple of the Holy Spirit. When influenced, as it can be, by the soul, and through the soul, by the spirit, it directs its efforts upwards. The eventual fate of the natural body is to be raised at the Resurrection into a spiritual body.[9]

Erasmus held that the tripartite division belonged not only to Man but to everything – all creation. Even the eucharist can be spiritual, 'natural' or carnal, depending on how the faithful approach it. In all things the Christian must seek out the spiritual and follow it.

The Christian, under grace, strives to purify his character in this world. Even in this life our souls and bodies can be brought under the purifying discipline of the spirit. That is part of our preparation for the life to come; then we shall not be disembodied spirits but full persons, embodied in our former bodies, duly spiritualized. Such a life, lived by Christian fools in accord with the absolute values, is contradicted at every point and at every stage by the worldly values of the worldly fool. That is why each laughs at the other. Erasmus's Christian fool never forgets St Paul's reminder that 'the things which are seen are temporary: but the things which are unseen are eternal'.[10]

For Renaissance Humanists that is the proper Christianizing of the essence of platonic philosophy. Men laughed at Socrates. They laughed at Christ. They will laugh at you. A legal scholar as influential as Guillaume Budé reminded his learned readers that Jesus was treated as though he were the same kind of fool as the legendary François Villon: a scamp, a silly mountebank, a deceiver.

According to St Matthew the authorities in the synagogue called Jesus a *planos*. By so doing they were treating him like the François Villon of fact and legend. The Latin word for *planos* is *impostor*.

9. I Corinthians, 15:44–46. The *sōma* (body) is shown as a *natural* body, that is it is *psychikon* (of the soul): it will be raised at the Resurrection to the highest state: it will then be *pneumatikon* (spiritual).

10. I Corinthians, 13:12. Erasmus rightly gives both 'temporal' and 'temporary' as the sense of the original.

'Our fathers saw in their time an outstanding *impostor*, François Villon. His name alone is as good as a definition.' When Jesus foretold the Resurrection, they called him by the abusive name of *impostor*, 'as though he had put forward certain artifices as miracles, mocking the people with his mountebank's trickeries'.[11]

The mockers laughed at Christ at his most spiritual. The carnal majority of mockers allow their bodies to taint their souls, and allow their souls to taint their spirits. Worst of all, they allow their bodies to pass on their taint via their souls to their very spirits. Seeing that, Christians may laugh at them.

11. Matthew, 27:63. Guillaume Budé, in *Annotationes in Pandectas*, Book XXI, § Ex. I iiij, *Nec gulosos nec impostores*; in *Opera Omnia*, Basle, 1557 (Gregg reprint, Farnborough, 1966), III, p. 255.

40

Caps and Bells Sneak In

There was not, even in Villon's case, the slightest hint of bauble, cap or bells. Yet that kind of fool sneaked in, and for centuries distorted the reader's understanding of what folly was for Erasmus and for Christian laughter generally. In their own way those caps and bells popularized aspects of Christian laughter.

Erasmus's mixture of laughing classical and Christian erudition expressed in zealous, elegant Latin foxed many of the first readers of the *Praise of Folly*. To help them, Erasmus wrote an explanatory letter to Martin Dorpius, which to this day is often printed as an appendix to the main work. Despite such efforts, misunderstanding remained.

Hans Holbein bears a great responsibility for that. He filled the margins of his 1515 copy of the *Praise of Folly* with pen-sketches of charm and power which were destined to become known the world over. They show us how a sensitive and friendly artist could see the *Praise of Folly* as a work akin to the *Ship of Fools*.

Hans Holbein's *Moria* is in Basle. After 1676, when his marginal sketches were discovered, copied and printed by a new editor, Holbein and Folly have normally walked hand-in-hand. Once they had appeared in I. B. Kan's elegant and learned text the assimilation of Erasmus's fools to Brant's fools was for a while complete. Holbein's first sketch shows Folly preaching to fools. She, and they, are in caps and bells. His last sketch shows Folly coming down from the pulpit; again, she and her congregation are all in caps and bells. There are similar fools in a few other sketches: even a little boy fool. None of Holbein's illustrations is copied directly from those of the

Ship of Fools; Holbein was too original an artist to copy. Nevertheless he was influenced in style and subject: for example, he was probably thinking of the *Ship of Fools* when he represented hypocrisy by a finger-post pointing the way but never going there itself. What probably remains in readers' minds up to this day are those two sketches of Folly mounting the pulpit to preach and, at the end, coming down from it.

One point Holbein clearly grasped: two types of fool embrace all mankind. The caps and the bells are not all on one side.

Holbein saw Erasmus's fools in the light of Sebastian Brant's; that was largely a private matter until his marginal sketches burst into print before a receptive world. But the same tendency can be seen working at the level of printers and publishers. At least two of them sought to clothe Erasmus's difficult and exacting *Moria* in the conservative and easier garb of the *Ship of Fools*.

It happened almost as soon as the *Moria* saw the light of day. In January 1512 Theodore Martens of Antwerp printed an edition of the *Moria* designed to make it seem a work similar to the *Ship*. The title-page is dominated by an elegant woodcut of Wisdom preaching; it derives from Brant. Perspicaciously, it does not borrow Brant's Fool but Brant's character, Wisdom. She is angelic-looking, with large wings, and she wears a crown. Beneath her crown a fool's bells are clearly visible. Her bauble is prominent, held firmly in her hand. Prominent too is the nearest of her congregation. Engrossed and apparently in an ecstasy of amazement, his gaze is fixed on Wisdom and his hand is raised in a gesture of astonishment. Behind his neck his fool's bells are visible. That brings the *Moria* firmly into the context of the *Narrenschiff*: we are shown foolish-wise Wisdom preaching Christian truth. We are left in no doubt that Wisdom is inspired: the finger of God points towards her bosom. But there is not the slightest suggestion of fool laughing at fool, madman at madman. The very title of the *Ship of Fools* leads one to expect laughter on every page: one does not get it.[1]

Erasmus's Folly has a different ancestry from the *Ship of Fools*,

---

1. The copy illustrated is that of the British Library, at 12316.f.37.

De contione ſapientię.
Quem ſacra delectat diuū ſapientia: quic̨
    Pectore flagrantí dogmata ſancta colit.
Híc cunctis prẹſtat: claroſc̨ meretur honores:
    In cẹlo datur & dígna corona ſibí.

De contío
ne ſapien-
tię.

Clamat voce graui populo ſapientía cuncto
O genus humanū ad noſtram concẹde cathedrā.   puer.i.& viii
Diſcite quíd recti doceant mea verba/bonic̨:
    Diſcite mortales caſte monumēta Minerṷ   e.í.

Wisdom preaching, from the Stultifera Navis *('Ship of Fools'),*
Io. *de Olpe, 1497*

MORIAE ENCOMIVM ERA✦ SMI ROTERODAMI DECLAMATIO

¶ Ad Lectorem

Habes hic lector laudē ſtulticiæ. Libellū oppido✦ q̄ facetum ab Eraſmo Roterodamo Germanorū decore concinnatum, in quo varii hominū ſtatus̃ mire taxātur, Hunc tu ſi emeris, & legeris, diſperea̅ ſi non impendio gaudebis. Vale.

Wisdom preaching, from Moriæ encomium *('Praise of Folly'),*
Theodore Martens, Antwerp, 1512

FOLIO

Veritatem obticere.
Quiſqs amore/metu/pretio:atqs fauore/minis ve
Non loquitur verum:ſed bene faƈta ſilet:
Qui populo vt placeat:ſupplantat vera palato.
Hic Anthicriſti/curſor/amicus erit.

Qui per ti
morem oc
cultat veri
tatē puo =
cat in ſe irā
deí. Meli⁹
ē enī p ve
ritate ſup=
plíciū p ati
q̃ bn̄ficiuz
habere p
falſitate.

xxxviii.diſ.
ſedulo.   Eſt anímus multis ſincerus:menſq parata
Pſ̄.xxxv.   Vt poſſint leges chriſti verumq fateri:
Prouer.xii.
Eccſ̄.xii.   Blanditiis tamen hi:verboq aliquando mínací:
Ad Roma. 1. Terrentur:línquuntq boni conamína veri.

*An ignorant fool preaching, hiding the truth, from the
Stultifera Navis ('Ship of Fools'), Io. de Olpe, 1497*

⸿Erafme Roterodame

De la declamation des louenges de follie/stisse fa=
cessieux et profitable pour congnoistre ses erreurs
et abuz du monde.

Stulto-
rum nu=
meras i=
finitus.

On les vend a Paris par Galliot du pre Mar=
chant Libraire/demeurant sur le pont nostre dame
a lenseigne de la Gallee/Et en la grãd salle du pal
lais au tiers pillier.

⸎Auec priuilege⸏

The title page of La Declamation des louenges de follie
('Praise of Folly'), P. Vidoue for Galiot Du Pré, Paris, 1520

LXXV

De cura cſtrologíę.
Eſt fatuus ſiquidem/vanuſcp:incredulus atcp:
Ex aſtris cupiens noſſe futura polí:
Ruſticus & quiuis índoctus:certat haberí
Aſtrologus:fatuas fingít ephímerídas.

Líbera fa=
ta homíní
tríbuít dí=
uína pote=
ſtas:
Sydera níl
cogűt:ſa=
píes dñabí
tur aſtrís.

Aſtrologos etíam decet huc arceſſere vanos:
  Atcp mathematícos/aríoloſcp ſimul:
Huc ades aſtronõe /atcp plãetíſta/augur/aruſpex
  Sortílege/& quiſquis ſydera ſola colís.   k.iii.

26.q.ſ. non li
ceat chriſtio.
&per toti.&
26.q.7.nõob
fuetiſ.&.c.ſe

The Fool and the Astrologer, from the Stultifera Navis *('Ship of Fools'), Io. de Olpe, 1497*

The Fool and the Astrologer, from Rabelais, Pantagrueline
Prognostication, *François Juste, Lyons [1532?]*

and very different literary aspirations, but the wording on this clever title-page suggests something close to what we find in Brant's book:

You have here, Reader, the Praise of Folly. A booklet exceedingly amusing, prepared by Erasmus of Rotterdam, the glory of the Germans, in which the various states of men are marvellously rebuked. If you buy this and read it, may I die if you do not greatly rejoice. Farewell.

As space-fillers at the end are several epigrams of Erasmus. Finally – so little has the nature of the *Moria* been understood – there is a light-hearted epitaph of a drunken fool who downs his last drink as he dies.

Erasmus had no desire to see his work appear in such company. Never again does any hint of the *Ship of Fools* appear on any title-page of the *Moria*, or anywhere else.

The *Moria* was allegedly translated into French (*allegedly*, since it was not translated but disfigured). A commercially-minded publisher wanted to make the *Moria* into something less demanding. To do so he too turned to the *Ship of Fools*. The entire work was changed. When he first heard of the 'translation', Erasmus was amused: now those ignoramuses at the Sorbonne would be able to read it and understand it![2] Once he had seen a copy he changed his mind: it was an all but different book; much had been misunderstood; much had been left out. Indeed, adapter and publisher had recast the *Moria* in the mould of the *Narrenschiff*. The *Moria* is here condensed, truncated and divided into sections. Each section is provided with a woodcut directly derived from the *Ship of Fools*: with some repetition, there are no fewer than thirty-five woodcuts in all, each accompanied by doggerel. The effect is to bring the work very close indeed to the artistic and mental world of the *Ship*. Erasmus had been betrayed.

The title-page reproduces a copy of Brant's preaching fool. He is not the wise, queenly, angelic Wisdom chosen by Theodore Martens

2. *Erasmi Epistolae*, ed. P. S. and H. M. Allen, no. 660, III, p. 83; no. 641, III, p. 63. George, Seigneur de Halewin, is known to have turned the *Moria* into French. It was perhaps his version which P. Vidoue printed for Galiot Du Pré: the work has a privilege from the Prévôté de Paris, dated 24 July 1520. The printing was completed on 2 August 1520.

for his Latin *Moria*. What we have now is a fool indeed, a reprobate worldly fool preaching beside the biblical maxim 'The number of Fools is infinite'.[3] In that woodcut those who have to endure the fool's preaching are not themselves fools, and they are hostile. In Brant's original the preaching fool served to illustrate the theme, 'Concealing the truth'. Hardly a responsible choice to liven up the title-page of what claims to be a French version of Erasmus's most subtle book, with its wise evangelical Folly.

A similar tendency can be seen at work between Brant and Rabelais. In 1530 Françoys Juste had published in Lyons a French version of the *Ship of Fools*. In 1532 he published the slim *Pantagrueline Prognostication* of Rabelais, and for the title-page he cut down a woodcut from his own French edition of the *Ship*.[4] The effect was again to make Rabelais's inimitable little evangelical comic masterpiece don the drabber clothes of a Brantian fool with cap-and-bells. Rabelais was an artist in words; words alone. He had no taste for illustrating authorized editions of *Gargantua* or *Pantagruel* with woodblocks. Had he exceptionally sanctioned the reproduction of that woodcut, or had printer and publisher taken a liberty? Probably the latter. He never allowed it – or anything like it – to be reproduced again on any of his works.

With its numerous woodcuts and its traditional morality the *Ship of Fools* was assured of a public wherever it was issued, whether translated or not. Yet there is little of laughter in it; the fools and their accoutrements add a feeling of fun which is not, however, borne out by the text.

A gulf separates the thought of the *Moria* from the *Ship* of Brant. It is not a matter of fine distinctions. As the *Moria* rushes to its close, Folly (good Madness) praises the ultimate madness of the Christian saint: ecstatic rapture. The primary model for it is the ecstasy of the three disciples at the Transfiguration. During his ecstasy as he witnessed the transfiguration of his Lord, Peter babbled, not

3. Ecclesiastes, 1:15 (Vulgate): *Stultorum numerus infinitus.*
(The Authorized Version reads very differently.)
4. See S. Rawles, M.A.S. *et al.*, *A New Rabelais Bibliography*, Geneva, 1987, no. 14, pp. 113–16.

knowing what to say. It is theologically important that Peter should not have known 'what he should say', rather than not remember what he had said. Platonic figures do not remember what they have said once they return from their ecstasies; Hebrew prophets and inspired Christians do.

As Erasmus treats ecstasy in the *Moria*. Folly draws dangerously close to the inspired Socratic fool who, in his enthusiasm, speaks things which he cannot remember once he has come back to himself. In a footnote added later to the *Moria* Erasmus took care to explain any such confusion firmly away: his Folly only *pretended* to have forgotten what she had said – it avoided a tedious recapitulation!

Ecstasy as Folly expounds it in the *Moria* may rise to that ultimate Christian ecstasy which brings a favoured few into union with God. Such ecstatics are 'beside themselves' with divine madness. There is nothing of that in Brant.[5]

Those who, firmly anchored in this life, place the interests of their neighbours above their own seem mad to those who accept the standards of this world: even more so, those who are 'beside themselves' as their spirits soar towards heavenly things.

Mad, too, seems the prophet touched by God. An unnamed Old Testament prophet suddenly commanded a neighbour to hit him hard. His reasons for giving such an odd and peremptory order were never explained. His neighbour refused to hit him. Like Elisha's naughty boys, he got his deserts: 'And as soon as he was departed from him, a lion found him, and slew him.'[6] As Erasmus noted, that prophet's command 'was not far from madness'. What showed it to be good madness, not the erratic activity of a mind organically insane, was the power of the Holy Spirit. But that would not stop the worldly-wise from finding it all laughable.[7]

---

5. The 'translation' of the French *Moria* mangles and distorts his text (cf. I. B. Kan, op. cit., p. 181 with the French *Louenge de la Folie*, fol. lxvr°). The translator has no idea of the real meaning of *meditatio*, and therefore parodies the theology of Erasmus. Even then some little of Erasmus does come across, something quite foreign to the *Narrenschiff*. 6. I (III) Kings, 20:35f.
7. Cf. M.A.S., *Erasmus: Ecstasy and the Praise of Folly*, Penguin Books, 1988, p. 231.

41

Obscure Men

Erasmus not only wrote satires of his own: he appeared in other people's. His name will be forever associated with the laughter aroused by the *Letters of Obscure Men*. He did not like it.

The *Letters of Obscure Men* are fictitious, deliberately written in appalling, workaday Latin. They are certainly funny, but for anyone with a sensitive taste for refined Latin they can pall. Their context was a series of letters in Latin, Greek and Hebrew written by illustrious men who supported Reuchlin in his battle against bigotry and ignorance. The 'Obscure Men' come to the defence of Reuchlin's enemies.[1] They write illiterate letters to each other attacking Reuchlin and all those who favour Humanism, and especially the study of Hebrew. In later expanded editions, Erasmus figures prominently as an enemy of the Obscure Men.

The *Letters of Obscure Men* are certainly worth a laugh. But the reader must understand Latin; much of the laughter is aroused by their complacent abuse of the language of culture. The humour barely survives translation into bad English from worse Latin.[2]

One might have expected Erasmus simply to have laughed at those

1. Both texts were often reprinted. Cf., for example, the *Clarorum Virorum Epistolæ Latinæ, Græcæ & hebraîcae variis temporibus missæ ad Ioannem Reuchlin Phorcensem Ll. doctorem*, Tübingen, 1514, and the *Epistolæ Obscurorum Virorum*, Nuremberg?, 1517. Both are often catalogued under *Epistolæ*.
2. A valiant and useful attempt to give some idea of the Latin in translation can be read in F. G. Stokes, *Epistolae Obscurorum Virorum. The Latin text with an English Rendering, Notes and an Historical Introduction*, London, 1909. In the following extracts I try rendering the text into English myself.

satires. (He was even suspected of writing them.)[3] Those fictitious clerical boobies complacently shriving one another are clerics such as Erasmus held up to mockery. The point was not lost on contemporaries. Erasmus was about to gain allies more troublesome than Brant in Strasbourg with his unwelcome and ambiguous praise.

When sending him a copy of the *Letters of Obscure Men*, a correspondent called Angst recalled how Erasmus had repeatedly read out a real document in such barbarous Latin which had fallen into his hands. He had done this secretly in order to joke about it – so often that he finally learned it by heart. The boobies Erasmus had read it to had thought he was citing it with approval; that is why they now sought to get in touch with him. Angst adds that those ignorant loons were 'of the same family as those whom the *Moria* had so zealously made famous'.[4]

Erasmus disliked any such comparison with his *Moria*. Angst begged him not to spurn those silly satires, but spurn them he did.

Thomas More too laughed at the letters, not least when the ignorant failed to recognize that they were satires: 'It is rewarding to see how the *Letters of Obscure Men* please everyone.' The learned got the joke, the unlearned took the letters straight:

When we laugh at those letters, the unlearned believe we are laughing only at their style, which they do not defend, maintaining that it is counterbalanced by the weight of the arguments![5]

Erasmus objected shrilly when his own name was brought in. One can see why. Those letters are attributed by their anonymous author to a real man and his circle. They are presented as though they had been either addressed to Dr Ortuinus Gratius, an influential theologian of Cologne, or written by him. Erasmus did not want to make enemies at second-hand. At first the *Letters* mainly concerned Reuchlin and the study of Hebrew; Erasmus did not feel directly involved. He was not a Hebrew scholar and had no taste for the

3. Cf. *Erasmi Epistolae*, ed. P. S. and H. M. Allen, nos. 808 and 961, III, pp. 262f. and p. 574.   4. ibid., no. 363, II, p. 153.
5. ibid., no. 481, II, p. 372. 'The fairest of swords' – the attacks on Reuchlin – 'can be hidden within a gross scabbard.'

cabbalistic studies which often accompanied them. The expanded *Letters* were another matter: in them his *New Testament* was put at risk:

Greetings honourably wished unto your Honour.

Venerable Herr Master: since you wrote to me recently that a certain poet in Germany add composed a lot of books and above all composed a letter to the Pope in which he commended Reuchlin: know ye that I of read that letter. but I of also seen an huge great book of his intituled *The New Testament* – he sent it to the Pope; and I opine that he would willingly wish the Pope to autentikate that book. But I hope he will not. Because the Maestro di Palazzo, who is a man notable and of good reputation, wants to prove that that Erasmus is an heretic.

What if – as Thomas More said they did – boobies took that straight, as bad Latin but good sense!

Because in certain passages he rebukes the Holy Doktor, and does not hold with Theologians. In addition he as produced a thing called *Erasmus' Moria*, wherein are many propositions scandalizing, hardly reverential and sometimes open blasphemies. Wherefore the Parisians want to burn such a book. Therefore I believe not that the Pope will autentikate that other big book.[6]

Erasmus exploded: 'The whole sodality of Basle knows that those epistles attributed to those obscure men displease me.' They mock a living man. It is not a question of having a poor sense of humour: Erasmus does not shudder at festive joking. What riles him is the smearing of a living person, Dr Ortuinus Gratius:

I cannot approve of the example they have set by harming a man's reputation[. . .]. I too once sported in the *Moria*, but no one's name was hurt by me.

Erasmus bitterly complains that things had become much worse now that the anonymous author had brought out a new edition

6. The above are my attempts to render something of the savour of the Latin text in F. G. Stokes, *Epistolae Obscurorum Virorum*, letter no. XLIX, p. 491.

which dragged in his name. Such action was ambiguous. Did the author wish him well? Then why stir up animosity against him? Did he wish him ill? Then why put him on the side of the good?

Tacitly Erasmus is again accepting for Christian laughter the counsel of Martial, the Roman satirist: laugh at error and wrong-doing; do not make the attacks personal. That is an important and authoritative limitation of the scope of Christian laughter: laugh at the sin, not, by name, at the living sinner.[7]

Erasmus also half-reveals a more private reason for placing the limits he does on Christian laughter: people were tracing back to him the *Julius Exclusus*, a satire he probably wrote before learning prudence. If he did write it, then it is the earliest of his *Colloquies*.

In a light and elegant dramatic dialogue, *Julius Exclusus* tells how Pope Julius II fulminates when he finds the gates of Paradise barred to him by St Peter. Erasmus later clearly mocked that bellicose pope in expanded editions of the *Praise of Folly*, but only after the man's death. While the butt of the satire is clear, names are avoided. Never in the *Moria* is any living man mocked by name. As in the case of Julius II, it is an instance of 'If the cap fits, wear it.' Erasmus was capable of caustic naming in private conversation and table-talk, but that is another matter. Writing to John Caesarius, he claimed that he had hurt no one in his *Moria*:

I myself sported about in the *Moria*, but without bloodshed. I wounded no reputation by name. I sported with men's *mores*, not their reputations.[8]

At the height of his fame, he says the same to Cardinal Wolsey – with an important concession. He has never published anything which does not bear his name; but, he concedes,

I once sported about in the *Moria*, without bloodshed, but perhaps too freely.[9]

---

7. Again the authority is the famous counsel of Martial in his *Epigrams*: 'To spare the persons: to sing of the vices' X, xxxiii, 10.
8. *Erasmi Epistolae*, no. 622, II, p. 45: '*Lusi quidem in Moria, sed incruente: nullius famam nominatim perstrinxi. In mores hominum lusimus, none in famam hominum.*'   9. ibid., no. 967, III, p. 592.

Twice 'without bloodshed'. Was that meant to counter the expectation of Sebastian Brant that bloodshed is precisely what the *Moria* would bring forth? Erasmus holds that any indignation at laughing in general at men's *mores* is misplaced; only personal satire is even metaphorically capable of shedding blood.

The mature convictions of Erasmus ruled out personal attacks from the territory of Christian laughter. He did not always live up to his ideal. Attacked by the likes of Noël Béda or Cardinal Prince Pio da Carpi, he replied in kind. He was right about the *Moria* and the *Colloquies*: living men are spared. Yet he never shied away from mocking dead men: Nicholas of Lyra and Hugo Carrensis are but two among the many whom he mercilessly pilloried.

Erasmus signed what he published. *Julius Exclusus* (if he did write it) was never published by him. In so far as it mocked Julius II during his lifetime, it had no place in Christian laughter as he ideally conceived it. That is a limitation to the doctrine that 'madman laughs at madman': the good madman laughs not at the person but the *mores* of the living madman (though he may well laugh at the dead). Beatus Rhenanus, in a letter to Erasmus, was speaking the language of Erasmus himself when he regretted the injection of Erasmus's name into the *Letters of Obscure Men*:

If they like being insane with such an insanity, let them not bring in anyone's name.[10]

Whoever laughed at those mad Obscure Men, it was not a counter-mad Erasmus. He even wrote a brief and wise letter to Ortuinus Gratius; however things turned out, it was genuinely a letter of peace.[11] And, in a remarkably frank letter to Jacob Hochstrat, the public enemy of Reuchlin, Erasmus cited the example of Origen. If ever Christian man had cause to write a bitter reply to an attack, it was Origen, faced by the onslaught of Celsus. Origen did no such thing: 'Yet Origen never inveighs against Celsus as you constantly

10. ibid., no. 581, III, p. 557: '*Si illis insanire libet hanc insaniam, nullius admisceant nomen.*'
11. ibid., no. 1022, IV, p. 84. It is best read together with the long letter to Hochstrat, no. 1006, IV, pp. 42–51.

do against Reuchlin.' Reuchlin has not been condemned, not yet at any rate. (He never was to be.)

Origen never strives to pile up what Celsus says, twisting it towards the worst of meanings; you, it seems to me, constantly do so with astonishing ardour; there is nothing you do not drag towards a case for heresy.[12]

In his calmer and more charitable mood Erasmus was aware that laughter can be cruel, not least the kinds of laughter authorized or exemplified by Scripture. As Christ was being crucified the multitude laughed. By the rules they ought to have been laughed at in return by the Son and the Father.

For Erasmus they were: God laughed at them from the heavens. But all was not lost. Some Jews had yelled a terrible imprecation: 'His blood be upon us, and upon our children.' There have been Christians over the centuries who ensured that it was. Erasmus in his *Paraphrases* sees things differently. There is no toning down of the mob's diasyrm; that crowd 'exulted over the Crucified'; they were 'hurling abuse, deriding him by wagging their heads':

'Hey! You up there, who would destroy the Temple, and rebuild it in three days! You promised to save others: now save yourself. You boasted you were the Son of God: come on down off that cross then!'

Pogroms have been started for less. But some of that mob were not destined to be divinely laughed at for ever in return. Erasmus interpolates at this very point words of charity which have no equivalent in the text he is paraphrasing:

They called down destruction on themselves and on their posterity. But Christ, more merciful towards them than they were to themselves, rejects no man from forgiveness provided that he repent. Many then in that crowd yelling 'Take him! Take him! Crucify him!' later came to venerate the Cross of Christ.

12. ibid., no. 1006, IV, p. 45.

42

Dutch Wit, Gallic Licence and the Liturgical Year

'I called you Father; if by your indulgence I might do so, I would also call you Mother.' The words are from the pen of Rabelais. They were addressed to Erasmus on 30 November 1532. Rabelais, a priest, a student of the law turned doctor, a Franciscan turned Benedictine, now living irregularly out of his cloister; the father of at least one child, called Théodule (Slave of God), was seizing an opportunity to write to the man he had never met but who had changed his whole life.

Rabelais, the principal physician at the great hospital of Lyons, the Hôtel-Dieu, was in fact acknowledging an immense debt. Erasmus was trying to get his hands on a manuscript of the Greek Josephus. Georges d'Armagnac, the powerful humanist diplomatist and Bishop of Rodez, wanted to get one to him. He entrusted the task to Rabelais. Hence this eye-catching letter, with its copious and very visible Greek, its elegant Latin, and the opening words: 'Georges d'Armagnac, Bishop of Rodez.' A letter beginning like that was sure to be read.[1]

What had led Rabelais to leave his cloister, with the connivance and support of his own bishop, Geoffroy d'Estissac, rapidly to graduate in medicine in Montpellier and to practise medicine in one of the greatest hospitals of France? What had led him to risk death as a doctor when the plague was raging? The influence of Erasmus:

---

1. *Erasmi Epistolae*, ed. P. S. and H. M. Allen, letters nos. 2743 and 2569: X, pp. 130f.; IX, pp. 380f.

You so educated me, so fed me from the chaste bosom of your divine doctrine that, if I did not attribute to you alone whatever I am and whatever I am worth, I would be – of all the men that ever were or ever shall be – the most ungrateful.

Erasmus was an example to follow. Rabelais too studied humanist Latin and had mastered Greek. Like Erasmus, he too had translated into Latin some works of Lucian. He too was to show that laughter can be allied to evangelical piety and evangelical religion. But the Christian laughter they raise is very different. Comedy is not wit.

Erasmus found that French culture was open to coarseness and over-free satire. He even cleverly exploited the fact. He pretended to see a joke where there was none. He twitted the great Budé over it. Already incensed with Erasmus, Budé had exploded with anger, sending off a letter headed, 'Guillaume Budé, until now a friend, greets Erasmus for the last time' – a stomach-heaving letter to receive.[2] Erasmus replied in a long placatory letter, affecting to believe that all had really been said by Budé in jest. He could see the joke. Would others?

I know there is a kind of Gallic jesting which is extremely free, gesticulating and a trifle too presumptuous, which to severe minds can seem close to impudence.

He had actually witnessed Budé enjoying such humour. But friendly jesting must be reciprocal. How could others understand? They 'will read those jests of yours, which are so very like violent abuse'. Erasmus is virtually alone in seeing the joke. (Was he appealing to a warning in Ecclesiasticus: 'He that casteth stones at birds will drive them away: so he that violently abuses a friend breaketh friendship'? He and Ecclesiasticus use the same Latin word for 'violent abuse'[3]) Elsewhere also Erasmus drew attention to the licence of Gallic wit. He did so when defending himself in the context of adverse judgements on the *Julius Exclusus* and the *Letters of Obscure Men*.

2. ibid., letter no. 896, III, pp. 434f.
3. ibid., letter no. 906, III, p. 450. Ecclesiasticus, 22:24 (Vulgate text). The common word is *convicia*. It means loud and violent abuse, insult, reviling.

Despite their great difference in style, Erasmus lumped those works together: both laugh at named people. Erasmus found it offensive that folk in Strasbourg should be attributing *Julius Exclusus* to him. The French had already laughed at something similar:

Some time ago I heard that a farce of that sort had been acted in France, where there has always been unrestrained licence for such trifles.

(That letter of Erasmus was seized upon and reprinted by Ortuinus Gratius, the very man most mocked as a correspondent in the *Letters of Obscure Men*.)[4]

If such a farce had been put on in Paris it was in good company. Quite outspoken college skits were common, though some were suppressed by the authorities. Under Francis I, students had even dared laugh at his sister Margaret of Navarre and her protégé Girard Roussel, the evangelical priest. If Erasmus wrote *Julius Exclusus* he probably had a version of it with him in his early days in Paris.[5]

There were currents of French laughter which Erasmus found himself swimming against. He conceived of Christian laughter as chaste laughter for chaste ears. His laughter is often cruel but never obscene. Whatever Rabelais owed to Erasmus it was not his idea and practice of comedy. Erasmus is chaste in both subject-matter and vocabulary. Rabelais is chaste in neither. Rabelais's laughter is at least as moral as that of Erasmus, but he does not tiptoe round moral quagmires. Erasmus can, it is true, name a Sorbonne professor 'Merdardus', but *merde* was already a word emasculated by usage and was not under a strong taboo.[6] It can remain condemnatory: Luther saw papal Decretals as *merdæ*, dung worse than all the silly

4. ibid., letter no. 622, III, p. 45. The letter is addressed to John Caesarius, 16 August 1517. Ortuinus Gratius printed it in his not unwitty reply to his attackers, *Lamentationes Obscurorum Virorum*, Cologne, 1518. Erasmus uses the word *fabula*, which can mean a tale, a *conte*, but also a play, a farce, which is I think its meaning here.
5. Thomas More, in a defence of his 'darling', Erasmus, alludes to a lampooning of Julius II staged in Paris when Julius died. *Julius Exclusus* may also have connections with the sojourns of Erasmus in Cambridge. Cf. More's letter of 15 December [1516] in *Erasmi Epistolae*, letter no. 502, II, pp. 418–21.
6. *Merde* ('shit') has little power to shock and a great power to amuse.

fables of Lucian.[7] In the colloquy *The Parliament of Women* the purely-named Candida risks a joke on the ambiguity of *coitus* in Latin (coming together either in an assembly or in carnal union). It is effective but hardly obscene. Yet even that astonishes in Erasmus: it would hardly be noticed in Rabelais.[8]

Self-imposed limits cut Erasmus off from some of the livelier stimulants to laughter. It even restricted the force of his satire of the monks, whose obscenities and blasphemies he could bring himself only to hint at.

There was so much laughter about, not least in France. There were comic sermons; the fun-and-games marked out by the liturgical year (Twelfth Night and Shrovetide) or by relaxations after harvest-time, *vendanges* or the autumn slaughter of cattle.

All levels of society rejoiced in the permitted licence of Twelfth Night and Shrovetide. Erasmus would have none of it. They were survivals of the ancient Bacchanalia. He was moved to write passionately against such excesses in his exposition of the psalm *Quam dilecta*.[9] The Gentiles celebrated the harvest with wantonness, 'in honour of their ridiculous Bacchus'. There were indecorous dancing, disorderly games and obscene words. 'We are grieved to find traces of such insanity even now.' Moses diverted irreverence towards the worship of God. Saucy games were replaced by prophets dancing: 'Even David danced before the Ark of the Covenant.' Moses turned the people away from irreverent songs and shameless talk towards mystical psalms:

In their festivals the Gentiles too had their contests, in which men, by no means sober, their faces bedaubed with wine lees, sang ridiculous songs

7. Cf. *Contra Papatum Romanum a diabolo fundatum*, translated by Justus Jona, 1545, sig. m.7ro, '*aut (quod deterius esse) qui papæ merdas et oleta legunt.*'

8. *Colloquia, Senatus sive* ΓΥΝΑΙΚΟΣΥΝΕΔΡΙΟΝ: Candida: 'Bishops have their synods; gaggles of monks, their conventicles; soldiers, their councils of war. Of all living creatures we women alone never coïte.' To which Margaret replies, 'Oftener than we ought.'

9. Psalm 84 (83), 'How amiable are Thy dwellings' (*De Amabili Ecclesiae Concordia*), LB, 5, 472D. (I first read it in the handy little edition of Johannes Maire, Leyden, 1613, *De Sarcienda Ecclesiae Concordia*, pp. 12ff.)

from their farm-carts. The victor's prize was a goat: 'a cover worthy of the pan'.[10]

Christians should be different. Even when those early Christians spoke ecstatically in tongues, they did so (Erasmus was convinced) without unruly contention. Too many Christians nowadays 'attribute sad things to God, happy things to the Devil'. They believe that they have amply served God if they live a little more austerely during Lent,

but when Lent approaches, what irreligious licence! Then, once the Easter festival is done with, how eagerly they return to their interrupted pleasures![11]

Erasmus was especially distressed by preachers who made concessions to the antics of the unlearned and the illiterate to be found in all ranks of society. There was a tradition of deliberately funny sermons on Easter Day. They formed part of what was known as 'Easter Laughter'. Erasmus judged such sermons to be shameless. Preachers tell 'manifestly made-up stories', so obscene that no decent man would repeat them even during a banquet. That is certainly not what is intended by the Easter psalm: 'This is the day that the Lord hath made: we will rejoice and be glad in it.'[12] True Christian joy should show as much religion as does Christian grief. That applies to the autumn festivals dear to country-dwellers. Isaiah says: 'They rejoice before Thee, according to the joy of the harvest.'[13] Those who rejoice will rejoice 'according to God, thanking Him with a good conscience for both sadnesses and joys'.

But those who in times of joy indulge in dice, drunkenness, dirty talk or whores may perhaps rejoice according to the world, but according to God they are insane.

Yes, according to God they are insane (*coram Deo insaniunt*): insane, therefore laughable.

10. LB, 5, 472E. He is citing one of his collected adages, *Dignum patella operculum*.
11. ibid., 472F–473A.
12. *Confitemini Domino*: Psalm 118 (117):24; LB, 5, 861CE.
13. Isaiah, 9:3; LB, 5, 473B.

But Erasmus breaks off. He has gone on too long. 'Would it were without good cause.'[14]

Erasmus's natural and chosen territory was wit, not comedy and certainly not seasonal fun-and-games. His crimped attitude towards seasonal licence severely limited the scope of Christian laughter for those who followed him. Many did, for he remained a good laugh-raiser.

Erasmus seems to have had objections to raw laughter that were almost physical. He objected to tickling: it is never right to encourage bodily pleasures. Tickling under the armpits affects the mind but is not of the mind. It resembles a fit.[15]

The wise avoid excessive laughter. In his explanation of 'Syncrusian Laughter' he says why. The Greeks used the term 'syncrusian' for the kind of effusive laughter 'which batters a man about'. It is 'vehemently unbecoming in a wise man precisely because it apparently proceeds from a weak mind'.

Just as it is ugly for a grave man to cry out like a woman if he is hurt, so too it is indecorous for him to burst out into guffaws from immoderate joy.[16]

The kind of joking he most detested is the kind often associated with friars and monks. The religious often make their jokes by misapplying biblical texts. (It is still called 'monastic humour' by French scholars, but it was certainly enjoyed by churchmen generally when I was a boy.) Erasmus was deeply offended when Cardinal Prince Pio da Carpi accused him of the very same thing in the *Moria*. His jokes, he retorted, are constructive and refined:

The *Moria* abuses scriptural texts! As though priests and monks did not select all their jokes from Holy Writ. For example, when they ask, 'What is Charity?' Back comes the answer, 'The monastic habit' – 'Why?' – 'Because it covers a multitude of sins.'

That answer plays about with a text of St Peter.[17] Harmlessly enough,

14. LB, 5, 473B.   15. *De tuenda valetudine*, in LB, 4, 32E.
16. *Adagia*, II, IV, XXXIX, *Risus syncrusius*.
17. I Peter, 4:8, 'Above all else be fervent in charity among yourselves, for charity covereth a multitude of sins.'

one might have thought. But not for Erasmus. He saw in such jesting the very token of monkish coarseness and brutishness.

Another example abuses the words of Christ in St Luke's Gospel:

Asked if he would like any wine, one says, 'Go up higher.' The other replies: 'Go up higher? Then thou shalt have glory!'[18]

(The monk is pointing his finger higher up the side of his goblet.)

In Luke, Jesus (in words to be interpreted spiritually) advises you to take the lowest place at table. Your host may then invite you to a more exalted seat: 'Friend, go up higher.' Jesus comments, 'Then thou shalt have glory.'[19] For the bibulous monk and his crony it meant splash wine higher up the goblet, followed by words to be irreverently twisted for a joke. Weak and harmless enough; but again, not for Erasmus. He did not object to that kind of joke on the grounds of casual blasphemy. What riled him was yet more proof of the coarseness of the monastic way of life. For him, monks are lacking in refinement and scriptural scholarship.

He was caught in a trap when he strove to condemn monastic laughter. How could it be done without citing examples? He conceded that excessive mockery delighted St Jerome.[20] The kind of ironical laughter found even in the mouth of Jesus was exploited by St Cyprian against idolaters. It was also exploited against the vanities of the Gentiles by Tertullian, Lactantius, Prudentius and Augustine. Jerome and Tertullian went too far. Nevertheless, 'there are some errors which are better refuted by jeering'.[21]

Erasmus does concede to preachers, even outside the periods of permitted licence, liberties which he would never himself adopt. A preacher may wake up a sleepy congregation by telling a funny story. Erasmus cites a Franciscan who did so. That friar spoke of a husband who had to go away for a while. He told his wife that she could do anything she liked, except wash her face in a certain liquid. Being a woman she could not resist doing so. Her complexion was ruined.[22]

---

18. See Erasmus's *Reply to Albert Pio*, in LB, 10, 1111D.   19. Luke, 14:10.
20. But in Jerome's case it was often scathing diasyrm.
21. *De arte concionandi*, LB, 5, 860D.   22. LB, 5, 860F–861C.

A typical *conte*; not very funny really. And there is nothing Christian about that laughter except that it was delivered from the pulpit.

Another example concerns a Dominican. (The tale which Erasmus tells was later retold with far greater success by Rabelais in his *Tiers Livre*.) A nun was found to be pregnant and her abbess called her to account for it. In excuse she said that the young man who did it was strong. The abbess was not satisfied: 'You could be excused if you had cried out, as Scripture counsels you to do.' (The allusion is to a legal principle laid down in Deuteronomy: a woman raped in a solitary place is presumed to have cried in vain for help. Otherwise she risked being stoned to death.) The pert nun had an answer ready: she would have cried for help, only it all took place in the dormitory; in order to shout for help there she would have had to break her vow of silence.[23]

Another typical *conte*. Even with that silly tale Erasmus felt he had gone too far: 'I stop lest by reprehending absurdities I make myself absurd.' Even before retelling the tale he warned that it was not without a 'kind of lewdness'. Erasmus cannot let himself go, and so his satire often loses its edge. He heartily disapproved of a particular sermon he had heard about, but his account of it lacks both the power to amuse and the power to shock. St Paul, when insisting that he was on a par with that of the other disciples, exclaimed, 'Are they Hebrews: so am I.' In Church Latin that is, *Hebrei sunt et ego*. But the word *hebrei* pronounced as the French do, dropping the *h* and sharpening the vowels, sounds very like *ebrii*, 'drunk'. Hence the sermon:

A certain preacher jumped into the pulpit half-asleep from a night's drinking. (Some judge even this to be erudite and ingenious!) He began with these words, as though taken from St Paul: *Ebrii sunt, et ego*, 'Are they drunk? so am I.'

He suddenly woke up to his mistake:

23. For the legal principle, see Deuteronomy, 22:27; A man raped a woman in a place where there was no one else about. 'But there is in the damsel no sin worthy of death'; because 'the damsel cried, and there was none to hear her'. LB, 5, 861BD.

With remarkable dexterity he took up and twisted what he had carelessly said: 'How great a drunkenness seized those wretched Jews when they strove to kill Christ our Lord.'[24]

For Erasmus, that was not an example of 'remarkable dexterity' but a cautionary tale, warning against rash and scurrilous preaching:

Our Church should be free not only from every kind of buffoonery but even from what is inept, laboured or impetuous. If anyone wants to be facetious, let him transgress elsewhere, though buffoonery should be directly excluded from the whole of the Christian life.

24. II Corinthians, 11:22; LB, 5, 863Dff.

43

Christian Wit and Christian Comedy:
'The Great Jester of France'

A contemporary of Erasmus – who greatly admired him – nevertheless thought that buffoonery has its rightful place in the spreading of the Gospel. That contemporary was Rabelais.

Erasmus is an exemplar of Christian wit; Rabelais, of Christian comedy. Whatever Rabelais meant when he called Erasmus his Father and Mother, it was not an avowal of artistic dependency. Rabelais exploited the works of Erasmus in all his French books, even in the minor ones, but he never wrote in his style. The Latin works of Rabelais are learned editions in which there is not much scope for elegance; his Latin is correct, routinely elegant in a Humanist sense – and totally devoid of artistic originality. (If ever we find the Latin translations of Lucian which he wrote during his years as a friar, that judgement may have to be modified.)

Rabelais is, if ever there was one, an artist in French. It is a form of the French language which he created, moulded, exploited and exemplified. What he did with the still pliant and living language of his country could never have been done with codified Latin. Latin remained, of course, his learned tongue. It was in Latin that he became an expert in the law; it was in Latin, with Greek, that he became a medical authority read far beyond France. Doubtless Rabelais learned from Erasmus that Christian truths can be defended by laughter, and that laughter is the means of reducing heresy and error to the kinds of worldly madness which Christians can contain. Nevertheless, when he wrote to Erasmus he had yet to develop – in his own spectacular way – Jerome's conception of the world as a madhouse divided between Christian maniacs and a multitude of worldly ones.

When Rabelais, now a Benedictine, left his new order to become a doctor, he had been influenced by Erasmus not as one author influences another but as one man influences another. Erasmus had taught and shown that better things could be done outside cloisters than within them. Rabelais did not even write to Erasmus as author to author. In his letter he does not present himself as a minor scribbler daring to address a towering one, but as a Humanist doctor who owes to Erasmus everything he is. Erasmus had changed his life.

I suspect, though, that he did slip into his packet a minor Latin work of his: an edition of the *Testament of Cuspidius*. If so, Erasmus apparently quickly read it and sent it on to Boniface Amerbach, a legal friend in Basle.[1]

Writing well in Latin could secure for a Humanist a wide audience made up of the intellectual elite. There were, however, disadvantages. Humanists did not look kindly on a flood of neologisms or grammatical innovations, so ruling out much of what Rabelais sought to do. If you wrote in Latin only a minority of your fellow-countrymen – and very, very few of your fellow-countrywomen – could read your work. King Francis could understand Erasmus only in translation, when presented through a courtier. That same king, hearing that Rabelais was being accused of heresy, could nevertheless judge the matter for himself. He summoned to Court the best public reader in France, Pierre Du Chastel, the Bishop of Macon. He did not ask the bishop for guidance or for his opinion: he ordered him to read Rabelais out to him. Having heard him, the king, on his own

---

1. In 1532 Rabelais published an edition of the *Testament of Cuspidius*. He saw it as an example of simple and elegant legal Latin. In Basle there is a copy of that work which had been sent to Boniface Amerbach. An inscription on the title-page reads: 'To the most honoured man, Dominus Boniface Amerbach doctor of both the Laws [Civil and Canon], Gilbert Cousin, the secretary of D. Erasmus, sent this as a gift.' The *Testament* was quickly reproduced in Basle, but it was soon recognized as supposititious. (See S. Rawles, M.A.S. *et al.*, *A New Rabelais Bibliography*, Droz, Geneva, 1987, no. 108, where the copy is illustrated.)

authority and following his own judgement, cleared Rabelais of all suspicion of heterodoxy.[2]

Erasmus could flatter a king; Rabelais could make a king laugh.

Incidentally, there is no word in Rabelais too common or too obscure to be read out in the royal court by an eloquent bishop. One suspects, though, that the bishop had to gloss quite a few passages as he went along: many of the jests in Rabelais demand more culture and erudition than the king ever had.

Rabelais came to his writing with few constrictions to limit the scope of his comedy. He wrote in a country renowned for its freedom of comment. He could, as a Humanist, delve deeply into ancient culture; he could as a Frenchman take note of what was making his fellow-countrymen laugh in lowbrow French literature as well as in the consciously highbrow; in satirical sketches staged in the inns of court or in faculty romps; in comic sermon, farce or pastiche: French abounded in laugh-raising writings at many intellectual levels.

French was already a language widely known outside France and French-speaking lands: in northern Italy, among literate Flemings and Germans, and among the English aristocracy, ever mindful of the Conquest. It was supported by great literary achievements, yet it had not been congealed by usage. Rabelais could mould it into the shapes he needed. He could ransack dialects and other tongues for new words and new meanings. He could summon up that special feeling which we all reserve for words in our own language.

In our Latin dictionaries we are cautioned about certain words: *archaic, poetic, vulgar*, we read; *not in decent use*; *obscene*. Without such warnings one Latin word risks looking much like another. Writing in French, Rabelais did not need, or have, a lexicographical nanny. If he used a verdant word, his readers or hearers would recognize it as such. Renaissance Courts were quite outspoken. Queen Margaret of Navarre in her *Heptaméron* shows us Court ladies laughing behind their fans when certain words and topics

---

2. Rabelais gratefully mentions this royal interest in his work, and his exoneration by his king, in the preliminary letter to the *Quart Livre* addressed to Cardinal Odet de Chastillon (See the TLF edition, p. 8, and the note to line 130).

crop up. There were few colourful French words which a French warrior king would not have heard. Ladies and gentlemen in the Courts of France and of Navarre would have known many a naughty word – French ones, not Latin. Even for the French gentlemen or the rare French lady who knew Latin, *cunnus* would never have the same effect as *con*. And neither would have the same arresting effect on a genteel English audience as would 'cunt' (or the four-letter verb that often goes with it). Only in a very restrictive sense can those three words be said to 'mean' the same thing. Apart from familiarity with one's own tongue, there are the differing tolerances of each language. In the case of English, a language with a huge vocabulary having roots in both Anglo-Saxon and French as well as massive borrowings from Latin and Greek, certain words have been isolated as 'obscene'. There are fewer such isolated words in Latin and fewer still in French. (English translations of Rabelais always risk making him sound more 'obscene' than his writings justify.)

The elegant members of the great European Courts and rich men's houses did not live in social isolation; there were domestics everywhere. From time immemorial there would always have been at least some servants whose language was rough and direct. Coarse oaths, coarse gestures, scribbled four-letter words – and 'four-letter' drawings as well – might be seen or overhead by anyone. Montaigne tells how a governess stopped his little daughter in her tracks when she was reading aloud. The cause of her fluttering was the French word for beech-tree, *fouteau*. It can lend itself to an obvious play on *foutu* (from *foutre*, a blunt word for sexual intercourse with a woman). Montaigne's comment is enlightening:

Unless I am mistaken the company of twenty lackeys would not in half a year have imprinted on her mind an understanding of what those naughty syllables mean, how they are used and what they imply, as did that good old crone by her one reprimand and prohibition.[3]

Graffiti were not invented yesterday either. Speaking as a male

3. Montaigne, *The Complete Essays* ('On some lines of Virgil'), Penguin Books, 1991, p. 967.

about the false ideas given to women by drawings of exaggerated penises, Montaigne comments:

What great harm is done by those graffiti of enormous genitals which boys scatter over the walls and staircases of our royal palaces! From them arises a cruel misunderstanding of our natural capacities.[4]

As for vocabulary, Montaigne was convinced, from a chance overhearing of ladies chatting, that 'there is no word' which they do not know 'better than our books do'.[5]

It is a priceless resource for a comic writer to be able to call upon any of the words his language contains; priceless too to be allowed to invent new ones. Rabelais, the consummate comic writer, knew how to put such resources to good effect.

Since Rabelais is our examplar of Christian comedy, it matters when conventional judgements deform his achievement, emphasizing his use of grosser words, especially scatological ones, and his dwelling at times on our bodily functions. It is an error to isolate such terms and themes. Rabelais has a greater vocabulary than any other French author and it covers a multitude of linguistic fields; it embraces scatology, but it is grotesque to think that it is limited to it or even dominated by it.

The saintly, platonizing sister of Francis I, Queen Margaret of Navarre, authorized Rabelais to dedicate his *Tiers Livre* to her. Both Francis I and his successor Henry II not only enjoyed Rabelais: they rated him amongst the greatest of all authors. They each gave him a *Privilège* to show their unstinting admiration and approval. Francis emphasized his 'utility' – that is, his worth as a moralist. Angered and depressed by vicious attacks, Rabelais gave up writing altogether. Those who begged him to resume writing his comic books were, as King Henry stated, 'the learned and studious persons of Our kingdom'. Horace taught that the highest category of author 'mixed the useful and the sweet', that is, mixed moral teachings with aesthetic delight. For his kings and his cardinals, Rabelais did just that.[6]

4. ibid., p. 971. 'Boys' here may mean servants or young lads generally – probably the former.   5. ibid., p. 967.
6. ibid. Both *Privilèges* can be read in Rabelais, *Tiers Livre*, TLF, pp. 3–6.

From his pinnacle of esteem Rabelais could laugh heartily in French at themes which Erasmus could but palely hint at or wanly smile at in Latin. Rabelais could also draw upon Latin, which is scattered through his French; he had to if he wanted to find matter for laughter in the higher reaches of Renaissance culture and Renaissance error. A few Latin words and phrases had anyway entered the public consciousness through the liturgical year. They might turn up anywhere. A romp written with students or the educated in mind could venture much further than that, and once his readers consisted chiefly or wholly in the 'learned and studious persons' of the kingdom there was no limit to what he could do: dozens of jokes in the *Tiers Livre*, as well as the whole structure of the book, presuppose a good knowledge of legal Latin.

When Renaissance Humanists were learned, they were learned indeed. Rabelais opened up the entire range of their culture and scholarship to Christian laughter.

44

Christian Laughter
at Shrovetide

Shakespeare, in *Twelfth Night*, has made generations appreciate the fun-and-games of the eve of the Epiphany, when increased merry-making marked the end of the twelve days of Christmas. At Twelfth Night Falstaff is a hero, not an old rake to be rejected. In medieval and Renaissance palace, city, village, college, church and chapel, such merriment was even more present at Shrovetide. A temporary goodbye was about to be said to eating flesh. The fastidious Erasmus loathed such periods of often coarse revelry, self-indulgence and riotous fun. He was not alone. Carnival and 'Easter laughter' were viewed by many as a pagan left-over, to be driven out of Christian lands. Many, on the contrary, saw Shrovetide revels as an occasion for good old Christian laughter.

Such periods of revelry were not always straightforward fun. A satirical society could use them for critical comments on Church and state. Students and budding lawyers might hone a cutting-edge on their laughter.

Attempts to clean up carnival did not always augur well for Jews or heretics. Outside a few historical centres, there were few Jews in France. In countries where Jews were numerous and where ghettos abounded, liturgical revelry could easily degenerate into Jew-baiting.

'Easter laughter', an excuse for innocent amusement, contributed much to the very basis of the laughter in Rabelais's *Pantagruel*. But Easter could give rise to sermons steeped in diasyrm. A chilling example comes from the pen of one of the most distinguished of the Reformers, the Hebrew scholar John Œcolampadius of Basle. In his short and unbending sermon entitled *On Easter Laughter* he condemned the practice of preachers who amuse their Easter congregations with joke-filled sermons. His own example of what a good Easter sermon should be is entitled *On the Joy of the Resurrection*.[1]

We are told how 'Christ brings great joy, but not to all, not to Jews and others who by their worst of lives do all they can to crucify Christ anew.' Responsibility for all the blood of the righteous shed since Abel the Just still falls rightly on those infidels. And on Pontius Pilate, too. And on his Emperor, and on all unfaithful kingdoms.

Easter laughter can be riddled with righteous hatred. It need not be, and rarely was, it seems, in France. Hatred and diasyrm are not of its essence.

In his first book, *Pantagruel*, Rabelais shows Shrovetide merriment at its best. There are some serious interludes, but the fun-and-games are fun-and-games, offensive to no one – at least in intention. Even the appearance of books can be part of the fun. The sober appearance of the earliest *Pantagruel* suggests laughter and merriment: it is done up to look like a learned law-book (many of its jokes would be best appreciated by students of the law).[2]

There is a joke in the very name of Pantagruel. The traditional name of that Celtic imp was Penthagruel. (By the prefixes Pol, Tre and Pen you can tell Bretons as well as Cornishmen.) Tongue-in-cheek, Rabelais claims that his giant's name is Graeco-Arabic, *Panta* meaning 'all' in Greek, and *gruel* meaning 'thirst' in Hagarene (the language of the descendants of Hagar the concubine). The educated would have laughed: the joke had topical relevance. Erasmus was ridiculing attempts of biblical scholars to find the etymology of a proper name in one language from roots in one or more others which had no linguistic connection with it.

Pantagruel had a literate audience in mind – one that could recognize and appreciate his list of comic titles of books and manuscripts allegedly in the great Parisian library of Saint-Victor. Many of the titles are in dog-Latin. A mock title such as *Braguetta Juris*

1. Œcolampadius, *De Gaudio Resurrectionis Sermo*, in *De Risu paschali*, Sigismund Grim Medicus and Marcus Wyrsung, Basle, 11 June 1521.
2. Cf. S. Rawles, M.A.S. *et al.*, *A New Rabelais Bibliography*, Droz, Geneva, 1987, pp. 65–72, for details and illustrations. The edition dates from 1532 (or 1531?).

('Codpiece of the Law') is worth a smile, provided that you recognize it as a deformation of *Brocardica Juris* (a standard little legal memory-book).

If you have a little Latin, and know how the theologians of Cologne hounded Reuchlin, the champion of the study of Hebrew, there is a well-directed smile of mockery in the imaginary treatise entitled (in Latin) *The Fuss and Pother of the Doctors of Cologne against Reuchlin.*[3]

There was at the Sorbonne a prickly theologian named Dr Sutor. He was a public opponent of Rabelais's hero, Erasmus. His taste for writing bitter attacks, counter-attacks and counter-counter-attacks was inexhaustible. Any Erasmian could enjoy a laugh at the expense of an imaginary book attributed to him: *Sutor, against someone who had called him a Ragbag: and that Ragbags are not condemned by the Church.* (The appalling Latin made it funnier for those in the know.)[4]

Traditionally Penthagruel was an imp whose task was to shovel salt into the gaping gullets of drunkards, so producing a morning-after thirst. During a prolonged period of appalling drought, Rabelais turns that imp into a kindly giant who arouses a good thirst for wine. Contemporaries would have enjoyed that without a footnote!

Some traditional Shrovetide jesting remains obvious enough, as when Rabelais gives Shrove Tuesday an ancestry. It includes, 'From Lord Guts Almighty sprang Saint Paunchy and Mardy-gras.' *Ventrem Omnipotentem* ('Lord Guts Almighty') is a fair example of carnival-esque licence, understandable to anyone who could recognize a comic distortion of the *Patrem Omnipotentem* of the Apostles' Creed.[5]

Familiarity, it is said, breeds contempt. No doubt. But is also breeds innocent humour within groups who share common knowledge and common assumptions.

3. *Tarrabalationes doctorum Coloniensium adversus Reuchlin.*
4. *Sutoris, adversus quemdam qui vocaverat eum fripponatorem, et quod frippo-natores non sunt damnati ab Ecclesia.*
5. *Credo in unum Deum, Patrem Omnipotentem* (I believe in one God, the Father Almighty).

The opening pages of *Pantagruel* make a tongue-in-cheek contrast between the selling-powers of the Bible and a little chapbook of tales of Gargantua (Rabelais was to borrow from it). Booksellers, we are told, will sell more copies of those chapbooks in two months than copies of the Bible in nine years. Virtually from the outset readers discover for themselves that *Pantagruel* is a send-up of Holy Writ in carnivalesque mood: knights and their ladies read that little chapbook with good faith. They believe in it. So too they should believe in *Pantagruel*, 'trusting it just as they do the text of the Holy Gospel'. The 'author', Alcofrybas Nasier, vouches for its truth: 'I speak like St John of the Apocalypse, *We bear witness to what we have seen*.'[6] Pantagruel has a genealogy going back well beyond the Flood. All good biographers provide one for their subjects, particularly Monsignor Saint Luke and Saint Matthew.

Rabelais's models are in fact genealogies in the Old Testament:

Who begat Sarabroth,
Who begat Faribroth,
Who begat Hurtaly, who was a great eater of sops and reigned
    at the time of the Flood.

We are back in that world of Jubal, the father of all such as handle the harp and the organ, and of Og, King of Basham, whose bedstead was a bedstead of iron, who have made numberless boys smile in quires and places where they sing.[7]

Back too to the world of Noah's Ark, and of that patriarch's lightning tipsiness which made François Villon invoke 'Father Noah, who plantest the vine' – 'Noah planted a vine, and he drunk of the wine, and was drunken.' Pantagruel's ancestor who was Noah's contemporary did not plant a vine and quaff its liquor; his excess was a surfeit of medlars, which turned all who gorged themselves on them into giants.[8]

6. *Pantagruel*, TLF, Prologue, pp. 3, 7. The reference is to the Vulgate text of John, 3:11, in which *Quod vidimus testamur* are words addressed by Jesus to Nicodemus. Alcofrybas Nasier is an anagram of Françoys Rabelais.
7. Deuteronomy, 3:11; *Pantagruel*, TLF, IV, 62ff.
8. Genesis, 4:21; 9:20; *Pantagruel*, TLF, I, 22–31.

But how could Pantagruel have giant ancestors who date from before the Flood? No giant entered the Ark when the whole world was drowned. The narrator has a reply which has delighted readers and illustrators alike: Pantagruel's ancestor, Hurtaly, was too big to enter the Ark, so he sat astride it and guided it with his feet, 'one leg one side, one leg, the other: like little children on their hobby-horses'. Grateful Noah 'fed him through a chimney, and sometimes they conversed together, as did Icaromennipus with Jupiter, according to the account in Lucian'.

With the name of Lucian the story originally ended. The tale does indeed read very much like something out of Lucian's amusing *True History*. What a surprise it is to discover that Pantagruel's Hurtaly is none other than Og, the *Hapalit*, the 'Surviving One', retold from a Hebrew work by Rabbi Eliezar.

Rabelais could put sound and rare learning to good comic effect.[9] Erasmus found rabbinical learning largely distasteful. Others found Rabbi Eliezar's story of Og, the King of Bashan, more worthy of the Arabian Nights than of a work of God's law; Sebastian Muenster condemned Jewish legends about Og as something stupid to laugh at: for Rabelais they were something delightful to laugh with. They enlarged the scope for Shrovetide comedy within the Old Testament. For Erasmus, Lucian meant dialogue and diasyrm. At first for Rabelais he meant jolly tall stories.

It is in the spirit of carnival to laugh for a while at what is normally admired or awesome. A great deal of the laughter in *Pantagruel* is evoked against a normally revered scriptural background. Rabelais's writings show him as accepting Scripture as the normative and inspired word of God. When less biblical ages fail to recognize either

9. The account of Og sitting astride Noah's Ark is taken from the *Pirkei de-Rabbi Eliezar ben Hyrcanus*, of which there is an English translation by G. Friedlander, London, 1916. When Rabelais wrote *Pantagruel* the work was available only in Hebrew. Rabbi Eliezar is mentioned in a book by Amaury Bouchard (a friend dating back to the Franciscan days of Rabelais), which might suggest that the *Pirkei de-Rabbi Eliezar* was discussed by Rabelais and his friends at Fontenay-le-Comte: *Τῆς γυναικείας φύτλης adversus Andrean Tiraquellam* Paris, 1522. Despite its partly Greek title, the work is entirely in Latin.

the normative scriptural allusions or the funny perversions of them, much of Rabelais's humour and wisdom slips out of focus.

Readers from a warm biblical culture can usually recognize Old Testament laughter for the fun that it is. Similar laughter has come to their lips, not least when children. But *Pantagruel* draws its merriment not only from the Old Testament but from the New, not excluding the very words of Christ. That too was understood.

Pantagruel receives his name after a 'nativity'. His ecstatic father is seized by the 'spirit of prophecy'. That was taken as a 'sign' – St John's word for a miracle.

Is anything sacrosanct from the beam of Shrovetide laughter? The Sermon on the Mount? No. *Blessed are the heavy, for they have stumbled.*[10] Christ's last words on the Cross? No. Rabelais's next book, *Gargantua*, reminds us that jesting on sacred subjects flourished in educated circles. We are treated to a series of clerical jokes from the Well-Drunken:

> 'I have God's word in my mouth, "I thirst".'
> 'The stone called *asbestos* is no less unquenchable than the
>   thirst of my Paternity.'
> '*Appetite comes with eating*, as Hangest Du Mans used to say.'

That is donnish or student laughter. Once it was simple enough, but now it needs footnotes.[11]

The Pharisees sought to flatter Jesus: 'Thou regardest not the person.' But the wine steward of the Well-Drunken is bidden to 'regard the person' and pour out a double ration for his friends. The joke falls flat nowadays: it demands too much analysis. Denizens of the Quartier Latin would have taken it in their stride.

---

10. *Pantagruel*, TLX, IX bis, 185–6, *Beati lourdes, quoniam ipsi trebuchaverunt.*
11. The *Bien-Yvres* forms ch. 3 of *Gargantua*, 1535 or 1534; cf. TLF edition, p. 43, variants. Those particular jokes were added to later editions from 1542 onwards. Evidently the public enjoyed them. *Sitio*, 'I thirst', is Christ's last word from the Cross in John, 19:28. The speaker refers to his 'Paternity' because his title as a priest is 'father'. The gourmand's saying, 'Appetite comes with eating', is cheekily attributed to Dr Jérôme de Hangest, one of the more austere theologians of the Sorbonne. Was he a good trencherman?

Again it was simple enough, but like all in-jokes it supposes common knowledge.

Christian laughter has in-jokes in plenty. The most firmly Christian are those which derive their laughter from the very texts which Christians venerate; without the veneration there would be no joke.[12]

12. Sometimes the scriptural allusion is an essential part of the joke, without being enough to explain it all. For example, Rabelais wrote, *Respice personam: pone pro duos: bus non est in usu.* Once we recognize the echo of Matthew, 22:16, *Non enim respicis personam*, there still remains the drinking-joke to cope with. *Pone pro duos* ('Pour out for two') is deliberately bad Latin; it should be *Pone pro duobus.* The speaker avoids the correct form, since it ends in *bus.* In French, *bus* – the past-historic of *boire* – means 'I drank', or here, 'I have left off drinking.' Good fun among student-friends, but caviar to the Latin-less general.

45

Seeking for Signs

Entire episodes in *Pantagruel* derive their fun from interlocked texts of Scripture. They remind us of a world of Christian laughter now largely lost. An example may serve to bring something of that world back to us.

All four of Rabelais's books are preoccupied with signs. Gestures are signs. Sounds, including words, are signs. Pictures are signs. Emblems are signs. Bodily gestures and bodily functions are signs. Signs have meanings. From where do their meanings derive?

Some signs, some gestures, have meanings which are 'natural' and so are understood from culture to culture. Touching your sphincter, pinching your nose and pointing at someone is a natural gesture indicating contempt: 'You stink!' Some have meanings which are entirely conventional: you have to learn what they mean. Deaf-and-dumb language today – or in former times the use of gestures to indicate numbers or concepts – have conventional meanings imposed arbitrarily upon them. You either know them or you do not. The meaning of the sounds we make when we cry are natural and do not have to be learned. The meanings of the sounds we make when we speak our own language, or any other language, are not natural to us and have to be learned. That is the common-sense point of view. It is also essentially the opinion of Aristotle.

From Plato onwards many held that words are signs which have, or may have, 'true' meanings. The senses which they have may be not merely arbitrary but correspond in reality. Such true meanings are recoverable from their etymologies (*etymos* means 'true'). Rabelais follows Plato in holding that at least some words (especially proper names) may have true meanings because those who imposed those meanings on their sounds had been divinely inspired.

Other sounds (including many proper names) have meanings imposed upon them quite arbitrarily; such words are then accepted by convention.

A few sounds convey their meanings directly, quite independently of linguistic conventions. Aristotle held that the meanings of all words are conventional, simple onomatopoeias excepted. *Rire*, say, or *ridere*, or *warau* or *lachen*, all mean 'to laugh': provided you know the relevant language. 'Ha, ha, ha' means laughter in all tongues.

Rabelais finds it outrageously funny when anyone confounds the categories, the true, meaningful sign, and the merely conventional one. He tells of Thaumaste, a learned Tommy who came from England to hold an esoteric debate with Pantagruel.[1] It is agreed to use gestures and signs other than words. By doing so the clack who attend debates in the Sorbonne will not be able to interrupt. The learned Thaumaste knows his esoteric and cabbalistic signs, but cannot recognize the most obvious natural ones. And so we laugh at him as Panurge the Trickster diddles him and mocks him. Thaumaste is in deadly earnest; Panurge, who stands in for Pantagruel, is not. Thaumaste makes an erudite sign, assuming that Panurge will understand it and reply in kind. The Trickster does no such thing:

Whereupon Panurge placed a left finger on his arsehole, drawing air through mouth as you do when slurping oysters in their shells.

Thaumaste, for once, can make no reply: his learning has let him down; he can only make an involuntary natural sign: he wheezes like a goose.

As Rabelais tells it the tale is as funny as can be. But what has this to do with Scripture or with Christian laughter? The general

---

1. Ever since Thomas Becket, 'Thomas' had been the nickname for an Englishman – not just a Tommy Atkins – as 'Taffy' is now for a Welshman or 'Jock' for a Scot.

context of Thaumaste's debate with Panurge is legal rather than scriptural: it was commonly asserted that sign language – misunderstood – caused the Greeks to bring law to the ignorant Latins. Rabelais, however, goes out of his way to make it scriptural. When Christ was asked for a sign – a miracle to prove his credentials – he condemned the 'adulterous generation' who sought signs, contrasting it with the Queen of Sheba who came from afar to learn from Solomon.

Here we meet ambiguity. Traditionally, Solomon and the Queen of Sheba (who could not speak each other's tongues) discussed hard enigmatic questions in sign language. What the queen did not do was demand that Solomon should give her a 'sign' to prove his status. Rabelais, continuing his carnivalesque spoof, makes Pantagruel even more clearly into a comic Christ.

Rabelais places the encounter of Thaumaste and Panurge in scriptural contexts. Plato held that, if men could see Wisdom personified, they would be moved to ecstasy. The Queen of Sheba bore that out, she 'who came from the limits of the East and the Persian Gulf to see the order of the household of the wise Solomon and to hear his wisdom'.[2]

But why that reference? Because Jesus was emphatic about *signs*: 'An evil and adulterous generation seeketh after a *sign*; and there shall be no *sign* given it – save the *sign* of Jonah the prophet and the Queen of Sheba.' The Queen of Sheba simply sought a wise man: Jesus is more than that. As he himself said, 'And behold, a greater than Solomon is here.'[3] In Rabelais's first Chronicle, the Queen of Sheba is to Panurge what Solomon was to Jesus. Thaumaste makes that point when acknowledging that he is beaten in the debate – beaten by a mere disciple of Pantagruel:

'My Lords, now I can indeed cite the Gospel saying, *And behold, a greater than Solomon is here.*'

2. Plato, *Phaedrus*, 250D; *Pantagruel*, TLF, XIII, 14–27; echoing Matthew, 12:42–43, with subsidiary echoes of I Kings, 10, the source of the reference by Jesus.
3. Matthew, 12:41–42.

That 'greater than Solomon' is Pantagruel, 'an incomparable treasure'. His disciple is Panurge.

Thaumaste concludes his praise of Pantagruel with another comic
misapplication of words of Jesus: 'A disciple is not above his Master':

You can judge what the Master would have been, seeing that his disciple
showed such prowess: for *The disciple is not above his Master.*[4]

Then – since Pantagruel's role is to raise thirst – they all drink,
thirsty as the soul in the psalm, longing for God 'as a land without
water'.[5]

The laughter arises from the tension created when texts and the
Godhead, recognized as awesome, are juggled with in contexts of
grotesque and relaxed fun. That comic tension was traditionally
exploited at certain seasons but could be at work at any time and
anywhere – in lecture-room, hall or monastery, as well as at table
with a drink in your hand. The laughter is Christian because its
references are Christian and the awe it presupposes is Christian. The
expectations aroused are Christian. Those who need footnotes to
point out the scriptural references will never savour such jokes as
do those who experience the sudden glory of recognizing the awesome
in the trivial.

Such jokes are a homage paid to Holy Writ.

Faint echoes of such laughter can still be heard: ordinands make
jokes on Scripture with other ordinands, and jokes about their
dearest liturgical or religious convictions. Some of those jokes are
risqué. Churchgoers are, of course, far more likely to make jokes by
citing words from liturgy or Scripture in unexpected contexts than
are those who know little of either.

As for those who know nothing of either, they are simply excluded
from the fun. 'Hang all the law and the prophets!' exclaimed out of

4. *Pantagruel*, TLF, XIII, 287–93; 314–15; citing Matthew, 12:42 (or Luke, 11:31),
and Matthew, 10:24 (or Luke, 6:40). As befits a gambol aimed at a literate readership,
Thaumaste cites his texts in Latin: *Ecce plus quam Salomon hic*, and *Non est
discipulus supra magistrum.*
5. Psalm 143 (142):6, 'My soul thirsteth after thee, as a land without water'. Rabelais
cites it in Latin: *sicut terra sine aqua*.

the blue is not funny. It is funny, though, if you experience the shared awe of Holy Communion. There they form part of Christ's summary of the law: Love God – the first and great commandment; and love thy neighbour: *On these two commandments hang all the law and the prophets.*

In the West Country when I was a child, a boy who had hoped to have broken wind so discreetly that no one noticed it might be twitted (if his fellows were olfactorily alerted) for 'spreading abroad a pleasant odour'. Our religion was Bible-centred. We would not have laughed if we had not known that we were misapplying a mystical text from the Book which we venerated above all others.[6]

That form of Christian laughter is part of a wider pattern of fun at the expense of what we hold dear. College sketches guy teachers and dons who are deeply respected, and laugh at subjects studied with earnest pleasure. Erasmus loathed his student days and had no truck with it. Rabelais enjoyed his. When studying in Montpellier he acted with other medics in a farce which sought its laughter at the expense of their Art: a doctor is begged to cure a beloved wife of her dumbness. He succeeds. Later the husband begs him to make her stop talking. But no one can make a woman do that! The doctor makes the husband blissfully deaf.

Rabelais saw that as a farce in the tradition of *Maistre Pathelin*, which had recently pleased the King of France. It is a lawyer's laugh at lawyers. Rabelais placed his qualification on the title-page of his *Tiers Livre de Pantagruel*: 'Master Fran. Rabelais, doctor of Medicine.' So we expect – and get – some guying of the medical profession: Panurge slips four coins into the hands of Dr Rondibilis:

Rondibilis firmly grasped them, then said, in amazement, as though he were offended, 'Hay, hay, hay, Sir, nothing was called for! Many thanks, all the same. From wicked folk I ever take nothing: nothing from good folk do I ever refuse. I am always at your service.'

'So long as I pay,' said Panurge.

'Yes, of course,' said Rondibilis.[7]

6. Ecclesiasticus, 24:25 (Wisdom is speaking): 'And as choice myrrh I spread abroad a pleasant odour.'   7. *Tiers Livre*, TLF, XXXIIII, 112–19.

Such laughter is not hostile and satirical; it is all part of professional fun-and-games. But it is open to jesters to move the laughter on to a more critical plane.

Limits are placed on Christian laugh-raisers, but they are hard to judge or to foresee.

Parisian cockney deformed *Jésus* into *Jarus*. Rabelais tried to bring that into his jests. He was obliged to take it out; the name of Jesus proved too holy to sport with in print. But one can suppose that that vulgar Parisian form appeared in Rabelais's tales told *viva voce* to his ailing Cardinal.[8]

Similarly, the Sorbonne objected to laughter at the expense of the genealogies of Jesus in the New Testament. Rabelais denied having used them as a basis for laughter. Would he ever have done so?[9]

Pantagruel delighted readers of French from the moment it appeared. Copies of Rabelais could be found in the libraries of many a convent and cathedral. Clergymen loved it. Yet it was examined by ecclesiastical censors in 1532. Those censors also examined *The Mirror of the Christian Soul*, a pious evangelical poem by Queen Margaret of Navarre! They were stopped in their tracks by her brother the king. The censors may have brought Rabelais and Margaret together. (He dedicated his *Tiers Livre* to her.)

Censors are always unpredictable, but especially when they do not reflect the current public mood. Pretending to vouch for the truth of his tall stories, Rabelais in *Pantagruel* had cited St John: *We testify to what we have seen.* That was removed. Béda and others at the Sorbonne often feared that any printed work of fiction might lessen the laity's trust in the historical truth of the Bible; they may even have been right.[10]

8. In the first version of the *Quart Livre*, Panurge twenty-seven times ejaculates *Jarus!* In every case *Jarus* was replaced by the anodyne *Zalas!* ('Alas!' in the dialect of Saintonge). See the *Quart Livre*, TLF, XVIII, p. 105, variants, and other variants during the 'Storm at Sea'. (*Jésus* and *Jarus* share much the same confusion as *chaise* and *chaire*.)

9. Cf. *Gargantua*, TLF, I, 4–44. (Rabelais used the Old Testament genealogies as the model for his fun in *Pantagruel*.)

10. *Pantagruel*, TLF, *Prologue de l'autheur*, 77–9: 'I speak as St John does of the Apocalypse, *Quod vidimus testamur.*' Cited from John, 3:11.

The only known copy of the first edition of *Pantagruel* has passed through the hands of a censor; he censored mentions of bosoms and female pudenda, but not anything religious whatsoever, except the oath *Par Dieu* ('By God'). Tellingly, he did draw a finger in the margin pointing to a joke against the Sorbonne.[11]

Rabelais expanded the Shrovetide laughter in later editions of *Pantagruel*. That shows that such laughter remained appreciated and understood. His own attitude towards Shrovetide laughter became more complex with the passage of the years.

But Christian laughter will never have it easy. Hovering in the background there remains a curious alliance of disapproving forces. There had long been Christian moralists who thought, like St Basil, that it was wrong ever to laugh in the Vale of Tears.[12] St Augustine revealingly associates laughter with that famous theft of pears which so harrowed his conscience.[13] In his treatise *On Free-will* he concedes that the ability to laugh is a genuinely human faculty, but notes that it belongs to the lower part of Man.[14] Despite his reputation for severity he knew how to enjoy a laugh; yet he still distrusted laughter. Asked what sin might conceivably have been committed by Abel the Just, Augustine concluded that he might perhaps have so forgotten himself as to laugh too heartily and even to have played practical jokes. *O felix culpa!*[15]

Theologians of many persuasions disliked the laughter which *Pantagruel* exemplifies. Could Erasmus ever have approved of *Pantagruel*? Literature redolent of student revels had many who would stifle it, among both the Reformers and the traditionalists.

11. S. Rawles, M.A.S. *et. al.*, *A New Rabelais Bibliography*, Droz, Geneva, 1987, entry no. 1. There were hardly any jokes at the expense of the Sorbonne in the first version of *Pantagruel*. From then on there are many.   12. *Regulæ*, no. 53.
     13. *Confessions*, II, ix.   14. *De Libero arbitrio*, I, viii.
     15. Peter Brown, *Augustine of Hippo*, London, 1967, p. 199.

46

Christian Laughter
for Faithful Folk

Between *Pantagruel* and *Gargantua* Rabelais made his Christian laughter much more accessible to a public (including a courtly one) which was not educated in Latin. Paradoxically, *Gargantua*, while accessible to a much broader pubic, is far more Humanist in its terms of reference. In the very first lines it evokes Plato and Socrates rather than the still popular medieval Romances and their popular or parodic successors. The change is not complete: Latin is less cited, but more than a little erudition is required to grasp fully some of the Christian jests.

One of the most fundamental oppositions among Christians is between those who see faith as a kind of good gullibility, and those who, turning to the Greek of their New Testaments, see faith as trust, as confidence in God and his promises.

The Reformation hinged on such matters. There were churchmen prepared to anathematize or kill over that question. Rabelais preferred to laugh, while making his point quite firmly: Christian faith is not the ability to swallow old wives' tales or tall stories. It is, as Mary showed, firm trust in the promises of God. The laughter here is not that of student revels but is akin to the laughter-filled sermons for which Franciscans were renowned. It is made all very funny in a Brueghel-like setting.

In *Gargantua* Rabelais set about propagating a doctrine which both Erasmus and Luther approved of, but which Thomas More denied. Rabelais contends that, in the Bible, faith never means the kind of credulity by which a pagan believer swallowed tall stories about his gods. It does not even mean giving intellectual assent to revealed truths about God. It means trust: trust in things which are unseen; trust in God.[1]

Central to Rabelais was a verse of the Epistle to the Hebrews:

Now faith is the substance of things hoped for, the evidence of things unseen.

But that translation in the Authorized Version has been digested for us. In the Greek it is not easy going.[2] In the once-dominant Latin Vulgate it was open to ignorant misunderstandings. If you know French better than Latin, the text can seem to mean that faith is believing things which have 'no appearance of truth' about them![3] Should Latin Christians, then, swallow anything they are told?

Laughter does not appear anywhere in St Luke's account of Christ's nativity or in the account of the aged Elizabeth's conception of John the Baptist. That did not stop a master of laugh-raising such as Rabelais from making them into the basis of a comic sermon. It finds its certainties in biblical texts rightly understood: it finds its laughter in biblical texts ignorantly wrenched out of context.

Rabelais tells of a strange 'nativity'. He again chose the term *nativity* rather than the everyday word *birth* so as to link the imposs-ible delivery of his baby giant though his mother's ear with the miraculous birth of Jesus and the miraculous conception of the aged Elizabeth. Birth 'through the ear' has amusing links with exploded

1. That is the common ground of all Evangelicals, of Luther and Rabelais and Calvin as much as of Erasmus. Thomas More was rare among Humanists in rejecting that contention as 'Lutheran', which is odd in the light of what he knew of Erasmus's scholarship. (Thomas More, *Dialogue touchynge Luther and Tyndale*, in *English Works*, London, 1931, pp. 287ff.)
2. Hebrews, 11:1. It was often cited as a *definition* of faith by experts on Roman law. Erasmus insisted that it was not a definition at all but a eulogy. It was also Erasmus who provided the interpretation found in the Authorized Version, for which faith is a matter of assurance and confidence in unseen spiritual truths and promises.
3. The Vulgate reading for 'of things unseen' is *rerum non apparentium*. That could seem to mean to French minds things *de nulle apparence* – things with no likelihood about them. And so (if you made such a mistake) it is things like that that Christians must believe in!

superstition: the Council of Lyons in the ninth century had to condemn the popular belief that, since Christ, the Word of God, having been conceived through the ear of the Virgin, he was also delivered through the Virgin's ear. It was not a current superstition, but it places Rabelais's story in a context.

Gargantua pops out of his mother's ear and yells for a drink.

You believe in the nativity of Jesus: why do you not believe in the nativity of Gargantua?

A good man, a sensible man, always believes everything he is told and everything he finds written down. Does not Solomon say in Proverbs 14, *The simple believeth every word*, and so on? Does not Saint Paul write in 1 Corinthians 13, *Charity believeth all things*? So why should you not believe it? 'Because' (you say) 'it has no appearance of truth.' But I say that, for that very reason, you ought to believe it with perfect faith, since the dons of the Sorbonne maintain that faith is an argument from things which have no appearance of truth.

The taunting of ignorance is gentle and refined. The (allegedly) ignorant professors of the Sorbonne are laughed at for not understanding a knotty verse of Hebrews. Solomon, however, did write, *The simple believeth every word*; but the alert Christian knows that he added, 'but the prudent man looketh well to his going'. (There is good and bad simplicity!) St Paul, in his famous praise of Christian love, did indeed write, *Charity believeth all things*, but not before emphasizing that Charity 'rejoices with the truth'.

Rabelais could count on his chosen public knowing things which are now the reserve of a few.

Is it against our religion or our faith; against reason or against Holy Writ? For my part I can find nothing in Holy Scripture which goes against it. But supposing the will of God were such, would you say that He could never do it? Ha! for grace's sake do not mingle-mangle your minds with such silly thoughts. For I tell you, that *with God, nothing is ever impossible*, and if such were His will, women would henceforth have their children through their ear-holes.[4]

4. *Gargantua*, TLF, ch. 5.

Notice the quotation from St Luke; recognize its source in Genesis: and that clinches the matter.

With God, nothing is ever impossible. With those words of St Luke's which echo God's assurances to the aged Abraham and Sarah, the angel Gabriel reminded Mary of God's promises and power. Mary had doubts about conceiving a child, since she has 'known no man'. Such doubts are banished when Gabriel reminds her that God's almighty power was still at work in the aged Elizabeth, as, long ago, it had been in the aged Sarah. The three most important conceptions in all Christendom, Sarah's, Elizabeth's and Mary's, all show that faith is trust – trust in God, for whom all things are possible.[5]

Theologians were to stress the point earnestly and heavily in treatise and sermon. It is never a case of what God *can* do – he can do anything – but what he wills and what he has promised. No argument from reason, no argument from the silence of Holy Writ will ever suffice. Nothing satisfies faith but God and his explicit promises. In them faith puts its trust; and in nothing else. To try to twist Scripture into another sense incompatible with that doctrine is ignorant and can be made laughable.

With his comic sermon woven into the woof and warp of the birth of Gargantua, Rabelais made a great stride forward. There is nothing like it in the first version of *Pantagruel*, where comedy may surround an evangelical letter or prayer but not pervade them. Lives would have been saved if rival Christians had followed Rabelais and found heretics funny in their misunderstandings of Scripture.

Funny: but Rabelais had not yet made them mad. He finds his way into that madness through schoolboy smut and Plato's schoolboy malice.[6]

Unlike Erasmus, Rabelais seems to have had a happy childhood. Nothing whatever in Erasmus takes us back to happy childhood memories: Rabelais makes the Picrocholine War in *Gargantua* – a war between giants and a comic Emperor Charles V – take place in and about the back garden of his childhood home at La Devinière.

---

5. Luke, 1:37; Genesis, 18:14. Gabriel in Luke, 1:37 follows the text of the Greek Septuagint.   6. Cf. ch. 16 above and Plato, *Philebus*, 49A–50C.

What strikes many readers of Rabelais – especially the majority who read *Gargantua* first – is the so-called schoolboy humour: all that revelling in wiping bottoms; all that glorying in eating, drinking, farting, peeing and galumphing about; all that hot-necked vulgarity about sexual intercourse. Much of it no longer seems all that funny – or even funny at all.

In Rabelais dirt and faeces have an artistic purpose. They are triggers of laughter: not laughter with, but laughter at. Since most of the faecal humour is centred on the young Gargantua, we are encouraged to see it as boyish. But there is also an aristocratic edge: the young prince Gargantua is presented as a peasant amongst peasants. As in Brueghel, bumpkins can be condescended to by their betters. Peasants work with dung. Rabelais's peasants – including Gargantua's mother – gorge themselves on tripe. You cannot wolf down barrels of tripe during the autumn cull without eating a firkin of cow-dung caught up in the folds. (Modern tripe is scalded and blanched.)

Laughter in *Gargantua* warns the great and good that if society is mad enough to leave a young aristocrat to his own devices in the hands of lubricious peasant women and ignorant, canting, snotty, syphilitic old dons, he can readily be turned into a yokel himself, mad and coarse.

There is a medical element too where faecal laughter is concerned. Renaissance doctors sought primary symptoms from urine and faeces. The symbols of their art were not white coats and stethoscopes but sample-bottles and enemas.

But above all the laughter is Christian. The aim of the reformed education of Gargantua is to get away from all that and to produce a young prince who is physically, morally and spiritually clean, pure and healthy.

Rabelais is indulgent to real peasants feasting. Their feasts are traditional, natural and cyclical, providing relaxation and merriment during a life of hard labour. In *Gargantua* their festive eating and drinking share a comic unreality with the vast ingurgitation of giants. One suspects that Rabelais himself has memories of such jollity when a boy at La Devinière. Certain foods and drink will not keep: tripe has to be eaten precisely when cheap *piquet* needs to be drunk.

But in giants or peasants, huge eating leads to huge stools; copious drinking means overflowing chamber-pots.

Gluttony is one of the seven deadly sins. Countless tomes thunder against it; most remain unread. Rabelais laughs at it, and remains a bestseller. The Renaissance was obsessed by education. Grammar-schools were founded or refounded; for the first time in centuries a great many noblemen aspired to see their sons as well educated as the sons of the professional classes. Earnest volumes were written on the education of the Christian prince, of the Christian boy, and even of the Christian girl. Rabelais prefers to make us laugh at a caricature of all that is wrong before giving an account of all that is right. Error is presented as old-fashioned, a thing of the past, some sorry remnant of old idiocies that the Renaissance has swept away.

What is wrong is not merely bad pedagogical theory but rampant ignorance, squalor and bad theology. Dirt and squalor can be powerful aids to laughter, when made ugly but unthreatening. King Francis was anxious that his princely sons should be educated in freedom, to overcome the effects of the restrictions they had been subjected to as hostages in Madrid.[7] He could have had a résumé made for him of *The Education of a Christian Prince* of Erasmus, or of many other Latin books on education. Or he could listen to Rabelais, read out to him at Court. There is little doubt which would be more effective. *Gargantua* could raise laughter at error in anyone who understood French, including kings, aristocrats, country squires and all their ladies. Listeners could also be swayed by an enthusiastic presentation of new positive ideals. Lawyers held that 'Opposites placed opposite shine forth more clearly'.[8] Rabelais exploits that: the medieval mad-and-bad is juxtaposed to an ideal Renaissance sane-and-good.

7. Defeated at Pavia, Francis was made prisoner of the Emperor Charles V. He was released after an undertaking was made to pay a huge ransom (against which Rabelais loyally protested in *Gargantua*). Meanwhile, the princes of the blood were held hostage in Spain. The king feared that now they had returned to France their royal sense of liberty might have been weakened by their captivity. He wanted them to receive a sound education, but in a spirit of noble freedom.

8. *Opposita juxta se posita magis elucescunt*, a legal brocard cited by Bridoye in ch. XXIX of the *Tiers Livre*.

What was a young boy like, when, in the ignorant past, he was left in the hands of the uncouth and the wrongly indulgent? We soon find out. Gargantua is the rustic son of a rustic monarch, living in some dark 'gothick' age before the invention of printing. Eventually, once we have laughed away the darkness and the dirt, we are bathed in the clean light of a Humanist education which will produce a wise and brave Christian prince. (There is of course no attempt to be fair to the achievements or difficulties of that gothick past.)

We see a princely baby giant turn into a foul if funny rustic loon, his giant stature allowing for a gigantic inflation of gothick error and contributing, by its very exaggeration, an element of charity to our laughter. No mean feat: charity and corrective laughter make uneasy bedfellows.

Children of monarchs, noblemen and squires were often placed as tiny babies in the charge of wet-nurses and their cronies. In Gargantua's case, his governesses – all moral sisters of Shakespeare's Nurse in *Romeo and Juliet* – deck out his little dick with ribbons; they work it through their fingers 'like dough in the kneading-trough', and cackle with laughter when it 'lifts up its ears'.[9] No woman – not even a good one – will get anywhere near Gargantua once his education begins anew.

Children do not at first know social conventions: they have to learn them. Many social graces concern the discreet screening of bodily functions. Children have to be taught not to laugh at a fart. Nobody taught any such thing to that happy, gigantic oaf who was Gargantua.

Social prudence is vested in the wisdom of proverbs. Gargantua goes against the lot: Rabelais piles up an increasing list of saws which Gargantua infringes or exemplifies: he never looks before he leaps, ever piddles in his shoes, shits over his shirt-tails, dribbles snot into his sops. This future knight is not given real horses to ride but wooden hobby-horses or a broken-down old mare.

The fault partly lies with Grantgousier, his indulgent, rustic 'medieval' father. 'Has the child been kept clean?' Grantgousier's simple

9. *Gargantua*, TLF, XXI, 5–6.

question, asked when he was having a tipple with those penis-kneading governesses, produces young Gargantua's own answer: a whole chapter devoted to the pleasure he obtained by wiping his bum in ingenious new ways. The 'most royal, the most lordly, the most excellent' way was to wipe it on the long downy neck of a white swan. Sadly, 'the most royal' had to come out; Rabelais's king did not tolerate jests on matters royal. One editor left the chapter out entirely, but he was an exception. After a few minor changes the comedy remained uncensored and appreciated.[10]

Comic authors read aloud to kings and their Courts have to learn prudence. Rabelais was no exception. Christian laughter always has to come to terms with the powers that be. The religion of Christ is not of the world, but until the end of time it remains fully in the world.

The giant's royal father is impressed by his son's divine ingenuity in bottom-wipery science. Why! the boy could become a don![11]

Other moralists might have thundered: Rabelais prefers to make us laugh as everything is stacked against any moral improvement in the boy-giant. There is a gulf between the standards to which society pays lip-service and the practices which society honours in the breach. The young giant whose penis was stimulated by his governesses and whose pleasure centres on his and others' arses is left alone in his jakes. There he is exposed to graffiti. On the walls are filthy poems in elegant verse-forms wallowing in a scatological approach to women and sex. The debasement of women and self is total. Women's genitals are coarsely named urinary ducts; during fantasies about sexual intercourse, the young giant's lady-love is imagined cleaning his anus with her fingers. The coarseness of the actions and foulness of the language are vital to the moral point which Rabelais is to make.

Physical faeces are accompanied by intellectual ones. Dirty, snotty, hacking old theologians teach the boy from antiquated books in bad

10. S. Rawles, M.A.S. *et al.*, *A New Rabelais Bibliography*, Droz, Geneva, 1987, entry no. 22; François Juste, Lyons, 1537. The chapter is found in all other editions, first numbered XII and then XIII.
11. *Gargantua*, TLF, XII, 114, 115.

Latin, such as Erasmus had already mocked out of the classroom. The boy becomes not only incoherent but 'mad, witless, totally raving and doltish'. Weakening of the import of words may once again mask the fact that we are laughing at madness.[12]

Such an education turns young Gargantua into a dirty, lazy, superstitious oaf – useless, bibulous, gluttonous and wenching. His pastimes are merely ways of passing time. His tutors are squalid theological dons with cant reasons to justify their laziness, ignorance and squalor. The young giant follows suit. Gargantua never combs his hair but, like old Dr Almain, a theologian of the Sorbonne, he simply runs his fingers through it. To do otherwise, his tutors opined, was 'to waste time in this world'. He gets up late, citing 'what David said: *It is vain for you to rise up early.*' David does indeed say such words, but to very different effect! 'Except the Lord build the house, they labour in vain that build it . . . It is vain for you to rise up early, to sit up late.' Know the context and you can laugh at the *tartufferie*. Even the Devil can quote Scripture.[13]

When the laughter turns more obviously condemnatory, the grosser physical functions become so too, and are given a clerical dimension:

Then Gargantua would shit, piss, fart, sneeze and dribble snot like an archdeacon.

His foods, all deliberately salty, increase his thirst:

Then – in order to counter the effects of morning dew and corrupt air – he breakfasted on rich fried tripe, rich grilled steaks, rich hams, rich goat-meat stews and monastical bread-and-dripping.

His huge meals produce – as produce they must – copious defecation.[14]

We have been laughing at a boy giant wallowing in some of the

12. The French words are *fou, niays, tout resveux et rassoté*. *Fou* (fool) speaks for itself; *niays* means witless, 'like a nestling'; *resveux* means, not dreaming, but raving or otherwise mad; *rassoté* means 'turned into a sot' – a dolt, an idiot. (*Gargantua*, TLF, XIIII, 5–6.)   13. Cf. Psalm 127 (126).
14. *Gargantua*, TLF, XXI, 30–34.

seven deadly sins: gluttony, lust, sloth. He has no knightly training. He learns no moderation, that Golden Mean of sage Antiquity. Instead he wallows in superstition, with much telling of beads and multiple masses; and over all, there is squalor, symbolic of gross error.

Then he would study a little – and, above all, his rosary. In order to speed through his beads in good form he would mount an ancient mule which had served nine kings. And so, mumbling with his mouth and with his head a-lolling, he would go and take some rabbit or what-not from the trap.[15]

That lolling head is pregnant with meaning. Already Gargantua showed that same symptom when his governesses woke him up by tinkling on wine-glasses:

Then, with his head a-lolling, he would strum with his fingers and baritone-it through his bum.[16]

The implications are spelled out in the next book, in which the giants have become sages. The butt of our laughter then is Panurge. He too is reduced to madness, melancholy madness; Pantagruel saw him in such a state, 'in the position of a madman, doting, with his head a-lolling'.[17]

Christian laughter may differ in its norms of madness, but madness remains the great stimulus to it.

Long before Panurge, the boy giant had been turned into just such a dolt. From *Gargantua* onwards, squalor such as this, and a concentration on bodily functions isolated in their physicality, are always laughable: but we laugh not with them but at them. Monks in the *Quart Livre de Pantagruel*, for example, display in their ablutions the same squalid delight as Gargantua did during his childhood:

They shat in their shitteries; piddled in their piddleries, gobbed in their gobberies, hacked melodiously in their hackeries; raved in their raveries –

---

15. *Gargantua*, TLF, XX, 251–4.   16. *Gargantua*, TLF, VI, 45–55.
17. *Tiers Livre*, TLF, XXXVII, 4–6: 'en maintient de resveur, ravassant et dodelenant de la teste'. Once more, *resveur* means, not a dreamer, but a madman; *ravasser* means 'to rave', but in a passive manner, like a dolt.

they had of course a cant reason for it all: 'so that nothing unclean be brought to divine service'.[18]

Such laughter-raising squalor was not limited to Rabelais at his most Rabelaisian. To remind readers of the literary dignity of scatology Rabelais later translated a grossly faecal poem – by Catullus, of all people – and placed it in a learnedly scatological chapter of his *Quart Livre*, which presupposes that his French reader could read Latin and Italian.[19]

Montaigne in his *Essays* did much the same, defending his outspoken sexual language with the examples of the Court poet and priest, Octavien de Saint-Gelais, and of the successor to Calvin, Theodore Beza. Certainly Luther had nothing to learn from Rabelais: to mock papal pretensions, a Lutheran engraving shows two Germans vividly farting in the face of the pope on his throne; another, entitled *The God-on-earth is Worshipped*, shows a man defecating into an upturned tiara, while another is dropping his trousers and preparing to join in.[20]

The acceptance of a mixture of the high and the low in Christian art means that you can come across what might seem to be obscenities or indecencies in the most surprising of places. The printers' ornament on the first page of the first edition of Erasmus's Greek and Latin *New Testament* shows a woman with her legs wide apart, revealing all she's got. A learned attack on Erasmus by Lopis Stunica sports a printers' ornament with a *mannequin-pisse* on one side and, on the other, a woman copiously, vigorously and vividly breaking wind. Are such things so routine that compositors set them up without a second thought, or is there a conscious mixture of the grossly earthly and the highly spiritual?[21]

---

18. *Tiers Livre*, TLF, XV, 62–6.
19. *Quart Livre*, TLF, LII, 9–12; translated from Catullus, *Ad Furium*, XXIII, 20f.
20. Montaigne, *Essays*, Allen Lane, 1991, 'On some lines of Virgil', pp. 1004ff. For the Lutheran prints, see the illustrations following Luther's *Wider das Bapstum zu Rom vom Teuffel gestifft* in the *Weimarer Ausgabe*, LIV.
21. Lopis Stunica, *Annotationes contra D. Erasmum Roterodamum*, Conrad Resch, Paris, 1522.

Rabelais exploited the themes which they illustrate for both moral and artistic ends.

Once reduced to squalid imbecility Gargantua is cured. For cured he must be; cured of madness, purged with hellebore by a thinly-veiled Dr Rabelais, who stands back from the comic character he has created and exercises his therapeutics. Behind the expert who cures him – 'a learned doctor of the time named *Seraphin Calobarsy*' – stands *Phrançoys Rabelais*. When he was obliged to drop that ana-gram because somebody else had pirated it, he replaced it by *Maistre Theodore*, a name which brings to the fore God and his gifts. Rabelais saw his medical profession as God-given.[22]

With the purging of Gargantua we finally realize – even if we have not done so before – that the way the young giant had been brought up is not simply wrong: it is mad. Being mad, it can be the subject of moral laughter. Christians will laugh most heartily since they are mad at the other extreme, mad with that good madness which will mark the new education.

Spontaneous laughter can be morally neutral or plainly immoral. We can laugh at simple-minded goodness at least as readily as we can laugh at the impostor who takes advantage of it. In a literary work laughter can be guided. Rabelais certainly guides ours. He creates a world of fantasy. Within that world the norms of right and wrong are those of elegant Christian Humanism. The power of madman laughing at madman, and of juxtaposed opposites shining forth more clearly, is shown by what happens once the young booby is purged of his lunacy. Food and drink are taken in healthy moderation; no time is allowed to go to waste. Books are not written out by him from dictation: they are printed. But those books are not silently read – you can have your eyes glued to a book while your mind is in the kitchen – those printed books are read aloud. All teaching is done orally. Now cleanliness is next

22. Gargantua is purged with hellebore – the cure for madness – by 'Seraphin Calobarsy' until 1542, when an unknown astrologer adopted that name for a series of slipshod and unscientific *Prognostications*. Rabelais then cut it out, not wanting, I suppose, to be associated with such shoddy work. Cf. *A New Rabelais Bibliography*, entries 115, 116.

to godliness. More, cleanliness becomes the companion and symbol of purity.

Now all is transformed. No cackling crone with her playful fingers comes anywhere near Gargantua. Never is he left alone to absorb graffiti on lavatory walls. There is no lingering, verbally, linguistically or practically, over urine, dung or defecation. Gargantua listens to the New Testament, heard as it should be heard – not intoned but read 'loud and clear, with a pronunciation appropriate to the substance'. That was no routine moment set aside for God in an otherwise busy day:

Depending on the drift and subject of the Lesson, Gargantua would give himself over to revering, adoring, worshipping and supplicating God in his goodness, whose majesty and amazing judgements and reading had revealed.

Then he would go to the privy to excrete his natural digestions. There his tutor went over what had been read, explaining points which were more difficult or obscure.

All that former glorying in faeces, urine, phlegm and filth is replaced by one tasteful and modest medical phrase: Gargantua 'excretes his natural digestions'. The adjective 'natural' recalls in this context the maxim, 'Things natural are not vile'. One can make them so or, as the new Gargantua does, one can take them for what they are: necessary functions which can be given their due but lowly place.[23]

Rabelais sees Man much as Erasmus does, as body plus soul, or body plus mind, with an intermediate area of things indifferent, which can be turned towards good or evil. 'The most divine part of Man' is his '*voῦς* or *mens*', his mind.[24] His body can be made healthy and handsome, capable of fulfilling a prince's obligations in peace and war. Or mind and body can together wallow in natural functions.

Scatological laughter can lead to understanding of the Pauline, tripartite division of Man. In *Gargantua* we are shown the endless fight between beauty and squalor, virtue and vice, good and evil,

23. *Naturalia non sunt turpia*. Cf. *Gargantua*, TLF, XXI, 28–41.
24. *Tiers Livre*, TLF, XIII, 73f.

the Gospel and the lavatory wall, the Humanists and the Sorbonne; a devoted and learnedly moral tutor and a gaggle of crones. Things outside the mind are indifferent – good or bad as we make them so. The mind itself is a battleground between good and evil spirits: it is not bound to the earth and to mere convention. For Rabelais, sound doctrine is a gift of God: true manna from Heaven. Such manna embraces Plato, Plutarch, Cicero, Papinian – indeed all the sound learning of Greece, Rome and Israel. That it was so readily available in Renaissance times was attributed to God: the Devil prompted Man to make gunpowder, so, as an antidote, God inspired man to invent printing. How comic it can seem to find men who prefer their anus to their most divine part, their mind, their '*νοῦς* or *mens*'.

For Rabelais, St Paul pointed the way when he told the faithful to be 'fully persuaded in their own minds'. Those who failed to do so risked being laughed at by Rabelais.[25] Those who decided aright risked being laughed at too. There have been critics who suggest that Rabelais was laughing at the New Testament when he has his tutor explaining its difficulties while his young charge 'excreted his natural digestions'. For Rabelais, the tutor is showing selfless devotion to his royal charge. To laugh at him shows that *madman laughs at madman*.

The graffiti which Rabelais laughed at are still with us. The gross anal-centred sexuality too: whole magazines are devoted to photographs and fantasies about the female anus. They differ from Rabelais in that such topics in sex magazines have a deadly earnest of their own. Any laughter in them is aimed against marriage,

---

25. *Tiers Livre*, TLF, XIII, 74; VII, 44ff.

Let everyone be fully persuaded in his own mind, especially in matters external, extrinsic and indifferent, which are neither good nor bad in themselves, because they do not come from our hearts and minds, which are the manufactory of all good and all evil.

Things are good when emotions are controlled by the 'clean spirit'; evil, when controlled by an 'evil spirit'. The wise Pantagruel is glossing St Paul's injunction in Romans, 14:5, tacitly cited without attribution in the first words quoted. Rabelais already calls 'good learning' manna from Heaven in *Pantagruel*, TLF, VIII, 106–7. Cf. *Gargantua*, TLF, LVI, 102–11, *variants*. For the invention of gunpowder and printing, cf. *Pantagruel*, TLF, VIII, 89–95.

monogamy, fidelity, Cupid, love, at husband and wife lost in a mutual embrace. Madman laughs at madman.

Fully to enjoy Rabelais's laughter on lavatorial and sexual topics the reader needs to share for a while in his Christian perspectives. C. S. Lewis did. Lewis, a good judge of the matter, held that 'almost the whole of Christian theology could perhaps be deduced' from two facts. First, 'that men make coarse jokes'; second, 'that they feel the dead to be uncanny'. No other animal does. 'The coarse joke proclaims that we have here an animal which finds its own animality either objectionable or funny.' Dogs and angels do not find their natures funny: human beings do. They are aware of a civil war or rebellion within them: their higher and lower natures are not in harmony; they are divided. That is relevant, as he asserts, to the pleasurable laughter aroused by the bottom-wiping chapter of Rabelais:

Once accept the Christian doctrine that Man was originally a unity and that the present division is unnatural, and all the phenomena fall into place. It would be fantastic to suggest that the doctrine was devised to explain our enjoyment of a chapter in Rabelais, a good ghost story, or the *Tales of Edgar Allan Poe*. It does so none the less.[26]

26. C. S. Lewis, *Miracles, A Preliminary Study*, Collins, 1947; 1980 edition, pp. 131–2.

47

Laughter at the
Philosophy of Christ

For Rabelais, as for Erasmus, Christianity is the 'philosophy of Christ'. It teaches men and women how to spiritualize their souls and to 'animate' their bodies. At its highest it does more. It teaches men and women to 'practise dying'. Socrates taught that truth. There is no saying more charged with redeeming power provided that 'what was said philosophically by a philosopher' be 'interpreted in a Christian sense by a Christian'.[1] Such practising of dying consists in striving towards God and the world of the spirit, in striving to separate soul from body in adoration, ecstasy and rapture.

When Rabelais turned to philosophical comedy in his *Tiers Livre de Pantagruel* such an idea, central to Christian laughter, finds its important place. For Rabelais's Dr Rondibilis the Socratic practising of dying is evident in the case of a man plunged in study. His brain is bent like a crossbow, striving to turn his vital spirits into 'animal spirits' (the spirits of the soul). In such a studious man 'all his natural faculties are suspended'. His external senses cease to function.

In short you will judge that he was not living within himself but abstracted out of himself by ecstasy, and will say that Socrates was not misusing the term when he said that Philosophy is nothing but practising dying.[2]

Not understanding higher things, the world laughs. From the dedicatory poem to Queen Margaret of Navarre onwards, the whole

1. Erasmus, *On Preparing for Death*, in LB, 5, 1295E.
2. *Tiers Livre*, TLF, XXXI, 96–115. The French term used by Rabelais, *meditation de la mort*, is often misunderstood. It is taken straight from the Latin *meditatio mortis*, that is, the practising of dying.

of the *Tiers Livre* is suffused with ecstasy and madness. To justify his marriage of comedy to dialogue, a genre once reserved for philosophy, Rabelais draws on Lucian, whom he copiously paraphrases.[3]

The first thirteen chapters of the *Tiers Livre de Pantagruel* are a dialogue. Two persons appear: Pantagruel, now metamorphosed into a wise and princely Christian Stoic; and Panurge, now a silly old fool, lusting to marry, but afraid of being cuckolded, beaten and robbed by a wife yet to be chosen. The rest of the book is dominated by talk: monologue; conversation, speeches, scenes of dramatic comedy and rhetorical elaborations.

The hesitations of Panurge are encouraged by his self-love, his *philautia*. For the Greeks self-love was the root of all error and self-deception. The teaching was widely known from one of Æsop's fables, *The Beggar's Wallet*. Beggars have a wallet thrown over their shoulders like a scarf. It has two pockets, one in front, one behind. All of us are tempted to be like beggars, hiding our own faults in the rear pocket, gloating over other people's, which are kept before our eyes in the front one.

Æsop's fables, at least from medieval times, form part of Christian teaching. (The first work translated into Japanese by the missionaries was not a Gospel but Æsop's fables.) The wise Pantagruel uses precisely this fable to condemn Panurge for his mad love of self.[4]

Christians of all persuasions welcomed such teachings. Self-love is another name for the 'old Adam', for the 'flesh', for that self-centred love which stops us from loving our neighbours as ourselves. It can be one of the ways in which the Devil works in Man. Panurge, seduced by the Devil and deceived by self-love, is reduced to melancholy-madness.[5] That is why we laugh at him. He superficially carried

---

3. Lucian defends his novelty in marrying comedy and dialogue in his treatise *To One who said to him, 'You are a Prometheus in Words'*. Rabelais paraphrases him at length in the Prologue to the *Tiers Livre*, TLF, 218–62.

4. *Tiers Livre*, TLF, XV, 97. Erasmus also made the lesson of this fable into an adage, and so spread it far and wide. Cf. *Adagia*, I, VII.XC).

5. *Tiers Livre*, TLF, XIX, 3–5: Pantagruel states that Panurge is 'seduced by the Evil Spirit'; XXIX, 8–15: Pantagruel accuses Panurge of self-love, '*Philautie et*

out all the consultations of experts and others which Roman law
laid down for a man faced with a legally defined 'complexity'. It
was no good. He twisted all the replies to suit himself. His conduct is
outrageously funny as he declines into madness. Panurge's cleverness
with speech and argument proved no match for the sobering prognostics of some, and the exacting moral demands of others. Panurge
becomes a rambling idiot, a madman 'with his head a-lolling'.[6]

Since madman laughs at madman, we expect other madmen to
appear. We have two. The first presents us with a great paradox in
the actions, role and significance of Judge Bridoye. There are fools
in plenty: Rabelais lists some two hundred of them, good and bad,
in one single chapter.[7] But two stand out.

Bridoye is a 'bridled goose' whose name suggests folly, silliness.
He decides all his lawsuits by casting dice. Roman law, as codified
by Christian emperors, did accept that lots could be used, but as
an absolutely last resort. There were safeguards. Such a recourse
to fortune was permissible only 'when there was no other way'
(St Augustine and canon law are called upon for support).[8]

Panurge's case is only apparently 'perplex' because of his folly.
(Sir Thomas More laughingly rejected the idea of choosing a wife
by lot, specifically reserving lots for when 'there was no other
way'.)[9]

Judge Bridoye finds every one of his cases to be what lawyers
called a *casus perplexus*. He allows lawsuits to grow in complexity
because he enjoys them. Eventually he casts his dice. He is mad! Yet
only one judgement, his last, is overturned by the Court of Appeal.
Dotty enough to believe that one of his legal *brocards* requires him

amour de soy vous déçoit.' The pun *de soy/déçoit* is a serious indication of the
meaning of *philautie*: self-love deceives.
6. ibid., XXXVII, 4–6: '*Panurge en maintien de resveur, ravassant et dodelinant
de la teste.*'   7. ibid., TLF, XXXVIII.
8. St Augustine is cited from his second sermon in psalm 36(31), verse 16 (Vulgate
text): *Thy lots are in Thy hands.* Consult also Gratian's *Decreta*, 26 Quaestio 2,
§ Sors, and Thomas Aquinas, *Opuscula*, XV, 5.
9. *Tiers Livre*, TLF, XII, 140–48; XLIV, 64–74; XLIII, 85 and notes. The key
text of Roman law is *Lex si duobus, C. de legatis* (a law of the Codex of Justinian).
Cf. Sir Thomas More, *English Works*, London, 1931, II, pp. 106–7.

to use his smallest dice, Bridoye does so. His eyesight is bad and he misreads the throw. He is so innocent that he believes that all other judges use dice exactly as he does. We laugh at the nice old fool.[10]

Then the tables are turned on us. Bridoye was right in the eyes of God and his angels. He was the kind of fool who is a bit 'touched' – touched by the Holy Ghost who guides him on his way. Readers had in fact been warned beforehand: the worldly-wise are preoccupied with amassing money: to the angels they merely seem daft. To appear 'wise and fore-wise' before those august agents of God, one must become a special kind of fool. Rabelais uses terms which recall St Mark and Erasmus: one must 'forget oneself', 'be beside oneself', 'empty one's senses of all earthly desire' and 'purge one's mind of all earthly solicitude'. One must despise all that is worldly. And that is 'commonly attributed to madness'.[11]

Pantagruel defends Bridoye on the grounds of his age, but especially because of his simplicity. Bridoye was aware of the complexity and ambiguity of the law. Clever barristers can make black seem white. Paul warned us that 'Satan often transfigures himself as an angel of light'. Rabelais cites that twice. The Vulgate text suggests to Rabelais that the 'transfigured' Satan works his wicked will through the judiciary, through 'ministers of justice'.[12] God must have been behind Bridoye's long run of right judgements. For God (with an echo of *Magnificat*) 'often wills his glory to appear in the stultifying of the wise, in putting down the mighty, and exalting the simple and the humble'.[13]

Was not Bridoye aware of the transfiguration of Satan and of the wiles of lawyers? Might he not have 'recommended himself humbly

---

10. Provided we are not put off by the flood of legal Latin which Bridoye pours out.   11. *Tiers Livre*, TLF, XXXVII, 31–6.
12. ibid., XLIIII, 47ff. (In the first edition, the speech in which Bridoye is defended was given to Pantagruel; in the second, to the learned Epistemon.) Rabelais twice cites II Corinthians 11:15. The first time (*Tiers Livre*, TLF, XIIII, 167) Pantagruel cites it apropos of the difficulty of telling good from evil spirits; the second time Rabelais translates *diabolos* from the Greek as the 'Calumniator from Hell', and *angeloi* as 'messengers'. He nevertheless returns to the Vulgate Latin, where Satan's wiles are exercised through 'Ministers of Justice', which Rabelais takes as alluding to legal officials.   13. ibid., *Tiers Livre*, XLIII, 37–45.

to God, the Just Judge'? Might he not have invoked the grace of God, turning as great authorities had to the 'lots' mentioned by the psalmist? We are left in little doubt. The answer is yes, not least since St Paul calls God the Father 'the Just Judge'.[14]

And so we have been caught out. When we laughed at Bridoye we were unwittingly siding with those earthbound madmen; we were laughing at a Christian fool. As in Erasmus, there is a warning here: the humble and meek in their madness, precisely when 'beside themselves', may be ministers of Christian truth and goodness. We really had been warned: what is done by the good man who is 'beside himself' is 'commonly attributed to madness'.[15]

Such innocence is not at variance with God-given wisdom. Pantagruel's wisdom and sound judgement is presented as a gift from God, the Giver of all good gifts. And Pantagruel champions Bridoye.

There are Christian fools who are madder even than Bridoye. Rabelais gives pride of place to a real-life one, a fool from birth who lived as a pet in the royal Court of France. His name was Triboullet. (He did not dress in cap-and-bells. His head, like a cone or a top, came to a point at the back. He was an excellent mimic.)[16] Panurge addresses that fool with useless rhetoric as he plays with his wooden sword. Triboullet is moved to answer Panurge's questions more fully than anyone else, however learned, however inspired. Triboullet 'whacked Panurge with his fist between his shoulderblades', 'thrust a bottle in his hands, bonked him on the nose with a pig's bladder, then in reply, very strongly jerking his head about, simply said, "By God! God! Raving fool. Beware monk. Buzançay bagpipes."'

Pantagruel interprets that as the fullest prognostic of the fate awaiting his mad friend. Panurge will be beaten, robbed and cuckolded by a monk. His wife will skirl at him with a voice like bagpipes. The cuckoldry will be scandalous: a monk is a 'Brother': those who affect to call themselves in their religious vocation 'Brother' or 'Father' never commit simple adultery: they commit incest.[17]

14. ibid., XLIIII, 64, and context.   15. ibid., XXXVII, 21–36.
16. Cf. Dr Ambrose Paré, cited ibid., XLV, 54. Triboullet was famous throughout France; Joachim Du Bellay, the poet, mentions his take-off of the reigning pope.
17. ibid., XLVI, 21–9; XLVII, 9–27.

That Triboullet is an inspired Christian fool is shown not least by his stuttering 'By God! God!'; but there is also a gesture, a movement, accepted as a sign of inspiration by Guillaume Budé, the very greatest legal mind of France. It is Budé's influential gloss that Rabelais follows. Everything depends on the strong 'jerking about of the head' which Rabelais attributes to Triboullet.

In his *Annotations on the Pandects*, Budé explains why the crucial comments concern that jerking of the head.[18] Roman law accorded privileges to 'fanatics' (inspired fools who inhabited the fanes). Men who were not inspired sought those privileges. The law established a criterion: 'If a slave amongst the fanatics did not constantly jerk his head' he was no true fanatic. The sign of inspiration lay in that 'jectigation', that jerking, wagging, tremulous movement of the head.

To Budé's legal knowledge Rabelais added his medical knowledge (he was renowned in both fields of study): that jectigation is brought on by the sudden rush of the prophetic spirit into the small human head. Doctors cite the analogy of the trembling caused by the sudden imposition of a heavy weight on to limbs really too weak to bear it; a 'manifest example' of that is the inability of a fasting man to carry a large goblet of wine to his lips without his hands trembling.[19]

Laughing at madness opens a gulf before our feet. Erasmus with his wit and Rabelais with his medical and legal comedy leave Christians in no doubt: genuine madmen, genuine fools, may be the chosen vehicles of God. The medically insane, the simple-minded, the Christian scholar, the philosopher and the true mystic in love with God, all have one thing in common: their souls, partly freed from the shackles of their bodies, may have glimpses of spiritual

---

18. The *Pandects* are the compendium of Roman civil law established in the sixth century A.D. by the Christian emperor Justinian. Consult Guillaume Budé, *Opera Omnia*, III, Basle, 1557, p. 251 (Gregg reprint, Farnborough, 1966). The gloss is on the law *De Ædilitio edicto* (*Digest*, 21:1.1.9), *Apud Julianum* (or *Apud Vivianum*). The phrase commented upon (Ex § *Exempli*) begins: *Si servus inter fanaticos non semper caput jactaret, et aliqua prophatus esset.*
19. *Tiers Livre*, TLF, XLV, 41–61.

realities denied to the earthbound, who by the standards of the world are thoroughly sane.

Christians practise dying, and men laugh at them, for they are, or seem to be, blundering fools. If we laugh at them with the laughter of the worldly-wise, we too are carnal fools. We first laugh – indulgently no doubt – at Bridoye or at Triboullet: but afterwards we change our judgements. Bridoye and Triboullet were fools blessed by God's angels with spiritual insight. That was no pious superstition reserved for thinkers in some theological ghetto: philosophy, medicine and the law all supported the same contention: Christ declared folly to be blessed.

Erasmus noted that the Venerable Bede, like most theologians, held that when Jesus said 'Blessed are the poor in spirit', he was referring to the simple – to those with slender mental abilities.[20]

---

20. *Erasmus' Annotations*, ed. Anne Reeve, Duckworth, 1986, I, p. 25; Cf. also Grotius, cited in Matthew Pole, *Synopsis Criticorum*, Utrecht, 1686, IV, 115, lines 1–20.

48

God's Coadjutors:
Deed and Words and
Christian Laughter

'We are God's helpers.' Or are we? Rabelais, when he was a Franciscan, had studied, and was ordained a priest. Among the authorities he would have pored over is St Bonaventura. That glory of his order had no doubts on the subject. His moral theology was a 'partly-partly' system: a system of collaboration between God and each individual man and woman. Good human endeavour depends 'partly on God's grace' for its beginning and increase, but also 'partly on the activity of free-will'. Free-will must actively be a 'fellow helper' with God's grace. As the Vulgate Latin puts it, St Paul wrote that 'We are God's adjutors' – God's *helpers*. That clinched the matter for many: God's grace is 'helped' by Man's efforts. Men are created to be 'coadjutors of God'.[1]

It was traditionally held by many that Man's free-will had not been entirely lost at the Fall: it was fatally weakened. Man was left with his *synderesis*, that innate force 'which goads him towards the good, and protests against the evil'. The strengthening of synderesis by moral and religious education is the theological basis of the Abbey of Thelema in *Gargantua*.[2]

A theology which allows for the working together of Man's free-will with the grace of God is called synergism. Rabelais was a

---

1. Cf. Bonaventura, cited in M.A.S., *Rabelais and the Challenge of the Gospel*, Koerner, Baden-Baden and Bouxwiller, 1992, p. 64. Bonaventura emphasizes the balance of the collaboration of God and Man by stressing the repeated term *ex parte*. The Vulgate text of St Paul reads *Dei sumus adjutores*. Bonaventura not only cites *Dei sumus adjutores* but uses for the collaboration of Man's free-will the verb *coadjuvari*. 2. *Gargantua*, TLF, LV, and notes.

synergist as a Franciscan friar, and remained so as a learned Evangelical laugh-raiser.

Not all agreed with a synergistic theology, particularly when St
Augustine was to the fore or when Calvinism was in the ascendancy.

Some denied that merit can ever be earned in the sight of God:
for them Christians do not act morally in order to earn merit and
so win God's favour; they do so because they love him. Many were
nevertheless determined to retain merit, at the very least as a driving
force towards morality. The doctrine of free-will – even weakened
free-will – endows Man with the dignity of causality. Where there
is free-will there is room for comedy, even at a cosmic level. Synergism
provides a rich field for Christian laughter.

Once it had all seemed so easy. The Vulgate speaks of 'help' and
'helpers'. Rabelais, in the 1530s, a Humanist priest educated in the
traditional Western catholic faith and open to Lutheran ideas, was
prepared to limit the help which God would accept from men. God
has business of his own: the spreading of the Gospel. In that domain
he requires 'no helper'. Or, rather, 'no helper, *except . . .*' In that
especially excepted domain the help that God demands is not human
might or soldiery; what he demands is the confessing of the catholic
faith and the ministry of his Word. By such things followers are won
for Christ.

That is a major exception, but it is an exception. In the vast
remaining domain of human morality, God demands that each of
us should be his active *adjutor*.[3]

Christian laughter gains immeasurably whenever it finds madness
to laugh at in human deeds and human errors, in human weaknesses
and human vices. It gains immeasurably too when it gladly accepts
itself as madness in the eyes of the world.

Both Rabelais and Erasmus were priests who had been long
apprenticed to the religious life. Both rejected that life, but clung to
its God-centred ideal. The height of wisdom for them both lay in

3. Cf. M.A.S., *Rabelais and the Challenge of the Gospel*, op. cit., pp. 37ff. The
keyword in Pantagruel's dense little sermon on this subject is 'coadjutor'. It links
the theology of Rabelais to both St Paul's *adjutores* and St Bonaventura's *coadjuvari*.
(For the text, see *Pantagruel*, TLF, XIX, 62–86.)

Christian madness, including the madness of God-centred ecstasy. That was the best and highest form of rapture. It went together with God-given wisdom and God-given knowledge, both of which can and will seem very madness to the world.

The exacting standards of Erasmus and Rabelais led them to value divine rapture till their life's end. But the majority of mankind, Christians included, must live out their lives firmly within this world. Even sound Christian laymen could not follow those great Christian laughers wherever they ventured. Montaigne, for one, could not. He loathed our 'being told to have our minds above the clouds, while our bodies are at the dinner-table'. Such a layman would not be swept off his feet with approval by Rabelais's counsel to have a lad seated on his jakes while going over the day's New Testament lesson. Nor did he think ignoring the body and practising ecstasy to be wise or feasible for all but a mere handful of mystics chosen by God. Where most of us are concerned, such excesses lead to Nature wreaking her revenge:

Our mind does not readily concede that it has plenty of other hours to perform its functions without breaking fellowship during the short time the body needs for its necessities. They want to be beside themselves, want to escape from their humanity. That *is* madness . . .[4]

Would-be Christian madmen practising rapture run great risks. If they rashly presume to be favoured with divine privileges beyond what they have actually been vouchsafed; if they believe that they have the grace of God as their coadjutor when they have not; if they think they can, without special grace, ignore Man's physical nature, then madness – medically attested madness – lies in wait for them. Christian synergism does not encourage human presumption. Men must work with grace, not presume to enjoy gifts of grace with which they have not been favoured.

Moral conduct concerns all mankind. Rabelais takes it as a field for Christian laughter. He had not studied only theology: he was a renowned expert in the law, the domain of morality. His synergism

4. Montaigne, *Essays*, Allen Lane, 1991, III, 13, 'On Experience', pp. 1267–8.

was at ease in just such a context. Students of civil and canon law were warned that their duty was precisely to ensure that they did indeed have the grace of God as their coadjutor. To do so they must take seriously the warning of Solomon in the first chapter of the Book of Wisdom: 'Wisdom will not enter into a malevolent soul': Rabelais laid the groundwork for that in his first work, *Pantagruel*. He was then equipped to adventure into the highest and widest reaches of Christian laughter.[5]

Legal authors often thought as Rabelais did on questions of moral responsibility. The same ideas are next exemplified by Rabelais in the context of monks and monasticism, but they apply to all mankind. Frère Jean in *Gargantua* has something to show us about laughter which spills out of the cloister into the world. He acts out a parable.

Frère Jean is a paradox. We laugh at him as generations before Rabelais had laughed at coarse and ignorant monks gadding about outside their cloisters. Knowing little save their breviary and the psalms which they chant without understanding them, they are at best drones and at worst foul-mouthed, lecherous gluttons. That aspect of Christian laughter was centuries old, and Frère Jean conforms to type: he was 'a true monk if ever there was one since the monkish world monked about with monkery'. Readers knew, or thought they knew, what to expect: 'the Monk' galloped through his masses; 'the Monk' sported an ample nose which indicated an ample sexual drive; 'the Monk' loved his food; he was dirty, with a ruby dripping from his nose; 'the Monk' was foul-mouthed and loud-mouthed. Precisely those 'monastic' jokes which Erasmus abhorred, and could scarcely bring himself to hint at, came readily to the lips of 'the Monk': for him his rampant penis recalled the

5. See, in the Apocrypha, the Wisdom of Solomon, 1:4. Cf. what Rabelais wrote at the end of Gargantua's letter (*Pantagruel*, TLF, VIII, 164ff.) and in Pantagruel's prayer before the battle with Loupgarous (ibid., XIX, 62ff.) with the teachings expounded in the beginning of *Tractatus de modo studendi in utroque jure . . . editus per famosissimum utriusque juris doctorem Joannem Gazalupis de Sancto Severino*. That little book of elementary advice to students of the law was written by Gazalupius, a law professor of Siena. It says in simple legal language much the same as Rabelais says more clearly still: without good morals, and a due exploitation of God's grace, study does not build up the soul: it ruins it.

words of the psalm, 'I lift up unto thee'! The Gospel duty to give water to your neighbour becomes for him a demand for wine:

'By the body of St James, what shall we poor devils have to drink in the meanwhile! Lord God, *Da mihi potum*, ' "Give me a drink".'[6]

St Paul's evocation of the 'stem of Jesse' becomes a text deformed into mild blasphemy and an evocation of thirst. For then, though not in modern French, *J'ai soif* ('I am thirsty') was pronounced *Jésé* – the same as 'Jesse'.[7]

But we are alerted from the outset. Frère Jean does not seize on any old weapon to save the vineyard of his abbey: he wields the butt of an ancient cross, covered with faded *fleurs-de-lys*. An evangelical symbol and a royalist one too. A royalist-Gallican one therefore. Rabelais is harking back to a faded, ideal world in which the Most Christian King ordered things well in his dominions.

The other monks are not pure hypocrites. That would be too simple. They are above all theologically obtuse, leaving to God things that require their active help. For them, words replace deeds. But few things are easier than to appear devout when devotion is measured by words, not deeds. In so far as those monks are hypocrites, they are obviously mad. Since hypocrites can deceive men, they are insane enough to believe they can deceive God.

At this point the other monks in the abbey of Frère Jean are not so much counterfeiting devotion as being superstitiously devout after their unlovely monkish fashion. The laughter is complex: for Rabelais those monks are theologically unsound, passive where they should be active. With the enemy at the gates and ravaging their vineyard, they merely stick to the ritual of their profession. They ring their bells to summon a chapter meeting and intone the litany with those 'vain repetitions' which Jesus condemned when he taught his

---

6. *Gargantua*, TLF, XXV, 52–3. *Da illi potum* ('Give him a drink') is said of our duty towards an enemy who thirsts. The Vulgate words of Christ to the woman at the well are *Da mihi bibere*, which probably means that they are not part of the joke here.
7. *Gargantua*, TLF, XXXVIII, 91–8; XXXVII, 84 (and note); XXXVIII, 74–5, etc.

followers the Lord's Prayer: '*Im, im, im, pe, e, e, e, e, e, tum, um, in, ni, i mi, co. o. o. o. o. o. rum, um.*' One can just pick out the words: *Impetum inimicorum*, that is, 'From the onslaught of our enemies, [Good Lord deliver us]'.[8]

But what do they do to help God? Nothing. They are in no way God's coadjutors. They are ignorant, servile, superstitious, passive and noddle-pated. Their worship is that mockery of God with its vain repetitions which Scripture, indeed Christ, condemns. So we laugh: but we laugh at them. In the case of Frère Jean – here at least – our laughter is quite different: we are laughing with him.

Yet all the pious language is on their side: the coarseness and blasphemy are all on his. But there are times when language matters much less than deeds.

Later in *Gargantua* the monastic claims are mocked less with comedy as with diasyrm. Any suggestion that monks intercede with God for men is peremptorily dismissed on scriptural grounds: the Spirit teaches us all how to pray. The Spirit himself intercedes for us. Monks are foul; venally occupied with auricular confession: 'they eat the shit – that is, the sins – of the world'. That is why good men 'toss them back into their jakes – their convents and abbeys – keeping them well away from civilized intercourse, just as close-stools are in decent houses'. All that is indeed redolent of diasyrm, but the wider context is one of comedy as Frère Jean, a descendant of the battling monks of medieval romance, runs the enemy through the bum with the shaft of his ancient cross. However much they grovel and call him 'Prior' as he pierces their posteriors, he dispatches them to Kingdom-come.[9]

'The Monk' is redeemed by two qualities. Normally monks are wet-blankets; they 'attract opprobrium, insults and curses': Frère Jean spreads fun and laughter.[10] True, he is ignorant, but he is active

---

8. The implied references are to 'God is not mocked' (Galatians, 6:7), cf. *Gargantua*, TLF, XXXVIII, 51ff., 229; the condemnation of 'vain repetition' by Jesus, just before he taught the Lord's Prayer to the faithful, ibid., XXV, 44ff.

9. ibid., especially chs. XXV; XXXIII; XXXVII, XXXVIII and notes.

10. '*Troublefestes*' (ibid., XXXVIII, 6–18); that is, they spoil the joys of a banquet by unseasonable chiding and gloom.

and well-intentioned. We do laugh at his theological obtuseness, but it is an indulgent laugh – a rarity in Christian laughter harnessed to the propagation of the Gospel. Frère Jean boasts that he would never have been weak like St Peter and the other Apostles in their moment of trial!

'How good of God to have given us this tipple! Had I lived at the time of the Apostles, the Jews would never have got hold of Him in the Garden of Gethsemane! I'd have seen to that! The devil take me if I hadn't snipped the hamstrings of Monsignor the Apostles who ran off so cowardly, leaving their Master in distress – after a good Supper too!'[11]

One can imagine Erasmus grinding his teeth at jokes such as that. But the laughter Frère Jean raises is the laughter of the comic parable. We all know how to pray thanks to the indwelling Spirit, as St Paul taught us. Rabelais concluded that monastic claims to intercede for mankind are irrelevant and impertinent:

All true Christians, of all estates and in all places, pray to God: the Spirit prays and intercedes for them, and God takes them into grace.[12]

Our 'good Frère Jean' is not like other monks: that is why everyone seeks to enjoy his company:

'He is no bigot; he is not down-at-heel; he is honourable, joyful, determined and a good companion. He travails; he labours; he defends the oppressed; he comforts the afflicted; he succours the needy; and he guards the close of the Abbey.'[13]

Parables are often surprising: traditional exegesis insisted that their message is to be sought not in their detail but in their conclusion. Jesus teaches truths about the Father by means of the parables telling

---

11. *Gargantua*, TLF, XXXVII, 65–71.

12. ibid., XXXVIII, 54–63. (The scriptural reference to the intercession of the Spirit is from Romans, 8:26: 'Likewise the Spirit also aideth our infirmities, for we know not what we should pray as we ought; but the Spirit himself makes intercession for us, with groanings which cannot be uttered.' That text was open to different interpretations, not all of which support Rabelais's theology.)

13. ibid., XXXVIII, 56, 64.

of an unjust judge and of a dishonest, worldly steward. Rabelais's developed parable, in its own comic way, follows the traditional practice: detail should be ignored; the moral is explained in the tail. Laughter first, moral later.

Frère Jean exemplifies the value of active virtue and practical charity over verbiage. Against such qualities shown when 'helping' God, even foul-mouthed verbiage weighs light in the divine scales. But we have come a long way from St Paul's condemnation of eutrapely.

Such laughter in its Christian context is positive and life-enhancing. Error is not hated; it is laughed away. The pious formulas and liturgical repetitions of the monks are laughed out of court, not as hypocrisy but as superstition, as attempts to bribe God with words. As Jesus hung on the Cross he fervently prayed, saying, 'Into Thy hands I commend my spirit.' It was an action requiring clarity of mind despite appalling agony; spiritual and physical courage; complete faith and trust in the Father. The words mean what they say: as he died, Jesus was commending his spirit to the Father. But there is nothing holy or magic about the words as such. They are not charms to ward off the evil eye. To utter those very same words as a means of warding off devils or avoiding danger is not religion: it is superstition. We are invited to laugh heartily at such folly. To do so is good theology and good Christian comedy.

Not all moralists or theologians willingly tolerate cursing and blinding in the manner of Frère Jean. For Rabelais his language pales into insignificance when set against his 'toil and travail' as he 'defends the oppressed, comforts the afflicted and succours the needy'.[14] Bystanders make grunts to encourage a woodcutter as he brings down his axe. On the bowling-green, men twist and turn to persuade a bowl to go where they want it to. Is Frère Jean's ripe swearing really any worse than that?[15]

Actions speak louder than words. For Rabelais they are infinitely valuable in the sight of God.

14. ibid., XXXVIII, 59–63.
15. *Quart Livre*, TLF, XX, 3–12 (Panurge suggests this to Frère Jean during the storm).

Christian laughter can be raised straightforwardly enough when the contrast is between selfless works of charity and self-serving cowardice, or between words of pious resignation and words congealed into magic spells and amulets. Laughter is aroused in *Gargantua* by Frère Jean as he breaks away from the dithering monks and battles for the vineyard against wilful, wicked, diabolical aggression. But where does God come in?

The battle for the abbey of Seuillé may not seem to leave much room for that 'partly-partly' theology which Rabelais had learnt from Bonaventura. But it does. The seeds of God's presence are sown in the detail. Frère Jean's weapon is that shaft of a neglected cross with its faded *fleurs-de-lys*. We are told that Picrochole was moved to treachery and military adventures by devilish fantasies which he could and should have questioned. God sweeps in later. But parables make one point at a time: the battle of Seuillé remains for Rabelais a parable teaching the need for a man to bestir himself as God's helper. The later discussion of monasticism emphasizes, rather, squalor, idleness and the sheer irrelevance of the monastic calling.

Synergism is a permanent feature of Rabelais's theology. It is fundamental to his comedy but antedates it. When he wanted to champion such things in his first book, *Pantagruel*, he left comedy aside for a while. The tone changes from banter to seriousness: in our dealings with the Almighty, it is never, we are told, a case of God helps those who help themselves; indeed, 'Help yourself, and the Devil will break your neck.' That does not mean that we leave it all to God. A wise king keeps strong means of defence. But even when his cause is just, a Christian king puts his trust in God, not in his big battalions.[16] In *Gargantua* the good king tries every means of honourable appeasement. Only after they prove useless does he fight a just war – for which he is already prepared. It is then his Christian duty to do so.

After the war in *Gargantua*, Frère Jean sinks into a minor role. He might never have come back into prominence: he had played

---

16. *Pantagruel*, TLF, XVIII, 25–35.

his part. But the theology of synergism did not stand still. The Renaissance was a period of theological ferment. In the *Quart Livre* Rabelais twice took up the theme again and to do so he brought back Frère Jean. In the first version (1548) he dominates the episode of the storm at sea. The monk, associated all along with that laughing parable in *Gargantua*, was needed again, to teach the same lesson.

In that age of great navigation Rabelais set his new dramatic parable on board ship. The parable is a simple one. The monk strives to save the ship: the coward tries to bribe God into saving him alone. Panurge is all servile cowardice, selfishness, mealy-mouthed superstition and inactivity. Frère Jean is all selflessness, all bustling, noisy, foul-mouthed and constructive activity. The drift of the laughter is much as in *Gargantua*, but Panurge, who befouls his trousers with servile fear and blubbers endlessly, is more immediately laughable than the fearful monks of Seuillé.

The first account of the storm at sea is really a cross between a fable and a parable. There are no paradoxes to be worked out; the moral is clear-cut.[17] Everything is in black and white: Panurge feeding the scatophagous fishes as he messes his breeches; the commonplaces of superstition and God-cheating:

'Ha! Frère Jean, my ghostly father,' said Panurge, 'my Beloved. Let us not swear. Thou sinnest! Jarus! Jarus! *be, be, be, bous bous*: I am drowning, I am dying, my friends. I forgive you all. Farewell. Jarus! *Into Thy hands* . . .

'*Bous, bous, bous, bouououous.* St Michel d'Aure, St Nicholas – do it just this once and I'll never bother you again! I vow to you and Our Lord that, if you help me now – by setting me ashore, I mean, out of danger – I will build you a great big little chapel or two between Candes and Monssoreau –'

(Rabelais's patrons knew that there was no land to build on between Candes and Monssoreau: the two villages adjoined.)

The language of Frère Jean is even more vigorous than in *Gargan-*

---

17. The episode first appeared in 1548 in the so-called 'partial' *Quart Livre*. That version has no royal *Privilège*. It is by no means certain that Rabelais authorized it to be printed and published.

tua. The actual name of Christ may pass unheard, but it is there in the immediate background:

'By the virtue,' said Frère Jean, 'of the blood, flesh, belly and head! If ever I hear you puling again, you damned cuckold, I'll wallop you like a sea-wolf! God Almighty! Why don't we chuck him down into the deep!'[18]

As is appropriate in an Æsopic fable, the implicit meaning is spelled out at the end in terms of the gods. The moral is put into the mouth of the wise Epistemon, who stands by, his palm scorched and bloody from restraining a hawser. He had never stinted his efforts, and he explains why:

'I consider that though our death is – as indeed it is – a fated and unavoidable necessity, dying in such-and-such an hour and in such-and-such a way lies partly in the will of the gods, partly in our own discretion. That is why we must implore them, invoke them, pray to them, making our requests and supplications unto them. But that is not the be-all nor the end-all: we on our part must bestir ourselves, helping them with the means and the remedy. If I am not talking in accord with the decrees of the matheologians, they will forgive me: I speak by Book and authority.'[19]

There is the 'will of the gods' on one side, and on the other the discretion, decision, *arbitre*, the will of Man.[20] They work together. Rabelais is giving the moral of his fable in terms of the 'partly-partly' theology of St Bonaventura. He is still happy to use the word *ayder*, to help. But there is a theological vagueness which weakens the moral and dilutes the laughter. *Mathéologiens* can be dismissed with

18. *Quart Livre*, TLF, XX, 79–82.
19. *Quart Livre*, TLF, XXIII, 22–34, variant text. *Mathéologien* is a portmanteau word, taken over from Erasmus's *mateologia*. It blends together *mataios* (vain, empty) with *theologos*.
20. *Volunté*, used for the 'wish' of the gods, would normally be translated 'will'. So too would *arbitre*, used for Man. It implies free-will, that is, the limited capacity of Man under grace to decide to do, or not to do, something – a decision which might well effect his salvation or eternal damnation. Rabelais does not seem, in his works as a whole, to make any vital difference between the two words; see the listings under *arbitre* in J. Dixon and J. Dawson, *Concordance des Œuvres de François Rabelais*, Droz, Geneva, 1992.

a jest; but what is their book? The Bible, no doubt. In that contentious age one expects a text to be cited. None is. Anyway, the Bible sits awkwardly in a fable about Man and the classical gods.

Rabelais, his patrons, or both, were not satisfied. Deep theological debates over Man's will, free or enslaved, had divided the Western Church between *Pantagruel* and the *Quart Livre*. Greater precision was needed. Æsopic fables are excellent for making moral points: they may prove inadequate to teach a specifically Christian theology. The laughter may be there, but ill-focused. So too, for parables. Powerful and authoritative in the mouth of Jesus, they may be inadequate in the mouths of men.

The first version of the storm episode is more than adequate to set us off laughing *at* and *with*: at superstitious, servile fear which inhibits all activity; with active virtue, however coarse and loud-mouthed. But theological imprecision will not do in a work encouraged by the King of France on the brink of schism, written at Le Mans in the palace of one cardinal and dedicated to another who sponsored and protected it. Cardinal Jean Du Bellay was a learned Humanist. Cardinal Odet de Chastillon, a royalist-Gallican, was dashing, cultured, princely, progressive, and committed to evangelical Christianity.

Christian theology demands the presence of Christ. Without him, Christian laughter, on theological themes, will be partial or flabby. It risks ambiguity or heresy.

Rabelais saw that. He fundamentally recast the 'storm' for the definitive edition of the *Quart Livre* in 1552. By bringing Pantagruel into the 'storm' as the Christian sage and making him echo chosen words of Holy Scripture an entirely new dimension is introduced. The episode acquires tragic and new comic depths. The laughter which now impregnates it is profoundly Christian.

Rabelais increases the magic nonsense of Panurge and the coarse language of Frère Jean. If that were all, the laughter would be more copious, but the moral remains unchanged. The language of Panurge is at times pious: but the true centre of his interest lies not in the ship, not in his comrades, not in God's commands, but in himself. He is self-love and servile fear personified.

Pantagruel played no part in the original 'storm'. Now he domi-nates, starting things off by imploring 'the aid of the great Saviour God' and leading 'public prayer in fervent devotion'.[21]

At the crisis of the storm, the ship's pilot, amidst a welter of nautical terms, emphasizes that the crew and the heroes can do no more. Human resources have been exhausted. Only then is the ship left to run before the wind. 'May God in his goodness come to our aid,' cries Pantagruel. 'Let every man think of his soul,' cries the Master: 'let all resort to prayer.' Even then Panurge can only blabber uselessly, hoping to bribe God by having a whip round to send someone off on a pilgrimage![22]

When all except Panurge have done all that brave men can, hope lies only in a miracle.[23] A miracle quietly comes, but not before a major interpolation makes the role of the three protagonists stand out in relief. As a result the laughter becomes theologically precise.

First the idea: Pantagruel, with his echoes both of the cries of the disciples when caught without Jesus aboard ship in a storm, and the cry of Jesus in Gethsemane:

Then was heard a piteous cry from Pantagruel, loudly saying, 'Lord God, save us, we perish. Yet, not according to our emotions, but Thy holy will be done.'[24]

The moment for prayer and resignation has come; no more 'working together' with God, until human efforts are required again, as soon they will be. Panurge, as ever, blubbers, bribes, and confounds creature with Creator:

'God,' said Panurge, 'and the Blessed Virgin be with us! Alas, Alack. I am drowning. *Bebebebous, bebe, bous, bous.*

'Into Thy hands . . .'

Frère Jean, the typical monk, resorts to his psalter – it is all he knows. But, once the miracle is worked, he remembers to thank God for having worked it. Panurge does not.[25]

21. *Quart Livre*, TLF, XIX, 1–3.   22. ibid., XX, 76–9.
23. ibid., XX, 65–75.   24. ibid., XXI, 44–6.
25. ibid., XX, 54–6; XXI, 21–2.

This is no longer an Æsopic fable. It is a mixture of dramatic comedy and high tragedy such as Shakespeare might have produced. The moral of the storm is re-written with theological precision, so that our laughter can be judged, weighed and, *post eventum*, explained aright. What we now have is God, truly almighty, granting to mankind the privilege of causality. As the wise Epistemon now explains:

'I consider that though our death is – as indeed it is – a fated and unavoidable necessity – dying in such-and-such an hour, and in such-and-such a way is in the holy will of God.'

Not of the gods but of God. As far as the formulation goes, St Bonaventura's 'partly-partly' is dropped. Instead of Bonaventura we hear St Paul:

That is why we must implore him, invoke him, pray to him, and make our requests and supplications unto him. But that is not the be-all and end-all; we on our part must bestir ourselves, and, as the Holy Ambassador said, be *co-operators with him.*

To compare what Epistemon says in each version of the 'storm' is revealing.[26] Bonaventura's lesson, well learned, has been inwardly digested and brought up-to-date.

Biblical scholars, Reformers and Counter-reformers were quarrelling over the complexities of free-will and synergism. Theologians like Rabelais continued to base themselves on the same text of St Paul, but they no longer talk of 'helping' God or of being his adjutors.

'Adjutors' served when the Scriptures were known mainly in Latin and when free-will was not everywhere challenged. 'Co-operators' is better: it is a more loyal translation of the Greek. Moreover it is the weak who need help; who can say that of God? Nothing, however, stops us from 'working together' with God, from 'co-operating' with him. Activity on the part of Man is still demanded and required.[27]

26. *Quart Livre*, TLF, XXIII, 22–34, and variants.
27. The key text remains 1 Corinthians, 3:9 ('We are workers together with God') in association with II Corinthians, 6:1 ('As workers together we beseech you . . .').

Fail to see that and you may be laughed at as a worldling, ignorant of Christian truth. The Christian laughter of the 'storm' is now on course.

When the danger is over, talking to a now cocky and irreligious Panurge, Frère Jean insists that the moral is still that of the parable of the attack on Seuillé in *Gargantua*:

'I give myself to the Devil . . .' said Frère Jean – 'I've already half-done so, myself!' said Panurge – '. . . if the close of Seuillé had not all been stripped bare and destroyed, if I had merely chanted *Contra hostium insidias* and so on – breviary stuff – as those monkish devils were doing, without bringing succour to the vine with the shaft of my cross, . . .'

The laughter was loud and lasting, no doubt, in the palace of Rabelais's bishop, patron and patient at Le Mans. Would anyone there fall into the vulgar error of equating catholic and Roman Catholic? Cardinal Jean Du Bellay had long been favourable to Luther. The Rabelais of *Gargantua* was influenced directly, or through his patron, by Melanchthon, the Lutheran Preceptor of Germany. The Rabelais of the *Quart Livre* was drawing directly on a satirical work of Luther and was encouraged and supported by another cardinal eventually to become an Anglican. In such circles, as in Roman circles too, synergistic Christian laughter is fully at ease.

Those who, like Calvin, denied that St Paul's words can bear the meaning which Rabelais gave them were moved to indignation and reproach. Calvin, following many traditional exegetes, maintained that free-will cannot be defended by St Paul's reference to men 'working together' with God. For him God works with Man as a gardener works with a spade. Man is a tool, not an agent with a degree of free-will. If that were so, the stream of Rabelaisian laughter would be reduced to a trickle.

Erasmus and Lefèvre d'Étaples opted to translate the key Greek words by *co-operare* and *co-operatio*. It was no longer a question of being God's 'helpers' but of being his 'fellow workmen', his 'collaborators'. God, as almighty, needs no help: Man cannot 'help' the Almighty, and the Greek original of St Paul never suggested that he can. Yet Man, it was claimed, can and must 'collaborate' with God on his terms. The two proof-texts both use the verb *sunergein*, 'to work together'.

It is not a coincidence that our two great exemplars of Christian laughter were pre-Tridentine catholic priests . . .

Rabelais shows how fables and parables can be adapted to provide richly Christian laughter. There is little room for laughter in classical determinism: there is immense scope for laughter in Christian synergism. Such Christian laughter can take most of Frère Jean's cursing and swearing in its stride – most, but not all. There are limits to indulgence. When the monk's ripe language helps him to strive for the good, it can be laughed at and condoned. It can in fact be enjoyed. But when indulged in for its own sake, just for a laugh, it is contemptible, and when blasphemous, intolerable.

The monk learns that to his cost. He tells a would-be funny story of a beggar whose gangrened leg brought in alms. His mate called that ghastly leg a God-send. Pantagruel rounds on the monk: to misuse the sacred name of God so abominably is enough to make a man vomit:

If such abuse of words is current within that monkery of yours leave it there; do not bring it out of the cloister.[28]

Erasmus would never have told the story in the first place.

28. *Quart Livre*, TLF, L, 28–42.

49

Laughing at Idolatry

Idolatry is a recurring and dominant theme in the *Quart Livre de Pantagruel*. It is the thread running through its most celebrated episode: the visit to the Isle of Papimanes. As their name shows, the Papimanes – Papimaniacs – are mad, maniacal.

Gallicanism was in the air. A French break with Rome seemed imminent and unavoidable. How better to hasten it along than to accuse the papacy of venal idolatry? Vatican lawyers had long since claimed that the pope was *quasi Deus in terris* – 'as though God on earth'. (In one infamous case they left out the *quasi*!) In 1546, after he had published his *Tiers Livre*, Rabelais fled to German lands. There he came across a Latin version of the virulent satire of Luther's entitled *Against the Roman Papacy, constructed by the Devil*. He read in it how the Vatican was propped up with true and false decretals – rescripts based on papal authority alone. (*Decrees* have the authority of catholic Councils.) The Vatican was said to be full of cynical atheists pretending to believe in Christ as a means of milking the purses of Christian simpletons.

The words those Roman cynics, sunk in their Vatican luxury, condescendingly use for such simpletons is *Bon Christian* – a plural term, though it looks singular: 'Good Christians'. Luther piles diasyrm upon diasyrm as he mocked the pretensions of the papal Court and the decretals, both authentic and forged, on which they were based. Today his book, with its torrent of bitterness, hardly seems funny. It was funny then – so effective that it was smuggled into unsuspecting hands under cover of a pro-papist treatise of

Cardinal Pole.[1] Now, it lies largely unread; yet the chapters of Rabelais which were inspired by it run on laughingly through the centuries.

Luther's mocking tongue lashed the Vatican, accusing it of cynical idolatry. It was built on the money-grubbing cult of the God-on-earth with the powers he abusively claimed over this world and the next. Rabelais is less hate-ridden and more devastating. He is also more charitable. Instead of homing in on the hypocrites of the Vatican with their God-on-earth, he invents a far-off island of Bon Christian, silly superstitious simpletons who swallow all the venal nonsense peddled by the Vatican.

Their bishop, Homenaz, is a booby of monumental proportions. Once again we are not laughing at hypocrisy – the Papimanes are nothing if not sincere – but at madness. Theirs is the worldly madness which goes right against the Summary of the Law, the very foundation of the religion of Christ:

Thou shalt love the Lord thy God with all thy heart and with all thy soul, and with all thy mind. This is the first and great commandment. And the second is like unto it, namely this, Thou shalt love thy neighbour as thyself.[2]

The Papimanes worship the wrong god, honour the wrong scriptures, and have the wrong policy towards their neighbour. We see from the outset how they trip up over the first and great commandment. The heroes draw near to the wharf. A delegation of representative Papimanes come out in a skiff, asking:

'Have you seen Him, O travellers? Have you seen Him?'

'Whom?' asked Pantagruel.

'The One-who-is-yonder.'

'Who is that?' asked Frère Jean; 'Golly! I'll batter him!' (He thought they were complaining of some thief or other, some murderer or blasphemer.)

'What!' they replied. 'Know ye not, O travellers, the One-and-Only?'

'Gentlemen,' said Epistemon, 'we do not understand such terms. Please

1. There is a copy of such a disguised book in the Codrington Library at All Souls College, Oxford.   2. Matthew, 22:37–8.

explain whom you mean: then, without dissimulation, we will tell you the truth.'

'We mean, the *I Am*. Have you ever seen him?'

'The *I Am*,' replied Pantagruel, 'by the teachings of our Theology, is God. With such words he revealed himself to Moses. Of course we have never seen him; he cannot be seen with the eyes of the flesh.'

'We are not talking about that High God who rules up in Heaven. We are talking of the God-on-earth. Have you ever seen him?'

'Upon my honour,' said Carpalim, 'they mean the pope!'

'Yes, yes,' replied Panurge, 'yes indeed, sirs. I have seen three of them. Didn't do me any good though!'

'What!' they cried. 'Our Holy Decretals chant that One alone is ever alive.'

I mean,' said Panurge, 'three in succession, one after the other. Otherwise I have seen but one alive at a time.'

'O people, thrice and four times blessed,' they said, 'be welcome, most welcome, among us.'

They then knelt down before us and wanted to kiss our feet. We would not allow them to, reminding them that they could do no more to the pope himself if he happened to visit them in person.

'So we would! So we would!' they replied. 'That is already decided between us. We would remove the fig-leaf and kiss his bum – and his bollocks too. For the Holy Father has got bollocks, you know; that is written in our lovely Decretals. Otherwise he would not be pope. There is a necessary consequence in subtle decretaline logic: *He is pope: therefore he has bollocks.* When, in this world, bollocks fail, then, in this world, there will be no more popes.'

The Papimanes insisted: they *would* kiss the travellers' feet. One of their exegetes and glossators of the Holy Decretals had written that

just as the Messiah, so much and so long expected by the Jews, came at last unto them, so too, one day, to this Isle the Pope will come. While awaiting that blessed day, if anyone should arrive who had seen Him in Rome or elsewhere, they would celebrate him and treat him with reverence.

– We nevertheless made polite excuses.

Reminded that popes have been seen parading in steel helmets rather than tiaras, the bishop of the island, Homenaz, has ready an unctuous reply:

'That was against rebels, heretics and hopeless Protestants, who do not obey the Holiness of our good God-on-earth. That is not only permitted and legal, but commanded in the Holy Decretals: all emperors, kings, dukes, princes and republics must put them to the fire – and to the sword – as soon as they transgress one iota of his commandments. They must despoil them of their goods, dispossess them of their kingdoms, proscribe them, anathematize them, and kill not only their bodies – and those of their children and their other relatives – but damn their souls deep in the hottest cauldron in Hell.'

Panurge ironically opines that these Papimanes are hand-picked Christians, not 'heretics as they are in Germany and England'.

'Gosh, yes,' said Homenaz, 'that is why we are all going to be saved. Now let's have a drop of holy water and then we can dine.'

Christian laughter is often nothing if not partisan – hence the favourable allusions to Germany and England. Royalist-Gallican Frenchmen were attracted by Luther's Germany and Anglican England. Rabelais himself once fled to German lands. Rabelais's latest cardinal-patron eventually fled to England with his wife. The laughter is less partisan and more universally Christian when it is truly anchored in deviations from the teaching of Jesus and the Apostles. In so far as any prelate goes against that teaching he deserves to be laughed at. No one ought to be offended at laughter directed at boobies who think that the pope is a god. Such laughter is more lasting and satisfying than Lutheran jokes about true Christians farting in papal faces. But Rabelais is more than a little marked by Lutheran attitudes.

At dinner, the Bishop of the Papimanes, at first in jolly and confiding mood, gives an unctuous, sermonical praise of the decretals, which he contrasts favourably with Holy Writ. (The Bible cannot get anything like as much money out of France as they can!) Epistemon suddenly leaves the room: the bishop's sermon had brought on diarrhoea.

The bishop replaces the Bible by the decretals. No one should study anything else. Such a study brings power in this world and salvation in the next. It could usher in the earthly paradise:

'Then there will be no more hail, no more frost, no more rime, no more storms. Then, O then, there will be an abundance of all good things in earth; then, O then, will come stubborn and unbreakable peace in all this Universal World. No more war, no more pillaging, no more forced labour, no more robberies or murders – except for heretics and cursed rebels.

'Then, O then, for all Mankind, will be joy, happiness, mirth, ease, delectation, pleasures and delights. But, O! what great doctrine, what inestimable learning, what God-made precepts there are, united together by the holy chapters of those Everlasting Decretals. Why! When reading but a demi-canon, one tiny paragraph, one single sentence of those Sacrosanct Decretals, you feel ablaze within your hearts the furnace of your love of God, and of charity towards your neighbour – provided he's not a heretic.'

Rabelais had developed a keen awareness of the cruelty of much laughter, especially in farces. The opening chapters of the *Quart Livre* form a practical study of such farcical cruelty, as we are led to laugh as bailiffs are, one after another, reduced to pulp, and as a silly pompous cleric is so battered by the heels of his mule that nothing remains of him but a sandalled foot, clinging to the stirrup by its fancy leather-work.

However much the readers may laugh, Pantagruel does not. He is the jester's worst audience: 'That tale had been a merry one, were we not obliged to have the fear of God ever before our eyes.' He is seconded by the wise Epistemon. One can laugh at the bailiffs; they are unreal characters in a comedy; but behind that comedy was a real abuse organized by the Prior of Saint-Louand against the Seigneur de Basché. In real life the blows should not have rained down on the heads of those wretched comic bailiffs but on the very real head of that fat, grasping prior.[3]

---

3. *Quart Livre*, TLF, XVI, 1–11; XII, 41–8.

Rabelais's distaste for cruelty helps to explain the charity with which the Papimanes are treated. They are stupid and gullible *Bon Christian*. The real villains are those who have abused their childish and ghastly gullibility. Ghastly it is, full of cruelty and maudlin sentiment. The one subject which sets Bishop Homenaz off is the thought of punishing heretics. Only the decretals can justify all the gold which France pours into Rome! Yet the heretics refuse to study those holy documents. The bishop knows what to do with those who despise his decretals:

'Burn 'em, tear 'em with pincers, snip 'em, drown 'em, hang 'em, impale 'em, thrash 'em, dismember 'em, disembowel 'em, fry 'em, grill 'em, slice 'em up, crucify 'em, boil 'em, brain 'em, quarter 'em, smash 'em to pieces, unhinge 'em, carbonize 'em! Wicked heretics! Decretalifugitives, Decretalicides – worse than homicides and parricides, murderers of the Decretals!'[4]

The decretals are made the centre of the mockery because they are the pillars of that papal power from which Rabelais and his political and ecclesiastical patrons intended to free themselves, which they knew to be abused, and which they may even have sought to topple.

Rabelais's laughter penetrates the theology of Hell. The Papimanes are simple folk with a simple view of Hell (such as was held by Villon's old mother). Hell for them is place of boiling cauldrons. Their ecclesiastical polity is a simple one too, in which – thanks to the Holy Writ of the Decretals – Heaven, Purgatory and Hell lie under the arbitrary sway of Homenaz's far-off God-on-earth, whom they have yet to see:

'O my good God, whom I adore yet have never seen, in our article of death, open to us, by special grace, at least the most sacred treasure of Holy Mother the Church, of which thou art Protector; Saviour, Keeper-and-Distributor, Administrator and Dispenser. And give order that, in our hour of need, those precious works of supererogation and those beauteous pardons fail

4. ibid., LIII, 16–24.

us not: so that the Devils may find in our souls nothing to nibble upon; and so that the horrendous mouth of Hell engulf us not. If Purgatory we must bear, we must forbear: within thy power and will it is to free us when thou wilt.'

At which Homenaz shed hot, fat tears, beat his breast, made a cross of his thumbs and kissed it.

Epistemon. Frère Jean and Panurge, on seeing that distressing climax, cried '*Miaow, Miaow, Miaow*,' behind their napkins, pretending to wipe their eyes as though they had wept. The girls were well trained: they presented everyone with brimming goblets of Clementine wine, and with an abundance of sweetmeats. Thus was the banquet restored again to merriment.

Clementines are decretals. The girls were dressed up as choirboys.[5]

Rabelais was writing with a definite public in mind. It was a public which knew its Bible and the force of the scriptural texts that strew these chapters. Such laughter in context is positive and enriching. Error, even the uncharitable yearning to persecute, is not so much loathed as laughed away.

Rabelais was a priest and a doctor. He valued laughter for its therapeutic powers. As he wrote to Cardinal de Chastillon, 'many who are languishing, ill, or otherwise troubled or desolate' had beguiled their benighted suffering with his jests, 'joyfully passing their time'; through him they were brought 'merriment and fresh consolation'.

Rabelais sought to make his patients laugh. He could not do that for other sufferers who needed his medical skill, but he could reach them through his books. He wrote to bring to patients whom he would never see 'such little relief as he could'. Hippocrates lent his weight to what he did. That great Greek doctor had conceived of the art of medicine as a 'farce played by three characters: the patient; the doctor; the illness'. A doctor should dress up for the part and act to please his patient, washing his hands and wooing him.

A laughter-raising doctor is good for his patients. The only ques-

5. ibid., LIII, 110; LIV, 8.

tion is the actual process by which joy is aroused. Does the doctor bring happiness by encouraging the patient to an optimistic view of his condition? Are the doctor's own happy spirits actually transferred to the mind of the sufferer? (Medical opinion allowed for either.) Whichever explanation is correct, a jolly doctor is a relief to those who suffer. His duty is, 'without offence to God', to make his patients happy.[6] As a doctor Rabelais brought physic to the body. As a priest he brought physic to the soul. In both cases his cures included laughter.

Such a conception of Christian laughter moves it right away from being an occasional concession to human weakness. It is a good thing in itself.

Rabelais was the private physician to Jean Du Bellay, who had moved to Le Mans for his health. Rabelais calls the new abode of his cardinal-bishop 'a paradise of salubriousness'. It was there that he lived, wrote, and looked after his patient. A bitter enemy complained that 'one of our foremost bishops in rank and scholarship admits Rabelais to the intimacy of his table and conversation'. Indeed he did. It is inconceivable that Rabelais should have written about the Papimanes in his palace (at the request of Cardinal Odet de Chastillon) without reading his book aloud to him before it was published. (The *Quart Livre* contains after all the highest praise of the bishop's brother, the Seigneur de Langey.)

The *Quart Livre de Pantagruel* is enough to make an ailing cardinal laugh. It did him good.

---

6. ibid., *Epistle Dedicatory to Cardinal Odet de Chastillon*, lines 19–61. Throughout this letter, the main medical authority for Rabelais is Hippocrates.

50

Laughter and
Christian Mythology

The introduction of Christian references into the storm-at-sea episode was not an isolated act. The *Quart Livre* widened the power and scope of Christian laughter by marrying Æsop and Lucian to specific scriptural texts. In that way the Christian religion, and the Christian God, could be introduced into fables, not merely inferred from the moral at the end.

During his years in Ferrara, and certainly before the *Tiers Livre* was completed in 1546, Rabelais had discovered Celio Calcagnini – or, rather, his works, published after his death by his admirers. Calcagnini was the greatest Christian mythographer of his age. By the time Rabelais had completed the *Quart Livre* he had absorbed much of Calcagnini's erudition as well as his concept of moral mythography, and (using a neologism) had even started calling his own writings *mythologies*.[1]

An outstanding example of such Christian laughter is the Prologue to the *Quart Livre*. It is a long and independent piece of writing in the spirit of Lucian's *Dialogues of the Gods*, and applied to a fable of Æsop which was widely known: *The Woodcutter and the Axe*. Rabelais intended to preach the classical virtue of moderation and to fuse it into Christian humility.

1. Celio Calcagnini's *Opera* were published in 1544. He was essentially the kind of don who gives his best ideas to his students. The book is composed of unpublished manuscripts found at his death. He was already famous as a lecturer of great depth and originality.

Rabelais uses the word *mythologies* for his works for the first time in his *Epistle Dedicatory to Cardinal Odet de Chastillon, Quart Livre*, TLF, 3.

Moderation had long been applied to Christian conduct generally. St Paul, in the Vulgate Latin, urges the faithful to let their 'moderation' be known to all men.[2] Rabelais teaches that such moderation applies to firm faith itself, or rather, to the demands we make upon the basis of it. In the fable the woodcutter who lost his axe was offered by Jupiter a golden and a silver one, which he refused, preferring his own. Choosing aright (though not entirely for the right reasons), he was given the other two as well. Should not that lesson apply to Christians faced with the mysteries of God's predestination?

We can enjoy laughing at a thoroughly Lucianesque Jupiter without losing the Christian thread leading to the Pauline moral at the end. The Prologue insists that God answers prayers made with firm faith, provided that what we ask for conforms to the Golden Mean. 'Go through Holy Scripture: you will find that the prayers of those who asked in moderation have never been rejected.'

The example cited from the New Testament is that of the little chap Zaccheus who wanted to have a look at Jesus. Too small to see over the heads of the crowd, he clambered up a sycamore tree. Jesus – that 'all-good God' – recognized the purity and moderation of his desire; he let himself not only be seen by Zaccheus but actually went home with him and blessed his family.

Rabelais relates the whole episode in a bantering tone which adds to its force. So too, very briefly, the tale of the Old Testament prophet whose borrowed axe was miraculously restored when its head fell into the Jordan – thanks to his moderate prayer for its return.[3] The advantage of introducing Christian authorities into Lucianesque and Æsop fables is that one can, as here, have a silly, bumbling, irascible, overworked Jupiter in the fable, yet apply the moral directly to the Christian relationship to the true God.[4]

2. Philippians, 4:5, *Modestia vestra nota sit omnibus hominibus.* Even after Erasmus had shown that *modestia* does not, in the original, mean 'moderation' in the sense of the Golden Mean, the text was often cited as though it did. The classical ideal was, at all events, deeply rooted in Christian morality.
3. Luke, 19:1–10; II (IV) Kings, 6:1–7.
4. *Quart Livre*, TLF, *Prologue de l'auteur*, 48f.

The moral preaches moderation. It is wrong to ask for more. 'But,' you might say, 'a million in gold is as little to God as a penny!'

'Hay, hay, hay! And who taught *you* to argue and talk about the power and predestination of God, wretched folk? Peace. *St, st, st*: humble yourself before his holy face and confess your imperfections.'

Rabelais is preaching St Paul through laughter: Man must stand in awe of God's power and his predestination of the elect. It is not a man's right to criticize it: 'Nay but, O man, who art those who disputeth with God?'[5]

Pray for health. Leave health *and* wealth to the shifty prayers of Genoese bankers! Cardinal Jean Du Bellay could say 'Amen' to that.

5. Romans, 9:20.

51

Gluttony

The episode of Signor Belly, Messere Gaster, shows the force of introducing Christian authority into myth. Rabelais sees fear of hunger as the driving force of all natural human endeavour in this sublunary world. The theme is an ancient one, strongly supported by a clutch of Erasmian adages. Messere Gaster himself dwells in the high, fertile uplands which, according to a famous myth of Hesiod's, is reached only after a long, tough, rugged climb.[1] Struggle upwards to those sunlit uplands and you are in the dwelling-place of manly Virtue.

Human endeavour in all fields is humorously passed in review to the refrain of *Tout pour la tripe!* ('All for the innards!'). In a culture which knew hunger and famine the seriousness behind the laughter is never completely absent. Without the drive of hunger, nothing in the world would get done.

But supposing men, prone to idolatry, were to mistake Signor Belly for a god, or even for God. The temptation to divinize creatures like ourselves ought to have been scotched by a famous quip in Antiquity. Erasmus lists it; Rabelais cites it. King Antigonus the First was called a god by a flatterer. He replied, 'The Gentleman Bearer of the Chamber-pot denies it.' Gaster also refers flatterers 'to his close-stool, to see, consider, contemplate, and philosophize upon his faeces'.

Such explicit moralizing can usefully be read back into the comic emphasis on faeces in the earlier books: our natural excreta keep us in our places, as creatures; to accept them as natural is right and proper: to glory in them is subhuman and mad.

1. *Quart Livre*, TLF, LVII; Hesiod, *Works and Days*, 289f.

Messere Gaster serves another purpose. By him we are reminded of the deadly sin of gluttony. Many thought that monks, however divided by rivalry and by distinctive and varied vestments, all wallowed in it. Such monkish gluttons are idolaters, truly worshipping their bellies:

They all held Gaster to be their God, worshipped him as God, and sacrificed to him as their Lord God Almighty; they had no other god before him; they served him and loved him above all things; they honoured him as their God.

Such idolatry is laughed at, but it demands more than the wry condemnation by King Antigonus the First. It requires St Paul. It gets him, and with him laughter turns to tears: 'You might say that Paul was specifically thinking' of monks, we are told, when he wrote thus to the Philippians:

For there are many, of whom I have often told you (and even now tell you weeping), enemies of the Cross of Christ, whose end is destruction, whose God is their Belly.[2]

When those gluttonous monks are held up to ridicule, we are being invited to laugh at madmen on the way to Hell. Is that why tears take over?

For Rabelais, Paul is the key to evangelical truth, and the trigger to much laughter. As a pathetic little devil complains elsewhere in the *Quart Livre*, students have discovered the Scriptures:

'That explains why we can no longer get even one of them to go to the Devil. If the hypocrites do not help us, tearing their St Pauls from their hands by threats, attacks, force, violence and burnings, I believe we will never nibble another again down under.'[3]

Rabelais's famous lists of food are not merely laughable; when the food is stuffed by the monkish Gastrolastres the laughter aroused implies far more than fun-and-games. Carnival and its feasting have

2. *Quart Livre*, TLF, LVIII, 48–65; citing Philippians, 3:18–19.
3. ibid., XLVI, 68–77.

their place, but monkish idolaters make the whole of their life into a perpetual Mardi Gras, wolfing down white bread, sops of all sorts, sausages, hams, capons, pigs' trotters, jellies, puddings, pies, pasties, pastries – the lot. All is swilled down with the local wine. Laughter is invited at their expense, but Pantagruel, the moral finger-post of the *Quart Livre*, is not amused. Seeing all those base offerings to Belly, and the 'multiplicity of their sacrifices', he grows angry and wants to leave. Epistemon persuades him to remain, to 'see the issue of that farce'. In so far as *farce* means 'comedy', he awaits the climax; in so far as *farce* means stuffing, the 'issue' is faeces.[4]

What do these monks sacrifice to their omnipotent Belly on fast days? We are given a fresh list, starting with caviar. If fasting means merely avoiding flesh, you can gorge yourself on eggs and oysters and dozens of kinds of fish. (True fasting for Rabelais lies not in fish-eating but in moderation.)

Rabelais's identifying of the excess of Lenten revels with the monks and their perpetual gaudies helps to explain the absence of any victory for Lent in one of the funniest of all of his creations: the war between the heroes and their former allies the Andouilles, the Protestant Chidlings. It recalls the annual battle between Carnival and Lent (well-known from the picture by Brueghel), but does not re-enact it. The episode turns into a mock-heroic Trojan War, enjoyed for the joy of laughing. The onset of Lent, *Quaresmeprenant*, is presented as ugly and laughable.[5]

Explicit censure is reserved for followers of *Antiphysie* ('Anti-Nature'), an invention of Calcagnini. They include three men who had attacked Rabelais viciously in print: Postel (the insane Orientalist), Calvin, and Putherbe (that 'Stinkweed' for whom Rabelais was the worst of heretics). Rabelais turns them all into descendants of *Antiphysie*: 'maniacal Pistols; demoniacal Calvins, impostors of Geneva; and raging Stinkweeds'.[6]

4. ibid., LIX.   5. ibid., XXX.
6. ibid., XXXII, 118–23. Gabriel Dupuyherbault, in Latin Putherbeus, had attacked Rabelais in his *Theotimus*. He wanted the works of Rabelais to be condemned as blasphemous. Rabelais turns his Latin name Putherbeus into Putherbe, 'Stinkweed', just as he changed Postel to Pistol.

Such enemies are laughed at much as Rabelais brought his patrons to laugh at the Council of Trent, so despised by Gallicans. The most that Rabelais seems ever to have hoped for is that the *Concile National de Chésil* (his name for the Council of Trent) might have reconciled the warring factions, schisms and rival Churches. A *concile* ought to reconcile; it preferred to denounce.

In any case, for Rabelais it was not a truly Catholic council: it was a merely national one, dominated by Italians. It made things worse. The factions were fighting it out again like cats and dogs. The nature of the error of the *Concile National de Chésil* lies hidden in its Hebrew name: *Chésil (Kesil)* means 'fool'. Bad, self-confident fool, of course. It is the most widely used word for fool in all Scripture.[7] Being foolish, Rabelais can laugh at it.

---

7. ibid., XXXV, 46–72. As Gallicans, Rabelais and his patrons were unimpressed by the long-sitting Council of Trent. *Kesil*, the Hebrew for a self-confident kind of fool, or for foolish, occurs over sixty times in the Old Testament.

52

Realist Laughter:
Laughter and Eternity

Fool can laugh at fool, madman at madman, because each has his certainties. Where does the Christian madman find his? Where does he find the strength to confront the mockeries of the world and, when occasion arises, to outface it with surer mockeries of his own? In revelation. In Scripture. Does that mean, in nothing but words?

No. Inspired words are vital: but words may be twisted. There are signs other than words which also bring their certainties – mainly, but by no means only, human certainties.

Not all of a Christian's certainties are higher spiritual ones. You can find concrete certainties in natural signs. The pangs of hunger sent by Messere Gaster are signs which can be neither faked nor ignored.

Panurge claimed afterwards that he had never been afraid during the storm. We know for certain that he had been: he had messed his breeches. Faeces are, in his case, a sign of servile fear. For doctors, faeces provide medical signs and symptoms; for moralists they are a sign of our humanity, or, when gloried in, a sign of physical or spiritual impurity, of error or perversity. They are also, when copious, evidence of recent ample eating; when sustained, of gluttony. Eat without moderation, drink without moderation, and your immoderate excreta will betray you. Even when given their due and a not dishonourable place in the life of Man, faeces are a sign of our corporeality. To find the divine spark or the spiritual, Rabelais turns to the mind.

A great deal of laughter is generated when, in Rabelais, such natural signs belie the speech or conduct of any human being, man, woman or child. Language can be twisted into patterns of lies, self-deceptions or obfuscation, but concrete signs cannot. A man's deeds, too, are signs that speak louder than words. Tension between words and deeds can always provoke laughter; within that laughter no one doubts which is the dominant trait of the character of Frère Jean: valiant he is, and bold.

Such natural signs are in sharp contrast with conventional ones. Monks learn to associate bells with kitchens and refectories. Bells are conventional, not natural, signs.

Such notions come to the fore when the companions lie becalmed. They are bored and restless. Pantagruel rejects discursive reason as a remedy for their boredom and as a means of raising the wind by natural 'sympathy':

'A hungry stomach has no ears: it hears nothing. By signs, gestures and deeds you will be satisfied . . .'

In the middle of expounding authoritatively a standard example of a meaningful sign, Pantagruel accidentally touches the rope of the ship's bell: Frère Jean dashes off to the kitchen. True monk that he is, he mistakes an accidental *ding* for a conventional signal calling him to eat.

The sign that Pantagruel provided to remedy the stagnation of his becalmed ship and his retinue was a happy banquet shared in warm comradeship. It raised the men's hearts and minds and, in sympathy, raised the wind in the sails of their ship, 'at which all sang divers canticles in praise of the Most Highest . . .'[1]

God works through signs, and to ignore that leads to error and laughter. But what about words? They too are signs. Is there any place for certainty in things so flighty, so transient, so easily misused, as words? Is even revelation and Scripture a matter of flighty words?

A Christian's way is manifestly fraught with difficulties. In the

---

1. *Tiers Livre*, TLF, LXIII, 72–82; LXIV, 53–65. (That there are secret 'sympathies' influencing apparently independent natural phenomena was a widespread conviction among the learned in many fields of study.)

Tiers Livre Pantagruel states that language is a human construct: to speak is natural; to speak this language rather than that one is a matter of education. In no language do words actually mean anything of themselves; they are sounds on which meanings have been arbitrarily imposed and accepted by convention. That contention is Aristotelian in origin.[2] Only those who have been taught know what words mean. Words have no natural (or supernatural) force of their own.[3] If that was all there was to it, then Rabelais might have been a nominalist. But he is not.

Two rival theories of knowledge divide scholars: Realism and Nominalism.

Realists hold with Plato that ideas or universals (abstract concepts) have a real objective existence. If we say *Goodness*, for example, or *Beauty*, or *Truth*, such words correspond to the most permanent of values. Those values really exist – for Christian Realists, often in the mind of God. The universal exists to some extent in each thing. With universals you can have a rational theology.

Nominalists, on the other hand, maintain that universals are the product of human reason: it may be convenient to talk of *Goodness*, *Beauty*, or *Truth*, but Goodness, Beauty, or Truth do not actually exist. It is useful to generalize from singulars and to call things good, beautiful or true, but philosophy (for Nominalists) does not admit that Goodness, Beauty or Truth are things which have any real existence, in the mind of God or anywhere whatsoever.

Renaissance Platonism encouraged thinkers to be Realists. Realism provides certainties. Beauty, Truth and Virtue are not generalizations based on deductions from particulars, mere notions imposed arbitarily upon sounds: they are absolute values, giving – among other things – direction to Christian laughter. Rabelais's laughter at ugliness, error and vice is full-blooded and confident because its butts are not deviations from opinion but deviations from absolute value.

Nominalism, insisting that universals have no existence outside

2. ibid., XIX, 37–44. 'It is an abuse to say that we possess a natural language. Languages arise from decisions to impose meanings and from the conventions of nations: words (as the dialecticians say) do not signify naturally by desire.'
3. *Gargantua*, TLF, LII–IX.

the mind, required philosophy and theology to go their own ways: theological certainty was found in revelation and authority, not in reason: rational philosophy and revealed religion are discrete studies. Realists denied that, though they did not deny, of course, either revelation or authority.

Rabelais is, or became, a Realist. He spells that out in the *Quart Livre*. He also emphasized revelation and authoritative truth. He gives us hints before providing his certainties.

Readers of Shakespeare and Rabelais find important topics treated comically or light-heartedly in the very same work that treats them seriously. Comic and not-so-comic hints abound that the serious solution to the problem of verbal certainty will lie in Plato's *ideas*. In the *Tiers Livre* Pantagruel is praised as the 'Idea and exemplar of all joyful perfection', but not before Panurge had ridiculously and perversely called the bugbear of the Humanists, the Sorbonne, 'the living Idea of Pantheology'![4]

The judgement on Pantagruel receives quiet recognition from readers: the judgement on the Sorbonne (among the readers whom Rabelais sought) produces guffaws; yet the same word, *Idea*, is used for both.

In the *Quart Livre*, Epistemon bought a painting depicting 'the Ideas of Plato and the Atoms of Epicurus'. The great flying sow worshipped by the Chidlings was the very 'Idea of Mardi Gras'. The Bishop of the Papimanes venerated a pretty poor painting in its reliquary as the platonic 'Idea of that God-on-earth for whose visit' he so devoutly yearned.[5]

After such sporting with platonic ideas, misused or misunderstood, we are prepared to find them used to unravel profound mysteries, to reach new heights and plumb hidden depths.

The ship ventures into a sea where frozen sounds and words thaw out. In that Babel, Plato held out hope. Proper names, when divinely inspired, carry true meanings. The source of that doctrine is the *Cratylus*, often cited, we are told, by Pantagruel, who calls its author

4. *Tiers Livre*, TLF, LI, 58; II, 59–60.
5. *Quart Livre*, TLF, II, 39–41; XLII, 44; L, 5–14.

'the divine Plato'. Christians saw Plato's contention borne out by the meaningful names found in the Old Testament. In the New Testament too, where the name of Jesus, *Yeshua*, comes from a root implying divine salvation. Even pagan literature may hold such revelations, though normally veiled from profane eyes.

Plutarch's account of the death of Pan which fascinated so many readers in Western Europe from the fifteenth century onwards contains a powerful example. The *dæmons* make a veiled allusion to a superior being who has died. They call him Pan.

Who is he? Pantagruel sees Pan as a veiled reference to Christ and the Crucifixion. He finds support in both the words *Pan* in Greek: Pan is the shepherd-god, Πάν – in the Bible is not Christ called 'the great Shepherd of the sheep'? In Plutarch's account Christ is veiled behind the pagan deity Pan. There is another Pan, too: Πάν; that Pan means 'All', and Christ is the faithful's All-in-All.[6]

Renaissance thinkers also found Christian truths 'veiled' behind the attributes of pagan gods. These truths were there by God's grace. Duly 'unveiled', they convey moral and spiritual lessons to the enlightened Christian. In Amyclæa, Bacchus, the god of wine, was called *psilax*, 'winged'. His statue showed those wings. Rightly so, since wine plays a heaven-sent role in sending the spirits of mankind winging aloft:

Birds fly high in the air lightly on their wings; so, too, with the aid of Bacchus (that is, of delicious and delightful wine), the spirits of human beings are borne aloft, their bodies clearly lightened, and what in them was earthy is rendered lissom.[7]

Wine is a sign. Its moral effects are a sign also: a sign of divine favour. The very name of *psilax*, which was properly imposed on Bacchus, bears that out. The monk, too, was not called Jean des Entommeures for nothing. His name was properly imposed. Frère Jean makes mincemeat of his foes: *entommeures* means mincemeat.

6. ibid., XXXVII, 44–5; XXVIII: M.A.S., 'The Death of Pan and the Death of Heroes in the Fourth Book of Rabelais', in Michael Heath (ed.), *Some Renaissance Studies*, Droz, Geneva, 1992, pp. 50–69.
7. *Quart Livre*, TLF, LXV, 75–88.

But not all names have been properly imposed: hence a new field of humour. It would be laughable to seek divine truths or prophetic meanings in all names. Making the Celtic *Penthagruel* into a Graeco-Arabic *Panta-gruel*, 'All-thirst', was a learned joke, not a learned revelation. Rabelais chose to call his dying great and good Erasmian poet Raminagrobis, as though he were a worldly fat-cat. He was not. Rabelais took the name of his powerful and learned legal friend Tiraquellus; he sported with it, as though it derived from *trinquamolle* (a silly boaster). If Rabelais meant to suggest that Tiraquellus really was such a man, then he would have made a powerful enemy for life. It is precisely because some names are indeed awe-inspiringly 'true' and others are not that such jests are possible. But to an age such as ours, which neither seeks that sort of truth in etymology nor true prognostics in a person's name, such playing about with personal names can never be as funny.

If words, and not only proper names, may be touched by the certainty of platonic ideas, then the verbal inspiration of Scripture and some other revelations can be guaranteed. As the *Quart Livre* and his own life drew to a close, Rabelais, inspired by the example and teaching of Celio Calcagnini, embarked on his most ambitious platonic myth: the episode of the thawing words. He bases it on a christianizing of a myth attributed by Plutarch to the philosopher Petron. It comes from the same work of Plutarch's in which he had found so much other material for his *Quart Livre*, including the beautiful account of the death of Pan. That work, *Why Oracles Have Ceased*, made a deep impression on him. In it he sought hidden Christian truths. The ship with Rabelais's characters aboard sails on into platonic mysteries. It comes to a region where frozen sounds thaw out.[8]

Most are sounds, not words: *bou, bou, bou*, say, or the noise of cartwheels, of gunfire and of clashing arms. In so far as they form part of any language they are onomatopoeias. We know what they mean. They carry their meaning in their sound. But some sounds

---

8. Plutarch, *Moralia*, 422B–C; attributed to Petron, 422D.
Cf. Rabelais, *Quart Livre*, TLF, LV, 46–65.

are words: it is in those words, if anywhere, that inspired meanings may lie.

Adapting Petron's myth, Pantagruel expounds a myth of his own: there are many worlds strung together, forming the sides of an equilateral triangle; Truth has her *manoir*, her dwelling-place, within that heavenly triangle (just as Virtue has her *manoir* on the rolling uplands of Hesiod's arduous mountain). Within that celestial triangle dwells Truth: Truth expressed in words: 'the Words, the Ideas, Exemplars and Portraits of all things past and future'. The terms *ideas*, *exemplars* and *portraits* all refer to the same thing: to ideas as Plato conceived them. They form the divine universals which guarantee the meaning of revealed truth to men on earth.

Around that celestial triangle stretches the *æon*. In Latin called *ævum* and in English 'Age' (or, liturgically, 'world'), it stretches to the end of time. That gives a markedly Christian twist to the myth: it is Christians who intercalate an intermediate *ævum* between time and eternity.

At great intervals, parts of those ideas-exemplars-and-portraits drip down on to mankind 'like catarrhs, and like the dew which fell on Gideon's fleece'. The catarrhs bring in Plato. Socrates at the end of the *Cratylus* uses catarrhs as a symbol for such truth as drips down on to our snotty world. Rabelais quietly echoes him. As for Gideon's fleece, it vouches not only for God's revelation in the Old Testament: it also vouches for the presence of the New Testament in the Old. That fleece and that dew were traditionally held to foreshadow the fecundating of the Virgin Mary, 'like dew upon the grass'.[9]

And what about Christ himself and his Gospel in the New Testament? That part of those ideas-exemplars-and-portraits which does not drip down on to mankind remains intact 'until the consummation of the age'. Those words of Rabelais echo the final promise of Christ at the end of St Matthew's Gospel: 'And, lo, I am with you, even to the consummation of the age.' Truth will be given to Christians in

9. *Quart Livre*, TLF, LV, 55–60; Judges, 6:36–42. (The dew first fell on to the fleece alone; then, anywhere but the fleece. That was God's sign.)

this world by a Christ whose fund of truth will have plenty left in it when he ends the present age during which he has promised to be ever with his Church.[10]

Truth from the Word of God dripped down on to Scripture. For Rabelais, Scripture has massive force. When properly cited it trenchantly puts an end to obscurity and verbiage. It is the best of guides to moral and spiritual laughter. By the spirit of Christ, Christians have been given throughout the ages truths enough to live by. The divine *ideas* vouch for them.

There are also special gifts. On his deathbed Rabelais's real-life hero, Guillaume Du Bellay, was vouchsafed the gift of prophecy. (Rabelais refers to it twice. How those episodes must have pleased his brother the bishop when Rabelais read them to him!)

Pantagruel enjoys the God-given gift of wisdom. Like Socrates, he is individually inspired. At the end of the *Quart Livre* Pantagruel explains how he felt at times 'an urgent withdrawal in his soul' counselling him not to go ashore. It never failed him when he obeyed it. The wise Epistemon replies, 'That is like the *dæmon* of Socrates.' In the end Rabelais turns Pantagruel into a Christian Socrates.[11]

The laughter of Rabelais is played out against a background of God, time, and eternity. There are two verses of the New Testament – two verses only – which theologians recognize as vouching for the end of the age and of created time. One we have met already: the last words of Christ in the final words of St Matthew's Gospel: 'I will be with you to the consummation of the *ævum*.' Rabelais cited that promise. The other comes from St Paul:

10. The standard English rendering of Matthew, 28:20 is 'even to the end of the world'. 'World' in that phrase has the old sense of 'time', 'period of time'. The Revised Version (margin), prefers 'to the consummation of the age'. That is as close as can be to the Vulgate and to *usque ad consummationem sæculi* – and to Rabelais's *jusques à la consummation du siècle*. The original Greek of Matthew uses the word *aion* – the same word as Plutarch uses for the age which surrounds the mystic triangle.

11. *Tiers Livre*, TLF, XXI; *Quart Livre*, TLF, XXVI; LXVI, 51–62. Cf. Plato, *Apology*, 31C–D.

... the end, when Christ shall have delivered up the Kingdom to God, even the Father.

Rabelais quotes that too. It comes in *Pantagruel*, with reference, correctly, to the Last Judgement, which will bring all life on earth, with its generation and corruption, to a close:

... when Jesus Christ shall have given back to God the Father his peaceful kingdom, free from all contamination from sin.[12]

Rabelaisian laughter wells up against the backcloth of eternity. The certainties of the Christian madman are in time, but not of time. Enlightened by revelation, the Christian can judge deviations from divine truth to be as mad as they laughably are.

The Scriptures provide their certainties both in the Old Testament, as interpreted by a Humanist Church, and in the New. In Rabelais one verse of Scripture, properly cited, can outweigh pages of ingenious rhetoric. All Panurge's amusing and windy words in praise of one-way debts which he intends never to repay are countered by a few words of St Paul: 'Owe no man anything, but that ye love one another.'[13]

A conclusive argument in favour of defensive wars is provided by God's title, *Sabaoth* ('of armies'). In Hebrew, Solomon's name means 'peaceful', so another argument is the mystic sense of a phrase of that 'peaceful Solomon' applied to the beloved in the Song of Songs: 'Terrible as an army with banners'. For Rabelais that military comparison alluded to 'the unutterable perfection of Divine Wisdom'.[14]

Scripture does not stand alone. There is the presence of Christ, promised to the end of the age. There are special inspirations, such as those of Judge Bridoye, or – more clearly awesome – that of Pantagruel.

Sound learning comes from God – all sound learning: – it is 'the heavenly manna of good doctrine'. The Renaissance itself, with its

---

12. *Pantagruel*, TLF, VIII, 24–30, from the letter of Gargantua to his son, Pantagruel. Cf. I Corinthians, 15:24.
13. *Tiers Livre*, TLF, V, 4–10.
14. ibid., Prologue, 144–7, citing the Song of Songs, 3:9.

restoration of ancient learning, is attributable to the goodness of God.[15] Within that Renaissance the 'divine' Plato plays a great part, but not an excluding one. Aristotle, Hippocrates, Roman law, Greek and Roman philosophers may all share in providing that manna. All were in varying ways inspired.[16]

In the early Church, Justin Martyr had not abandoned the doctrines of Plato when he became a Christian: he could accept them in so far as they shared in the Word of God, whose seeds are sown so widely. Rabelais, centuries later, found it quite natural to state a truth 'following the advice of Plato in the *Gorgias*, or, better, the teachings of the Gospel (Matthew 6)'. He cites at the same time Plato, Socrates, Aristotle, David and Paul.[17] The Renaissance Christian had no need to crouch in an intellectual ghetto. His laughter could beam widely into stupidities revealed by the manna to be found in Roman law, in Greek medicine, in ancient philosophy – indeed, in all areas of learning.

But the Christian will always be wary of words in the void. During the fair weather following the significant happy banquet in the *Quart Livre* which banished idleness and raised the wind, Panurge, for a moment calm and replete, talks for a while like a saint or sage:

'Without fail we should indeed praise God in his goodness, our Creator, Saviour and Defender, who, with this good bread, this good cool wine and these good viands, has cured us of those perturbations of body and soul – quite apart from the pleasure and delight experienced when eating and drinking them.'[18]

Can that foolish coward and servile God-mocker be really reformed? Not for long. Not really. He will wear his character-mask to the end.

The heroes come to the final island, the Isle of Thieves. Should they land? The very idea brings back Panurge's servile fear: '*Ha! da, da!*' The other characters resume their roles: Frère Jean des

15. *Pantagruel*, TLF, VIII, 103–4.   16. ibid., VIII, 77–9.
17. *Almanach pour 1535*, in *Pantagruéline Prognostication* [and other texts], TLF, 1974, pp 45–7.   18. *Quart Livre*, TLF, LXV, 30–39.

Entommeures wants to dash ashore and make mincemeat of the enemy; Panurge skulks below-decks in the bread-store while others do the hard and dangerous work, going ashore to fill the water-butts. Frère Jean suggests giving Panurge a good fright – just for a laugh. Pantagruel agrees, and orders a canon to be noisily fired (and then to be instantly re-loaded, as an act of prudence).

The canon-fire reverberates below decks. Panurge misinterprets that sign: for him it is not a friendly canon being set off but the sign of an enemy attack. He is beside himself with fear. His teeth chatter madly, like a baboon's when it is searching for fleas. He staggers up on deck, his beard strewn with crumbs. He is bespattered and streaming with blood. He has one foot thrust through half of his breeches while he uses the other half as a mitten to hold on to the ship's cat with her sharp claws. ('You need a mitten to catch a kitten.')

In real life the anguish of Panurge would be intense. He is mocked, humiliated and running with blood. But in comedy the pain is made light of. Panurge is akin to Carabba, that wretched lunatic mocked in the course of theological reflections on the sufferings of Christ; he is like Christ himself in the eyes of those who found Jesus mad and therefore funny.

So why do we laugh at the blood-streaked Panurge, but not at that Man in garments gory, triumphing on Bozrah's way; not at the blood-streaked Man of Sorrows? Because, for Christians, Jesus was not mad, except in the eyes of the worldly and the spiritually blind; because he is indeed God. Because Christ in his manhood on earth was good, kind, blameless, sinless, but bore infinite pain to redeem mankind; because his blood was real blood; his wounds, real wounds; the mockery of him, real cruelty.

Make the pain seem trivial and everything changes. Panurge's pain has been made to seem so. Panurge is inglorious, unheroic, condemned by all the signs, natural and divine: Frère Jean pinches his nose and points to the shirt-tails on which Panurge had noticeably squittered. (The pinching and the pointing – and the faeces-stained shirt – are all signs.)

The wise and inspired Pantagruel, our guide to the Good, the

Beautiful and the True, is not moved to pity by that suffering. He has not laughed once throughout two whole books; he condemned laughter-filled tales of comic cruelty on the grounds that we should 'have the fear of God ever before our eyes': yet he does laugh now. He cannot help it. Panurge's plight was as irresistibly laughable as Carabba's was to others. Pantagruel saw Panurge 'emotional, dazed, all a-tremble, speechless, and be-shitten'. He noted his skin, lacerated by the claws of the cat; and 'could not restrain his laughter'.

Panurge babbles on about the Devil. Then, after that inescapable laugh, Pantagruel replies with words of God and of purity:

'What are you doing with that cat?' asked Pantagruel.

'Cat!' replied Panurge. 'The Devil take me! I thought it was some scraggy boy-devil I'd sneak up on and grabbed in the great hutch of Hell. The Devil take the devil! It's herring-boned my skin, lacerating it like the beard of a crayfish!'

'Go,' said Pantagruel, 'on behalf of God, go, bathe yourself, wash yourself, calm down, find a white shirt and clothe yourself anew.'

Cleanliness, good in itself, is also a sign of purity, and so indeed is next to godliness.

Characters in comedy do not change. Panurge answers Pantagruel's invitation to godliness, cleanliness and purity by evoking dirt and the Devil, and glorying in the foul physical sign of his disgrace:

'Ha, ha, ha! Hooray! What the devil is this? Do you call it squit, dung, shit, lask, droppings, faeces, excrement, pellets, turd, mute, manure, brown-stuff, *scybalon* or *spyratos*? It is, I believe saffron from Hibernia:

> *Ho, ho, hie!*
> *Sapphran d'Hibernie!*
> *Sela,*

Let us drink.'[19]

Messer Gaster had made the point with a moral smile, referring the gluttonous idolatrous monks to his chamber-pot. Rabelais is

---

19. The closing words of the *Quart Livre*.

touching upon matters which, for Platonists, go to the roots of our
humanity. Platonists have a deep and primitive loathing of dirt. It
is not simply because we fear germs that we find it repugnant to be
spat upon, or shat upon. For a platonizing Christian, loathing of
dirt may be classed 'among the elementary constituents of human
mentality', with, say, our sense of moral value or of beauty. Dirt
pollutes.[20]

And so dirt may be hated, or feared, or laughed at. What we hate
or fear can be tamed by laughing. We laughed at young Gargantua
as he revelled in filth, brought up as he was; that laughter distanced
and condemned. We transfer that laughter to Panurge, now that the
giants are exemplars of cleanliness and purity. If we side with
the pure and the true, again our laughter distances and condemns
as the polyglot Panurge learnedly revels in his own excreta. Such
laughter does not imply indulgence. To see, smell and stand close
to a real-life Panurge would be no laughing matter! That we can
laugh at Panurge we owe to Rabelais's art. And it is attributable to
his art that we have no desire to throw Panurge away like a broken
toy, and even less desire to send him – a human being who has made
us laugh – to eternal perdition.

Yet that glorying in his faeces matters. It anchors Panurge in
squalor and error. As he finally revels in filth, we do not even get a
hint of Man's 'most divine part, his νοῦς or mens, his mind', and
we do not catch a glimpse of the spirit.

A human being nailed to a cross would, during his long agony,
befoul himself. I can think of no work of art which faces that fact.
Christ was fully incarnate as man. But our laughter is guided by art,
and so are our horror and tears. Art takes us from some of the
features of the ghastly pain, squalor and horror upwards to the
Spirit.

Then, if anyone is being laughed at, it is not Christ on the Cross
but – from the Father and the Son in the heavens – those who laugh
at him.

20. Cf. the excellent ch. 8, on 'Dirt', in Edwyn Bevan's *Hellenism
and Christianity*, London, 1921, especially pp. 146–54.

53

Charity and Joy

The climactic last pages of the *Quart Livre* were Rabelais's farewell to laughter. The book appeared on 1 January 1552. Soon after 18 April 1552 he had a cancel inserted to flatter his conquering king. From then on he sent nothing more to the printers. Twelve months later he was dead, and was buried as an honoured cleric in Paris.[1]

When he wrote his first two Prologues he adopted a comic mask: he switched round the letters of his name and became Alcofrybas Nasier (later just Alcofrybas). Not so when he wrote his dedicatory epistle to Cardinal Odet de Chastillon: that is signed 'Franç. RAB-ELAIS, Medicin'. It was not as a jester but as a priest and doctor that he condemned in it *agelastes*, 'non-laughers'. The 'calumny of certain Cannibals, misanthropists and *agelastes*' had determined him never to write again. Only the support of his king, his cardinals and his learned readers led him to change his mind.

Non-laughers are condemned in the strongest of terms; yet, in the *Quart Livre*, until the final page, the wise Pantagruel is just such an *agelaste*. Chapters given over to uproarious slapstick within the comedy of cruelty leave him quietly watching from the sidelines, mildly disapproving, never joining in. On the other hand a monastic joke of Frère Jean's which goes too far brings down sharp and immediate condemnation.[2]

Only at the eleventh hour does Pantagruel laugh: he has no option.

---

1. For the cancel, see *Quart Livre*, TLF, Prologue, 69; and S. Rawles, M.A.S. *et al.*, *A New Rabelais Bibliography*, Droz, Geneva, 1987, entry no. 46.
2. *Quart Livre*, TLF, XVI, 1–3; L, 36–7.

That laughter was not checked by Panurge's abject fear, trembling hands, spouting blood and lacerated flesh: it was caused by them.[3] His laughter is, inevitably, cruel and without pity. But as soon as charity prevails the laughter is over. Or is it vice versa? Does laughter banish pity, or pity banish laughter? The two seem incompatible.

That is a characteristic of Rabelais's laughter. Only puppets, clowns and other dehumanized people are heartily laughed at. The more they are dehumanized, like the soldiers of Picrochole in *Gargantua* or the battered Chicanous of the *Quart Livre*, the more easily they can be smashed to pieces for our amusement. When the objects of our laughter remain fully human, things are different. Fictional human beings can be laughed at as we witness their destruction, but the slightest feeling of sympathy or pity must first be eliminated. That calls for the well-established tricks and art of the comic writer. The deaths of the soldiers who invaded the vineyard at Seuillé were dehumanized and trivialized by language: 'Some died laughing: some laughed dying'; a lance through the guts gives one of marauders an upset stomach, and so on.

Tappecoue ('Smack-tail'), the spoilsport sacristan of the Franciscans, refused to lend his vestments to Villon so that he could be God the Father in a play. Smack-tail met a fate akin to the tragic death of the innocent and handsome young Hippolytus, who was kicked to a pulp and dragged behind his steeds in full view of Poseidon. But the priest is not innocent, handsome and young: he has offended against the often subversive norms of comedy. Smack-tail is no name for a hero; Smack-tail had been a spoil-sport; Smack-tail had set himself up against the archetypal trickster Villon, whose very name, for Budé, sufficed to define his role;[4] Smack-tail was kicked to death by his convent's virgin mule, frightened not by Poseidon but by Villon and his band dressed up as devils and tossing firework-powder about. And Smack-tail's runaway mule copiously broke wind as she kicked and galloped, unseated her rider and smashed him to smithereens:

3. ibid., *ne se peut contenir de rire.*
4. Budé is cited in ch. 38.

Thoroughly scared, she started to trot off, farting and jumping and gallop-
ing, prancing, bucking, kicking with both her feet and letting loose a volley
of farts.

Not thus do epic steeds kill their noble masters. Nor was Hippolytus
reduced to a foot caught up in his stirrup by a fancy lattice-work
sandal. Hippolytus shows the preordained triumph of evil and the
vengeance of awesome gods who delight in tricking good men.
Smack-tail is awesome in another way: he reminds us of what comic
cruelty can do to the madmen who transgress its norms.[5]

It is surprising how few of the good characters in the mature
Rabelais ever laugh at anything at all. Yet even the great, austere,
generous, divinely wise and divinely prompted Pantagruel of the
Quart Livre can laugh. Not to laugh at all is to cease to be human;
nevertheless, Rabelais's mature definition of Pantagruelism emphasizes gaiety, not laughter. It is, with a glass of wine in your hand, 'a
certain gaiety of mind, pickled in contempt for things fortuitous'.
As a philosophy, Pantagruelism is not laughing but joyful. A joyful
mind and joyful conversation can be long sustained: a good guffaw
is a rare indulgence, at least for the wise.[6]

There is a moral tension in Rabelais which is characteristic of
Christian comedy generally. It is fun to laugh; laughter is potentially
a powerful moral force; it can be directed to good theological and
moral ends: yet the wise man controls it. The uproarious episode of
the Papimanes never shows Pantagruel giving way even to smiles. It
is the Bishop of the Papimanes who dribbles, sweats and farts as he
guffaws at his own joke. For Pantagruel, the Papimanes evoke not
laughter but charity: he offers rich cloth to curtain their reliquary;
money for the fabric-fund; dowries to marry off the servant choir-
girls.

In the name of a higher conception of Christian folly he finds
room for generosity and Christian charity even in the case of those
papimaniacal *Bon Christian*, even indeed in the case of their silly,

5. *Quart Livre*, TLF, XIII, 67f. and context.
6. ibid., Prologue, 14–17.

drunken, bloodthirsty, verbose, maudlin, bumptious and blasphemous old booby of a bishop: all fools cruel and cruelly misled.[7]

Both Erasmus and Rabelais shared in their culture's conviction that self-love, *philautia*, is a source of all evil, and can therefore instigate good moral laughter. Nevertheless, neither man seemed good at laughing at himself.

Such laughter is rare in literature. It demands the condemnation of your very self as a fool. Pope Gregory was one character who laughed; but Dante made him wait for Paradise before he did so! Gregory had dared to write with originality about the celestial hierarchies and to disagree with St Dionysius the Areopagite. Dante (who had no doubts at all on this score) tells how Gregory was brought to laugh at himself:

> Dionysius with such a desire
> Set himself to contemplate those hierarchies:
> He named them and distinguished them as I do.
> But Gregory afterwards dissented from him;
> So that, as soon as he actually opened his eyes
> In that Heaven, he laughed at himself.

Fancy thinking that his earthbound scholarship could rival Dionysius's revealed knowledge! He must have been mad!

There is one exception to laughter at oneself. 'Sympathetic' laughter can produce an appearance of such rare self-condemnation. Janotus de Bragmardo shows that in *Gargantua*. That doddering, senile, vicious and cruel old Dean of Theology started to laugh with the heroes who were laughing at him. Their laughter was contagious, and contagious laughter was classified as 'sympathetic'. It worked in the same way as yawning: by a natural transmission of feelings your yawning can cause others to yawn. Your laughing can cause others to laugh:

The theologian had no sooner finished than Ponocrates and Eudemon burst out into laughter so deep-seated that, through laughing, they nearly gave

---

7. ibid., LIV, 55–63.

up the ghost to God. [...] Master Janotus vied with them until tears came to their eyes from the vehement concussion of the substance of the brain, by which those lacrimatory fluids were expressed and then transmitted via the optic nerves.[8]

Even within the individual, the transmission of the impulse to laugh from the head to the limbs was seen by many as a matter of natural sympathy.[9]

But true Christian laughter stems from the conviction of absolute certainty. Christ on the Cross can easily be made as laughable as Carabba or Panurge if you think him simply mad and deluded. If that pseudo-Areopagite gentleman was what so many Christians once thought he was, then Gregory was indeed a madman to oppose a rival scheme to his. Gregory's was not a kindly laugh. It marked the rejection of a long scholarly endeavour. He had been insane enough to differ from a pupil of St Paul, the one apostle who knew the heavens since he had been enraptured into them.[10]

In those few lines Dante shows the way that Christian laughter was to go on its triumphant way; laughing at the world, certainly, but less than you might expect; laughing rarely at oneself; very, very often, laughing at other Christians in their error.

It was so much better than burning them.

Father Rabelais was a physician, providing cures and palliatives for the ills of body, soul and spirit. He was unusual in his deep concern for physical cleanliness in a doctor; before attending his patients he spruced himself up, washed his hands, and (as Galen insisted) cleaned his nails. For such a man, wallowing in the dirt of

8. *Gargantua*, TLF, XIX, 5–17.
9. Cf. the passage from Nicholas Nancel's *De Risu* (Paris, 1587) cited in note 17 to the same passage of *Gargantua*. For yawning, cf. the *Quart Livre*, TLF, LXIII, 54–8, when Rhizotome makes the others yawn 'by natural sympathy'. The notion derives from Alexander of Aphrodisius (III, 1) and was commonly held. Dr Nancel explains in *De Risu* that laughter arises from an agitation within the brain (not the heart). The body then reacts in sympathy.
10. Dante, *Paradiso*, III, 28, 135. Dante accepts that Dionysius was the Greek who had been taught by St Paul. Paul, having enjoyed a quite exceptional rapture, was able to tell him truths otherwise unknown. (Acts, 17, 34; II Corinthians, 12.)

the body was laughable and, at worst, diabolical. Much more than Erasmus, Rabelais was aware of the power of the Devil. Even such phrases as 'those devils of monks' often convey more than may first appear. Precisely because cleanliness and purity are next to godliness, dirt and impurity are signs of something radically wrong. They are signs of the kind of madness which, from the bastions of their unshakeable certainties, Christian fools can laugh at.

Paul's condemnation of eutrapely could easily have thrust laughter right outside the Christian pale. The Humanists, encouraged by eutrapely as Aristotle conceived of it, ransacked the happier writings of Greek and Latin comedies, and drew widely on the Latin satirists. Lucian for all his laughing at Christians was taken to the Humanists' bosoms. Rightly so, he is a natural ally for Christians who can tell religion from superstition, and charlatanism from fervour.

Rabelais (unlike Erasmus) rejoiced also in the kind of laughter found among the non-Humanist majority in village, town, guild, college and Court. But the greatest debt was due to Socrates and to Plato. They provided the structure for the high wisdom of Christian rapture, ecstasy and madness. They provided madness, *anoia*, as the cause of moral laughter.

Madman laughs at madman . . . There is no kindness, no charity, in that equation: a madman's laugh is unfeeling and cruel.

Rabelais did bring in kindness. He built his mature philosophical comedy around a sustained contrast between Pantagruel's gift of wisdom, with its normative self-knowledge, and Panurge's self-loving madness and ignorance. The laughter of wisdom at folly could have been stark. By making Panurge – a friend, not a foe – the vehicle for our laugher at self-deception and cowardice, Rabelais was putting into practice the 'schoolboy malice' of Socrates in the *Philebus*.

Characters in traditional comedy wear their masks (real or residual) from beginning to end. Panurge is an elastic trickster. He will not change. However distorted, he bounces back. By the standards of madness, *anoia*, he deserves to be laughed to destruction, just as Christ would deserve to be laughed at if the verdict of the worldly were right. If Panurge had been less human he could have been reduced to pulp and laughed at as he died, just like Picrochole's soldiers.

Something did soften the diasyrm of Erasmus, too. Something distinct from Lucianesque laughter led him to wish to save at least some of those vulgar madmen who were railing and jesting at Christ and his 'foolish' Cross. Something other than all his classical sources led Rabelais to have qualms about the comic cruelty he so masterfully exploited, and to reserve a fate other than comic dismemberment for cruel old heresy-hunting fools.

Erasmus held that Christians could express their happiness even from the pulpit when their thoughts turned to the unspeakable joys awaiting the elect. A pleasant, happy style is right when a preacher speaks of the happiness of the angels and souls who gaze in rapture at the Father, or when he tells 'what the life of the pious will be after the Resurrection'.[11] But Erasmus works mainly through diasyrm. Some, not altogether unfairly, see his laughter as akin to Voltaire's cackle. Charity and diasyrm make hard bedfellows. But so too do charity and comedy while the laughter lasts. Charity is by no means always to the fore. Sometimes justice is – the harsh justice of comedy, where fools get their deserts.

Is there still room to laugh at Carraba? Perhaps. Perhaps not. But unless Rabelais has lost his touch – and we our sense of humour – there is still room for a climactic laugh at a man with lacerated flesh and streams of blood – on the deck of Pantagruel's ship, though not on Bozrah's way. But then, that man, carefully deprived of our pity by Rabelais's art, gloried not in God and things spiritual but in the copious products of his bum.

What brought kindness trickling into the laughter of Erasmus, and flooding into that of Rabelais, was indeed charity. With charity comes a deeper understanding of the mercy of God and the redeeming power of Christ. Neither laugh-raiser revelled in the endless and ingenious torture of the damned.

Some think of the Christian revelation as above all a deposit

11. Erasmus, *De Ratione concionandi*, LB, 6, 860Af., cited in M.A.S., *Erasmus: Ecstasy and the Praise of Folly*, Penguin Books, 1988, pp. 132–3.

dutifully guarded by an infallible man, institution, or Church. Others
see the revelation of the fullness of Christ's truth as primarily a
winding road, leading members of a fallible Church – however
fitfully – towards a deepening of her understanding of divine truth,
justice and mercy. Christian truth may be at any time revealed – in
his own way and at his own choosing – by the risen Christ. Christ
is the *Logos*, the living Word, the very Idea of right-reason. He
approaches man and addresses him in ways he can understand. It
may all seem very mundane. The *Logos* does not smother the
personality of those whom he chooses to address, but he does expect
to elicit a response. One response had been a quiet rejection – despite
Fathers and Councils and encyclicals and synods – of the notion of
a celestial Belsen where wretches suffer infinite and everlasting
torment, partly in order to add to the joy of the elect. When in 1553
the Church under Edward VI drew up her Forty-two Articles, the
forty-second read: *All men shall not be saved at length.* Edward died
almost at once, and those articles were immediately abrogated under
Queen Mary. The forty-second was never restored under Elizabeth.
So the Church left even the universalism of Origen an open question.
Origen (the favourite theologian of Erasmus) held that, in the end,
all rational creatures will be saved: all mankind, and even all devils.
The Church, by never restoring Edward's forty-second article, leaves
the door of God's redeeming power wide open: all of us may
eventually be saved. If so, there will be no human beings left in Hell
to laugh at, not even unbaptized babes. Leibnitz said of the doctrine
of the damnation of unbaptized infants, 'It is not to my taste.' It
seems not to be to the taste of many theologians nowadays. It was
to the taste of many of them, though, for a millennium and a half.

The Reverend Frederick Farrar's sermons in Westminster Abbey
during 1877 led to the rapid rejection by many Christians of the
crudest and vilest doctrines of the eternal torment of the damned;
he opened wide the gates to charity. He deserves a place in the
liturgical Kalendar as a merciful Doctor of the Church. But there
was a price to be paid. His mercy restricted the scope of Christian
laughter, though not of Christian joy. Christians may no longer
be certain that they will enjoy, from a belvedere in Paradise, the

ingenious tortures inflicted upon the damned. Is there any room at all now for diasyrm in Paradise?[12]

But not all laughter is directed at enemies. Charity opens the floodgates to joy, and joy can lead to ample laughter. It is joyful rather than mocking laughter which dominates Rabelais's letter to Cardinal Odet de Chastillon.

The Church, not the philosophers or prophets of old, made joy a moral quality. What brought St Augustine from doubt to the Church was not simply her dignified face, but her 'serene and not dissolute joy'.[13]

12. Cf. Evan Daniel, *The Prayer-Book: Its History, Language and Contents*, twenty-first edition, 1905, pp. 552–3; Frederick W. Farrar, *Eternal Hope. Five Sermons preached in Westminster Abbey, November and December, 1877*, London, 1878; 1892, p. 85; D. P. Walker, *The Decline of Hell*, London, 1964, p. 38.

13. Migne, *Patrologia Latina*, XXXII, col. 761: '. . . *dignitas continentiae, serena et non dissolute hilaris, honeste blandiens ut venirem* . . .' Cf. Dean Inge (of St Paul's): *Outspoken Essays*, I (1933), p. 226: 'But we must add a third characteristic – the cheerfulness and happiness which marked the early Christian communities. "Joy" as a moral quality is a Christian invention, as a study of the usage of χαρά in Greek will show. Even in Augustine's time the temper of the Christians, *Serena et non dissolute hilaris*, was one of the things which most attracted him to the Church.'

Index

God – *cont.*
punishment by, 34
scornful laughter of, 51–2
see also Christianity; God; Jesus
Christ
Goldsmith, Oliver, 7
Gosling, J. C. B., 66n.
Gratius, Ortuinus, 206–7, 209, 213
and n.
Greek language,
Bible translations, 9–12
classical authors as source of
laughter, 142
Erasmus on
bad translations, 162–6
essential study for learned man,
10, 152
eutrapelia, meaning of, 132–5 *and*
n.
Franciscans' hostility to, 9
Humanists' study of, 8
ignorance of, 13–14
mataiologia, 178
moros 'fool': use of word, 176–7
Orthodox scholars of New
Testament, 98
Septuagint, 11–12
verbs used for mocking of Christ,
24–6
Greek philosophers,
anticipating Christian truth, 14
bringing Greek mind to Christ, 15
elegant jesting of, 137
Gregory of Nyssa, 76, 112n.
Grotius, Hugo, 94 *and n.*, 100
Guainerius, Antonius, 109
guilds, 141

Ham (son of Noah), 48
Handel, George Frederick, xv, 30, 95
Harmoniae evangelicae (Vossius),
78–9
harmonies and concords, 21
Heath, Michael, 22n., 297n.
Hebrew language,

parallelism in poetry, 50–51
and scholarship, 10, 152
Henry VIII, King of England, 72
Hermes Trismegistus, 14 *and n.*
Herod (of Judaea), 52
Hilarius, Saint, 50–51
Hippocrates, 285n.
Hochstrat, Jacob, 209
Holbein, Hans, 194–5
Holy Ghost,
inspiration by, like drunkenness,
111–12
prophesying under influence of, 100
Homer, 45, 152
Horace, 46, 49, 73, 113
Hugh, Cardinal, of Saint-Cher, *see*
Hugo Carrensis
Hugo Carrensis, 96–7, 100–101, 103,
162, 164–5, 169–70, 209
Humanists,
Christian, 9–14
devoted to *litterae humaniores*,
9–11, 311
Lucian's influence, 142
Renaissance Humanism, 9
Socrates as hero, 127

ideas, 295–6
idolatry,
of gluttonous monks, 289–91
pope 'as though God on earth', 278
theme of *Quart Livre . . .* , 279–81
norance,
about oneself, 66n.
confusion of *agnoia* and *anoia*,
64–6 *and n.*
Socrates on, 61–3
Index librorum prohibitorum, 144
irony, 52–3, 54–5
Isaac, xix–xi

James of Compostela, Saint, 154, 160
Jansen, Cornelius, of Ghent, 21, 103,
120
Jansenists, 68–70

Printed in Great Britain
by Amazon